D0296214
TINGHAM
LIBRARY

WHO WAS WHO IN EGYPTOLOGY

A BIOGRAPHICAL INDEX OF EGYPTOLOGISTS; OF TRAVELLERS, EXPLORERS AND EXCAVATORS IN EGYPT; OF COLLECTORS OF AND DEALERS IN EGYPTIAN ANTIQUITIES; OF CONSULS, OFFICIALS, AUTHORS AND OTHERS WHOSE NAMES OCCUR IN THE LITERATURE OF EGYPTOLOGY, FROM THE YEAR 1700 TO THE PRESENT DAY, BUT EXCLUDING PERSONS NOW LIVING

By

WARREN R. DAWSON

F.R.S.E., F.S.A.

Hon. Fellow of the Imperial College of Science and Technology

Membre Associé de l'Institut d'Égypte

LONDON
THE EGYPT EXPLORATION SOCIETY
2, HINDE STREET
MANCHESTER SQUARE, W.I.
1951

PREFACE

Egyptology, as a science, dates from the time of Champollion and, as is the case with all the comparatively young branches of learning, its history is very much bound up with the lives of its personnel : we still speak of the discoveries of Mariette, Brugsch, Maspero and Erman, for instance, by their personal names rather than by those of the discoveries themselves. For many years I have collected biographical notes of the scholars, excavators, travellers and writers whose names are connected with research in Egypt or are associated with important collections, monuments or papyri, and at the suggestion of my colleagues I have now extended what was originally merely note-book material for my own use into a general biographical index of all the names I have met with in the course of my studies concerning whom any facts of interest could be discovered.

In addition to Egyptologists in the strict sense, there are many names that have an association with Egypt. In the formation of the great museum collections of Europe and America, many travellers, both of pre- and post-Champollion date, have played an important part, and the consuls of the European Powers, as well as physicians, missionaries and other officials or residents in Egypt, have played no less important a role. In the latter connection such names as Drovetti, Salt, Anastasi, Mimaut and Sabatier are significant examples among consuls ; Abbott, Clot-Bey and Grant-Bey among physicians ; Lieder, Lansing and Murch among missionaries, and Maunier, Edwin Smith and Insinger among independent residents. It is therefore hoped that this book will be a convenient source of reference not only to Egyptologists who take an interest in the subject, but also to librarians and museum officials, who may thus be assisted in tracing the history of some of their earlier acquisitions (received in the days when registers were not so carefully kept as they are now), by a record of the dates, activities and movements of the persons whose names are associated with such specimens.

Of the "lions" of Egyptology, there are usually adequate biographies or obituary notices in existence (although it is surprising that some, even of these, have disappeared without record), but of the lesser-known names it is often very difficult to collect data. It is upon the latter that I have mainly concentrated my efforts, and I have made use of every source of information available to me, both printed and manuscript. In some cases I have succeeded in getting into touch with descendants, relatives, or others who possess knowledge that is nowhere to be found in print. I have also had much verbal information from some of the Egyptologists whom I knew personally but who are now no longer with us—Naville, Budge, Sayce, Griffith, Newberry and others ; I have had access to the correspondence of some of the earlier scholars and travellers in various collections, public and private, and have made copies of large numbers of letters, and I have consulted many diaries and note-books. In summarizing the results, I have aimed at the greatest brevity, but in nearly all cases references are given to sources where fuller information can be found ; in the few instances where no references are quoted, I have obtained the information by direct enquiry and research.

The term Egyptology has until recently been understood to comprise not only the study of Pharaonic Egypt, but that of two other branches that are tending to separate themselves from the parent stem and to take on an independent and specialized existence of their own, namely Coptic and Greek. Most of the earlier Egyptologists concerned themselves not only with ancient Egypt, but equally also with the Graeco-Roman and Christian periods. Of purely Coptic scholars, therefore, I have included only the pioneers such as Peyron and Tattam, and such of the later scholars as have been definitely connected with the Egypt Exploration Society, the Institut Français d'Archéologie Orientale or other bodies operating in Egypt, or who have themselves undertaken excavations or have visited Egypt in order to procure manuscripts. The same applies to students of Graeco-Roman Egypt whose main study is that of the numerous Greek papyri that have been found there. These scholars have labelled themselves "papyrologists," a term which seems to me a usurpation, ignoring as it does the great mass of far more ancient papyri of Pharaonic times, and implying that the significance of papyri is confined to those that are written in Greek. Be this as it may, I have applied the same selection as in the case of Coptic scholars : thus, such names as Grenfell, Hunt, Jean Maspero and Jouguet are included whilst many others are omitted, chiefly those of "savants de cabinet" not directly connected with work or institutions in Egypt.

In addition to the names set forth in this book, I have a considerable list of travellers, collectors and others who ought to have taken their places with the rest, but concerning whom I have been unable to obtain any information. I shall be grateful for any additions or corrections sent to me at the office of the Society.

Whenever the present location of papers, drawings or diaries of the earlier Egyptologists and travellers is known to me, I have stated the names of the museums or libraries that contain them together with their official registration numbers if ascertainable. I have also noted public sales of antiquities, some of which were anonymous but which I have identified. Sale catalogues are often a valuable aid in tracing the history and provenance of antiquities. Within my limits of space, it has been impossible to name publications except to a small extent, but references to bibliographies of the works of particular authors are given whenever they exist : most of the works of authors can be traced by the aid of two general bibliographies, neither of which, however, is absolutely complete. These are, for the older authors and publications up to 1887, *The Literature of Egypt and the Soudan* by Prince Ibrahim Hilmy, 2 vols., London 1886–7, and for later writers up to 1941, *Ancient Egypt : Sources of Information in the New York Public Library*, by Ida A. Pratt, N.Y., 1925 and *Supplement*, 1925–41, N.Y., 1942.

It gives me great pleasure to record my sincere thanks to the many colleagues, friends, and even strangers, who have assisted me by answering queries, looking up references and supplying a variety of information by correspondence. Many of these have put themselves to infinite trouble on my account. The names of my correspondents and helpers are too numerous to set out in this preface, but I trust I have adequately thanked each and all of them either personally or by letter. The work has been, not only to me, but to all who have participated in it, a labour of love and my deepest gratitude is due to an old and valued friend who has defrayed the cost of printing and to the committee of the Egypt Exploration Society who have undertaken the publishing and distribution of the book. I trust that critics will not be too severe on this pioneer effort, carried out under difficult conditions, and indeed I can wish this little book no happier fate than to see it superseded by a better, undertaken by an author whose knowledge and facilities for research are greater than my own.

WARREN R. DAWSON

15*th August*, 1951

ABBREVIATIONS

(Periodical Publications are marked by an asterisk.)

AAA*—*Annals of Archaeology and Anthropology*, Liverpool.

ASA*—*Annales du Service des Antiquités*, Cairo.

Athanasi.—*A brief account of the researches and discoveries in Upper Egypt made under the direction of Henry Salt Esq.* By Giovanni d'Athanasi. London, 1836.

Barker.—*Syria and Egypt under the last five Sultans of Turkey: being the experiences during fifty years of Mr. Consul-General Barker, chiefly from his letters and journals.* Edited by his son, Edward B. B. Barker. 2 vols. London, 1876.

Belzoni.—*Narrative of operations and recent discoveries in the Pyramids, Temples, Tombs and Excavations in Egypt and Nubia.* By G. Belzoni. 3rd ed., London, 1822.

BIBIB.—*Biographical Index of deceased British and Irish Botanists.* By James Britten and George S. Boulger; 2nd ed., revised by A. B. Rendle. London, 1931.

Bibl. Ég.—*Bibliothèque Égyptologique, contenant les oeuvres des Égyptologues français* . . . Publiée sous le direction de G. Maspero. 40 vols. Paris, 1893–1915. [Those most frequently quoted are the volumes containing biographies of Mariette (Vol. 18), De Rougé (21), and Lefébure (34).]

BIFAO.*—*Bulletin de l'Institut Français d'Archéologie Orientale.* Cairo.

B.M.—The British Museum.

Bonomi Diary.—The manuscript journal of Joseph Bonomi, for the years 1829–33. [I have used my own abstract compiled from a copy in the Griffith Institute, Oxford.]

Budge, N & T.—*By Nile and Tigris: a narrative of journeys to Egypt and Mesopotamia on behalf of the British Museum between the years 1886 and 1913.* By Sir E. A. Wallis Budge. 2 vols. London, 1920.

Budge, R & P.—*The Rise and Progress of Assyriology.* By Sir E. A. Wallis Budge. London, 1925.

Cahiers.*—*Cahiers d'histoire Égyptienne.* Cairo.

Carré.—*Voyageurs et Écrivains français en Égypte.* By Jean Marie Carré. 2 vols. Cairo, 1932.

Chabas.—*Notice Biographique de François Joseph Chabas.* By Frédéric Chabas and Philippe Virey, Paris, 1898. [Also reprinted in *Bibl. Ég.* Vol. 9.]

Champollion.—*Lettres et Journaux de Champollion.* Ed. H. Hartleben. 2 vols. Paris, 1902. [*Bibl. Ég.* Vols. 30, 31.]

Chron.*—*Chronique d'Egypte.* Brussels.

DAB.—*Dictionary of American Biography.* 20 vols. 1928–36.

Dawson MSS.—My own manuscript collections bound in about 100 vols. These are quoted as they are ultimately destined for the B.M.

DBF.—*Dictionnaire de Biographie Française*. Ed. Balteau, Barroux and Prévost. 1933 (in progress).

DNB.—*Dictionary of National Biography*. 63 vols. and supplements. London and Oxford, 1885–1940.

EB.—*Encyclopaedia Britannica*. 12th ed. 32 vols. 1922.

E.E.F.—Egypt Exploration Fund.

E.E.S.—Egypt Exploration Society.

Enc. It.—*Encyclopaedia Italiana*, 36 vols. Rome, 1935 &c.

E.R.A.—Egyptian Research Account.

Erman.—*Mein Werden und mein Wirken*. By Adolf Erman. Leipsic, 1929.

Finati.—*Life and Adventures of Giovanni Finati*. Dictated by himself, translated from the Italian and edited by W. J. Bankes. 2 vols. London, 1830.

GM.*—*Gentleman's Magazine*. London, 1731–1868. 224 Vols.

Goodwin.—*Charles Wycliffe Goodwin, 1817–1878, a Pioneer in Egyptology*. By Warren R. Dawson. Oxford, 1934.

Hartleben.—*Champollion : sein Leben und sein Werke*. By Hermine Hartleben. 2 vols. Berlin, 1906.

Hay Diary.—The manuscript diary of Robert Hay, for the years 1824 to 1827. [I have used my own copy made from B.M. Add. MS. 31054, supplemented by extracts from other Hay manuscripts, and a partial copy, fuller than the original, made by Bonomi.]

Henniker.—*Notes during a visit to Egypt, Nubia . . . and Jerusalem*. By Sir Frederick Henniker. 2nd Ed. London, 1824.

Hilmy.—*The Literature of Egypt and the Soudan : A Bibliography*. By Prince Ibrahim Hilmy. 2 vols. London, 1886–7.

Hincks.—*Edward Hincks, a selection from his correspondence and a memoir*. By E. F. Davidson. Oxford, 1933.

Irby.—*Travels in Egypt and Nubia, Syria and Asia Minor, during the years 1817 and 1818*. By the Hon. Charles Leonard Irby and James Mangles. 2nd ed. London, 1844. [The 1st ed. was privately printed, 1823.]

JAI.*—*Journal of the Anthropological Institute* (later, *Royal*). London.

JEA.*—*Journal of Egyptian Archaeology*. London.

JMEOS.*—*Journal of the Manchester Egyptian and Oriental Society*. Manchester.

JRAS.*—*Journal of the Royal Asiatic Society*. London.

Kürschner.—*Kürschners Deutschen Gelehrten-Kalender*. Berlin, various years.

Larousse.—*Grand Dictionnaire Universel du XIXe. Siècle*. 17 vols., Paris, 1866 ; and ditto, *XXe. Siècle*. 6 vols., Paris, 1928.

Legh.—*A narrative of a journey in Egypt and the country beyond the Cataracts*. By Thomas Legh. London, 1816.

Lelorrain.—*Notice sur le voyage de M. Lelorrain en Égypte et observations sur le Zodiaque Circulaire de Dendereh*. By P. Saulnier, Paris, 1822.

Lepsius.—*Letters from Egypt, Ethiopia and the Peninsula of Sinai.* By Dr. Richard Lepsius, transl. by L. and J. B. Horner. London, 1853.

Light.—*Travels in Egypt, Nubia and the Holy Land . . . in the year 1814.* By Henry Light. London, 1818.

Lindsay.—*Letters on Egypt, Edom and the Holy Land.* By Lord Lindsay. 4th ed. London, 1847.

Madox.—*Excursions in the Holy Land, Egypt, Syria,* etc. By John Madox. 2 vols. London, 1834.

M.M.A.—Metropolitan Museum of Art, New York.

NBG.—*Nouvelle Biographie Générale.* By H. Hoeffer. 46 vols. Paris, 1855–66.

Newberry Corresp.—The Correspondence of Prof. P. E. Newberry, in the Griffith Institute, Oxford.

OFRS.*—*Obituary Notices of Fellows of the Royal Society.* London.

OLZ.*—*Orientalistische Literaturzeitung.* Berlin.

PEFQS.*—*Palestine Exploration Fund, Quarterly Statements.* London.

Petrie.—*Seventy Years in Archaeology.* By Sir Flinders Petrie. London, 1931.

PSBA.*—*Proceedings of the Society of Biblical Archaeology.* London.

QR.*—*Quarterly Review.* London.

Rec. Champ.—*Recueil d'études égyptologiques dédicés à la mémoire de Jean-François Champollion.* Paris, 1922.

Rec. Trav.*—*Recueil de travaux relatifs à la Philologie et à l'Archéologie égyptiennes et assyriennes.* Paris.

Richardson.—*Travels along the Mediterranean and parts adjacent, in company with the Earl of Belmore, during the years 1816, 1817 and 1818.* By Robert Richardson. 2 vols. London, 1822.

Romer.—*A pilgrimage to the temples and tombs of Egypt, Nubia and Palestine.* By Mrs. [Isabella Frances] Romer. 2 vols. London, 1846.

Salt.—*The Life and Correspondence of Henry Salt, Esq., late H.B.M. Consul-General in Egypt.* By J. J. Halls. 2 vols. London, 1834.

Sayce.—*Reminiscences.* By the Rev. A. H. Sayce. London, 1923.

Sherer.—*Scenes and Impressions of Egypt, India,* etc. By Moyle Sherer. 2nd ed. London, 1825. [1st ed. pub. anonymously, 1824.]

Tresson.—*Le Voyage archéologique de M. le Comte Louis de Saint-Ferriol en Égypte et en Nubie.* By P. Tresson. (*Bull. Acad. Grenoble,* 1828), 33 pp.

TSBA.*—*Transactions of the Society of Biblical Archaeology.* London.

Valentia.—*Voyages and Travels in India . . . Abyssinia and Egypt in the years 1802 to 1806.* By George [Annesley] Viscount Valentia. 3 vols. London, 1809. [The 8vo. ed. of 1811 is here quoted.]

Vapereau.—*Dictionnaire Universel des Contemporains.* Paris, 1878.

Vyse.—*Operations carried on at the Pyramids of Gizeh in 1837.* By

Colonel [Richard William] Howard-Vyse. 3 vols. London, 1840-2.

Walpole.—*Memoirs relating to European and Asiatic Turkey and other countries of the East, edited from Manuscript Journals.* By Robert Walpole. London, 1818.

Westcar Diary. The manuscript diary of a tour in Egypt and Nubia in 1823–4, by Henry Westcar. [The references are to the original MS. in the possession of Dr. L. Keimer of Cairo.]

Wilbour.—*Travels in Egypt (Dec., 1880, to May, 1891); Letters of Charles Edwin Wilbour.* Ed. by Jean Capart. Brooklyn, 1936.

WWW.—*Who Was Who,* 3 vols. London, 1929–47. [Vol. i., 1897–1915; Vol. ii., 1916–28; Vol. iii., 1929–40.]

WWWA.—*Who Was Who in America,* Vol. i., 1897–1942. Chicago, 1942.

WZKM.*—*Wiener Zeitschrift für die Kunde des Morgenländes.* Vienna.

ZÄS.*—*Zeitschrift für ägyptische Sprache und Altertumskunde.* Leipsic.

ZDMG.*—*Zeitschrift der deutschen morgenländischer Gesellschaft.* Berlin.

ABBOTT, Henry (1812–1859)

Medical practitioner and collector of antiquities; born 1812; as a youth joined R.N. and served as orderly to a ship's surgeon; he left his ship at Alexandria and entered the service of Mohammad Ali, becoming a physician to his fleet; resigned about 1830 and settled in Cairo as a medical practitioner, but although he is often called M.D., he apparently held no medical diploma; in 1852 he founded, jointly with Prisse, a Literary Association in Cairo, where he received Wilkinson, Lepsius and others; he formed a considerable collection of antiquities, catalogued by Bonomi in 1846 (about 450 items); his family removed to America in 1851, and he joined them there bringing with him his collection for sale; it was exhibited in New York in 1853, but the exhibition was financially a failure, and Abbott returned to Egypt in 1854, when he bought from A. C. Harris the famous papyrus that bears his name with the intention of re-selling it at a profit; in 1857 it was bought by the B.M. through the mediation of Sir Gardner Wilkinson; after many ineffectual attempts had been made to sell Abbott's main collection, it was eventually bought by the N.Y. Historical Society, and in 1948 it was transferred to the Brooklyn Museum; Abbott died in Cairo in 1859.

Bull. N.Y. Hist. Soc. 4 (1920), 8–15; *Brooklyn Mus. Bull.* 10, No. 3, 17–23 (Portr.); *Romer*, i, 103, 368; ii, 113.

ABDERRASSŪL (*fl.* 1871–1891)

A family of Gurneh consisting of three brothers, Mohammad (who was in the service of Mustafa Agha, Consular Agent at Luxor), Ahmed and Soliman; dealers in antiquities; they discovered about 1871 the famous cache of Royal Mummies at Dêr el-Bahri and sold papyri and other small objects from it, the appearance of which on the market aroused the suspicions of Maspero; as the result of his enquiries and action, Mohammad A. in 1881 disclosed the secret, and all the contents of the tomb were removed to the Cairo Museum; the same family discovered another tomb, the contents of which had also been exploited for some years before it was known; Mohammad A., who was then in the employment of the Antiquities Service, disclosed the secret to Grébaut in 1891, and about 105 coffins and mummies of Dyn. 21, with their funerary furniture, were taken to the museum.

Maspero, *Momies Royales*, 511 ff.; *ASA.*, 1, 141–5; 8, 3–38; *Wilbour*, 33, 74 and often (*see* index).

ACERBI, Giuseppe (1773–1849)

Austrian Consul-General in Egypt; born Castel Goffredo, 3 May 1773; naturalist and litterateur; founded *Bibliotheca Italiana*; resided in Milan 1816–1828; in Egypt, 1828–34; a friend and supporter of Champollion; died 25 Aug. 1849.

Barker, ii, 192; *Hilmy*, i, 14; *B.M. Add. MS.* 25663, f. 42–107; *Champollion*, ii, 234, 244, 245.

ACWORTH, Joseph John (1853–1927)

Collector of antiquities ; born 9 Feb. 1853 at Rochester ; Ph.D., F.I.C., F.C.S. ; visited Egypt many times ; formed a large collection of Eg. antiquities by purchases in Egypt and at sales, particularly the Meux sale of 1911 ; retired in 1919 and devoted all his time to the study of Egyptology and adding to his collection ; after his death, his widow presented the major part of the collection to the B.M., and the remainder to the Museum of Archaeology and Ethnology, Cambridge ; Dr. Acworth died in London, 3 Jan. 1927.

Inf. by Mrs. Acworth.

ADAMS, Andrew Leith (1820–1882)

Surgeon and naturalist ; born 1820 ; Army surgeon, 1848–73 ; Prof. of Zoology, Dublin, 1873–78 ; Prof. of Nat. Hist., Cork, 1878–82 ; visited India, Egypt and Canada and pub. accounts of his travels ; travelled in Egypt with Alex. Henry Rhind ; his *Notes of a Naturalist in the Nile Valley,* 1870, besides natural history, contains much information of the persons he met, such as Edwin Smith ; died 1882.

DNB. i, 94 ; *Hilmy,* i, 15.

ADANSON, Jean Baptiste (1732–1804)

" A French Diplomatic Interpreter in the East whose name is mentioned in some early books of Egyptian travel. The tale of his sufferings and scientific endeavours is very touching. He would be classed along with Sonnini and Denon had not his portfolios and notebooks perished ; with the exception of a few drawings preserved in the Bibliothèque Nationale all his work was lost."

E.E.F. Arch. Rep. 1899–1900, 38 ; Hamy, *Comptes Rendus,* 1899, 738.

AFFRE, (*Evêque*) **Denis Auguste** (1793–1848)

Born 27 Sept. 1793 ; educ. for the priesthood at St. Sulpice ; Archbishop of Paris, 1840 ; studied Champollion's works but considered them insufficient to explain hieroglyphic writing ; pub. *Nouvel Essai sur les Hiéroglyphes Égyptiens,* Paris, 1834, a scholarly though mistaken work ; died Paris, 27 June 1848.

L. Alazard, *Denis-Auguste Affre, Archevêque de Paris,* Paris, 1905 ; *Hilmy,* i, 16.

AGOUB, Joseph (1795–1832)

A Copt, Armenian by birth ; born Cairo, 18 Mar. 1795 ; taken to Marseilles by his father, 1801, and to Paris, 1820 ; Prof. of Arabic at the Collège Louis-le-Grand ; published translations of Arabic songs, *Discours sur l'Égypte,* 1823 ; *Littérature Orientale et Française,* (posthumous), 1835 ; a friend of Champollion ; died Marseilles, Oct. 1832.

Champollion, i, 285 ; ii, 421 ; *Hilmy,* i, 21.

AHMED KAMAL (*Pasha*) (1849–1923)

The first native Egyptian to take up the scientific study of Egyptology ; he was a pupil of H. Brugsch, and was attached to the Antiquities Service, first as Secretary-Interpreter, and afterwards as

Assistant Curator of the Museum from which post he retired in 1914 after 30 years' service, when he was made Hon. Curator ; carried out numerous excavations for the Service, reports of which he pub. in the *Annales* ; his works are numerous and include contributions to the great *Catalogue Général* of the museum ; he was a member of the Inst. Ég., and lecturer on Ancient Egyptian in Cairo Univ. ; having had the title of Bey from the Khedive, he was made Pasha shortly before his death, and was also nominated Director of the School of Egyptology established on his suggestion by the Eg. Government ; died 4 Aug. 1923.

JEA. 9, 241 ; *Bull. Inst. Ég*. 6, 171.

AINSLIE, (*Sir*) **Robert** (1730–1812)

Diplomatist and numismatist ; Ambassador at Constantinople, 1776–92 ; Knighted, 1775 ; created Baronet, 1804 ; formed a large collection of ancient Eastern and N. African coins, which were published by Sestini in 11 vols. ; made a collection of drawings of Egypt executed by Luigi Mayer of which 48 were published in colour in 1801–2 and a further series in 3 vols., 1804 ; died 21 July, 1812.

DNB. 1, 189 ; *Hilmy*, ii, 26.

AKERBLAD, Jean David (*c*. 1760–1819)

Swedish scholar ; born about 1760 ; studied oriental languages and was attached to the Swedish Consulate at Constantinople ; from here he visited Palestine and Asia Minor ; attached to the consulate in Paris about 1800, and studied Coptic MSS. there ; soon after, under the patronage of the Duchess of Devonshire he settled in Rome to continue his studies ; published works on Phoenician (1802) and Runic Inscriptions (1801) ; is best known by his *Lettre à M. de Sacy sur l'Inscr. de Rosette* (1802), in which he studied the demotic text and drew up an alphabet of demotic characters, some of which were adopted by Champollion and Young ; died suddenly in Rome, 1819.

Hartleben, i, 108, 125, 364–72 ; *Hilmy*, i, 26.

ALEXANDER, (*Sir*) **James Edward** (1803–1885)

General in the Army ; born 16 Oct. 1803 ; H.E.I.C. Army, 1820 ; British Army, 1825 ; saw much service, including Russo-Turkish War, 1817, and Crimea, 1855–6 ; retired, 1877 ; was largely responsible for the preservation and transport to England of Cleopatra's Needle in 1877, on which he pub. a descriptive work in 1879.

DNB. Suppl. 1, 31 ; *Hilmy*, i, 24.

ALEXANDER, William (1767–1816)

Artist ; born Maidstone, 10 Apl. 1767 ; student at R.A. ; Keeper of Prints, B.M., 1808–16 ; Prof. of Drawing at Marlow Military Academy ; made drawings of the Egyptian antiquities in the B.M. collected by Napoleon's Commission, which were engraved by Medland and published in 21 plates, 1805–7 ; died 23 July, 1816.

DNB. 1, 281 ; *Hilmy*, i, 24.

ALLBERRY, Charles Robert Cecil Austin (1913–1943)

Coptic scholar ; born 1913 ; Christ's Coll. Camb., M.A. ; first Lady Budge Scholar ; edited Chester Beatty Manichaean MS., and other Coptic texts ; editor of *JEA.* ; in 1940 joined the Royal Air Force, and attained the rank of Flying Officer ; he was killed in action over Germany in April 1943, having previously been reported missing.

The Times, 11 May 1943.

ALLEMANT, E. (*fl.* 1872–1885)

French dealer in antiquities ; dragoman to Sultan Abd-ul-Aziz until he was deposed in 1876 ; was much in Egypt where he carried on excavations and made purchases of antiquities, from about 1872 to 1885 ; a collection of antiquities was purchased from him by the Antwerp Museum in 1872, and a further collection by the Louvre in 1882 ; in 1878 he published *Collection d'Antiquités Égyptiennes : description historique et religieuse des monuments découvertes sur les lieux par l'auteur,* in which 832 objects are described ; the catalogue was pub. in London, although his business was carried on in Paris.

Wilbour, 7, 253 ; *Rev. de l'Art,* 43, 170.

AMÉLINEAU, Émile (1850–1915)

Born 1850 ; educated for the Church, and was ordained in the Diocese of Rennes ; was attracted to Egypt by Félix Robiou whose lectures he attended ; went to Paris to study Egyptian and Coptic under Maspero and Grébaut ; in 1882 joined Miss. Arch. in Cairo where he remained four years ; seceded from the Church, 1887 ; excavated at Abydos 1894–8 ; the results were important but his methods unscientific and provoked severe criticism from Maspero, and from Petrie who followed him on the site ; the antiquities he collected were sold in Paris, 8–9 Feb. 1904 ; published reports on his excavations and a bulky but inferior work on funerary customs, but his principal output is the great mass of Coptic texts contributed to *Rec. Trav., ZÄS.* and other journals ; he also published *Pistis Sophia* and the Bruce Papyrus ; professor of the Hist. of Religions in the École des Hautes Études ; died in Paris, Jan. 1915.

Rev. Arch. 24, 333 ; *JEA.* 2, 188.

AMHERST, (*Baroness*) **Mary Rothes Margaret Cecil** (1857–1919)

Eldest daughter of Lord Amherst of Hackney ; born 25 Apl. 1857 ; married 1885 Lord William Cecil ; frequently visited Egypt and excavated at Aswân, 1903–4 ; many antiquities found or acquired by her were incorporated in her father's collection ; pub. excavation reports in *ASA* ; *Bird Notes from the Nile,* 1904 ; succeeded as Baroness Amherst on the death of her father in 1909 ; died 21 Dec. 1919 ; generally known as Lady William Cecil.

Newberry Corr. ; *WWW.* ii, 20.

AMHERST, (*Lord*) **William Amhurst Tyssen-Amherst, first Baron Amherst of Hackney** (1835–1909)

Born 25 April, 1835 ; educ. Eton and C.C. Oxf. ; M.P. 1880–5 ;

created Baron, 1892; a keen collector, notably of Incunabula and Egyptian antiquities, and his museum at Didlington Hall, Norfolk, was one of the most notable private collections; he purchased the collection of the Rev. R. T. Lieder (q.v.) in 1861, and the entire collection of Dr. John Lee (q.v.) in 1865; made frequent additions when in Egypt, and from excavations he supported, including those of Petrie and Lady William Cecil; numerous purchases were also made for him by P. E. Newberry; he published volumes on the Eg., Coptic and Greek papyri and Cuneiform Tablets in his collection; the papyri were acquired by the Pierpont Morgan Library, N.Y., in 1913, but the rest of the collection (965 lots) was sold at Sotheby's, 13–17 June 1921, producing £14,533; died 16 Jan. 1909.

Norfolk Notabilities (1893), 67–75 (Portr.); *WWW*. i, 14; *Newberry Corr.*

AMIOT, Jean Joseph Marie (1718–1793)

Jesuit missionary in China; born Toulon, 1718; went to China, 1750; pub. a dictionary and valuable works on the history and culture of the Chinese and a Life of Confucius; wrote an elaborate work on symbolic writing with 39 plates in which he compared Egyptian with Chinese writing (Brussels, 1773); died Pekin, 9 Oct. 1793.

Bibl. de la Cie. de Jésus, i, 294–303; *BIFAO*. 5, 83; *Hilmy*, i, 35.

ANASTASI, Giovanni (1780–1857)

The adoptive name of an Armenian merchant settled in Alexandria; born 1780; went to Egypt to assist his father about 1797; after the death and bankruptcy of his father, by great efforts he re-established himself and became one of the most considerable merchants in Egypt; Swedish-Norwegian Consul-General in Egypt, 1828–57; in addition to his commerce, he carried on a large trade in antiquities, employing agents to buy from the natives in Sakkara and Thebes; he sold a large collection to the Dutch Government in 1828; another was sold in London in 1839, and the residue (1,129 lots) in Paris in 1857; he bequeathed a part of his fortune for Swedish charities, and a large granite sarcophagus to Stockholm Museum; died in Alexandria early in 1857. Anastasi's name is chiefly associated with the numerous important papyri from his collections now in B.M., Leiden, Paris and Berlin.

JEA. 35, 158; *Champollion*, i, 94, 210, 326, 346; ii, 25; *Lepsius*, 39, 43.

ANCESSI, (*Abbé*) **Victor** (1848–1879)

French priest; a pupil of Maspero at École des Hautes Études, 1869–73; studied the relations of Egypt to Biblical History and published several works thereon, 1872–7; a correspondent of Chabas; died young in 1879.

Maspero, *L'Égyptologie* (1915), 7; *Chabas*, 118; *Hilmy*, i, 36.

ANDERSON, John (1833–1900)

Anatomist and naturalist; born Edinburgh, 4 Oct. 1833; educ. Edinburgh University; M.D.; LL.D.; F.R.S.; Superintendent Calcutta Museum and Prof. of Anatomy, Calcutta, 1864–86; made two scientific expeditions to China and to Arabia and Egypt ; pub. *Reptiles and Batrachia,* 1898 (*Zool. of Egypt,* part i), a work of great value to Egyptologists in view of the importance of snakes, etc., in the Eg. texts and monuments ; died London, 15 Aug. 1900.

WWW. i, 15.

ANGELIN, Justin Pascal (*fl.* 1830–1839)

French naval surgeon ; born at Marseilles ; accompanied, as surgeon of the vessel *Louqsor,* the expedition led by J. B. A. Lebas (q.v.) to remove and transport to Paris the obelisk now in the Place de la Concorde ; pub. an account of the expedition, with plates, Paris, 1833 ; also pub. reports on cholera in Egypt (*Annales maritimes,* t. 46, Paris, 1831, and a separate thesis, Paris, 1834) ; afterwards went to the W. Indies and pub. a report on yellow fever in Guadeloupe (Toulon, 1839).

Wernich-Hirsch, *Allgemeinen Lexicon der Aertze,* i, 148 (1884) ; *Hilmy,* i, 37.

ANNESLEY, Arthur Lyttelton (1802–1882)

Born 30 Nov. 1802 ; son of Major-Gen. Norman Macleod and Hester Annabella, d. Arthur Annesley, Visct. Valentia and 1st Earl of Mountnorris ; in 1844 assumed by royal licence the name of Annesley in lieu of Macleod ; he inherited Arley Castle, Staffs. ; in 1854 presented to B.M. fourteen stelae which had formed part of Lord Mountnorris's collection sold in 1852 ; died 24 Oct. 1882. [B.M. 350, 354, 356, 426, 479, 506, 536, 663, 698, 702, 1085, 1093, 1095, 1096.]

Burke's Peerage.

ANNESLEY, George, Visct. Valentia and 2nd Earl of Mountnorris (1770–1844)

Born 4 Dec. 1770 ; succeeded as 2nd Earl, 1816 ; travelled in the East 1802–6 with Henry Salt as secretary and draughtsman ; F.R.S. 1796 ; formed a large natural history collection and a collection of Eg. antiquities at Arley Castle, Staffs., the latter mostly obtained for him by Salt in 1817–20 ; mostly sold in 1852, the majority being bought by Joseph Mayer of Liverpool, but some were given to the B.M. in 1854 by his kinsman Arthur Lyttelton Annesley (q.v.) ; died 23 July 1844, his son George Arthur having predeceased him in 1841, the earldom became extinct.

Salt, i, passim ; *BIBIB.* 8 ; B.M. *Add. MS.* 19348.

ANTONIADIS, (*Sir*) **John** (1818–1895)

Greek Merchant of Alexandria ; born Lemnos, 1818 ; came to Egypt 1833 and established himself at Alexandria ; in 1857–8 as a *favori* of Said Pasha, he became a famous public character ; Knighted by Queen Victoria, 1865 ; he presented to the Municipality his palace and garden, and was a great benefactor to the Museum of Alexandria, one of the galleries being named in his honour " Salle Antoniadis," and contains a fine collection of Egyptian antiquities ; died 1895.

Breccia, *Alexandrea,* ed. 1914, 172 ; *Inf. by Dr. T. D. Mosconas.*

ARAGO, Dominique François Jean (1786–1853)

French physicist and astronomer ; born 26 Feb. 1786 ; interested himself in the decipherment of hieroglyphs and published several memoirs thereon in support of Thomas Young ; died in Paris, 2 Oct. 1853.

Autobiography, transl. Rev. Baden Powell, 1855 ; *Champollion*, ii, 214, 250 ; *Hilmy*, i, 41.

ARBUTHNOT, (*Lady*) **Ann** (*d.* 1882)

Daughter of F.M. Sir John FitzGerald, G.C.B. ; married 20 Mar. 1828, Lt.-Gen. Sir Robert Arbuthnot, K.C.B. (1773–1853) ; she and her husband were staying in Cairo at the time when Howard-Vyse was exploring the Pyramids, and he named one of the newly-discovered construction-chambers of the Great Pyramid " Lady Arbuthnot's Chamber " in her honour ; she died in Florence, 6 Mar. 1882 and is buried with her husband in the Protestant cemetery there.

Vyse, i, 239, 256, 259, 264, 265 ; *Inf. by W. FitzGerald Arbuthnot* (*grandson*).

ARDEN, Joseph (1800–1879)

Of 27 Cavendish Square and Clifford's Inn, Barrister-at-Law ; born 1800 ; much interested in archaeology ; F.S.A., 1847 ; travelled in Egypt 1846–7 and purchased at Thebes the Hypereides papyrus pub. by Churchill Babington (q.v.) ; also purchased two mummies, one of which was unrolled at Worcester by Pettigrew (*J. Brit. Arch. Assn.* 4, 337) and the other by Birch in Lord Londesborough's house (*Arch. Journ.* 7, 273) ; died Rickmansworth, 10 June 1879.

JEA. 35, 162 ; *Dawson MS*. 23, f. 142.

ARMITAGE, (*Rev.*) **Elkanah** (1844–1929)

Congregationalist Minister ; born Manchester, 16 Dec. 1844 ; educ. Stuttgart, Owens Coll. and T.C.C. ; M.A. ; Theological tutor in Philosophy and Comparative Religion in the Independent Colleges of Rotherham and Bradford ; visited Egypt in 1881 and obtained two important papyri which he gave to Aquila Dodgson (q.v.) which were pub. by Griffith ; died 23 Dec. 1929.

WWW. iii, 33 ; *PSBA*. 31, 289.

ARUNDALE, Francis (1807–1853)

Architect and painter ; born London, 9 Aug. 1807 ; pupil of Augustus Pugin whom he accompanied to Normandy and assisted in the *Arch. Antiquities of Normandy* ; visited Egypt 1831 and accompanied Bonomi to Palestine, 1833 ; remained nine years in the East then travelled in Greece and Italy ; although trained as an architect, he never practised ; exhibited some large paintings made from his oriental drawings ; pub. *Jerusalem and Mount Sinai*, 1837 ; *Selections from the Gallery of Antiquities in the Brit. Museum*, 1842, in collaboration with Bonomi and Birch ; died Brighton, 9 Sept. 1853.

DNB. 2, 136 ; *Hilmy*, i, 43 ; *Bonomi Diary*.

ASHBURNHAM, Bertram, Visct. St. Asaph (1797–1878)

Born 23 Nov. 1797 ; succeeded as 4th Earl of Ashburnham, 1830 ; visited Egypt 1824–5 ; carried out excavations at Thebes under the direction of Bonomi ; was a keen collector of ancient coins and engraved gems ; died 22 June, 1878.

Hay Diary, 1824, Dec. 5 ; 1825, Jan. 2, Feb. 22, Feb. 24.

ATHANASI, Giovanni d' (1799–1837+)

Son of a Greek merchant of Lemnos who settled in Cairo ; born 1799 and went to Egypt in 1809 ; whilst still a boy, he entered the service of Col. Ernest Misset, Brit. Consul-General, on whose retirement, in 1815, he became servant to Henry Salt ; excavated at Thebes for Salt 1817–27, and thereafter on his own account ; he sold many important antiquities, and brought to England a large collection (some of which were engraved by Visconti), which was sold at Sotheby's in an eight-days' sale in 1837 ; Athanasi, or d'Athanasi (properly Ἰωάννης Ἀθανασίος), was well known to all travellers in Egypt as Yanni, and he is frequently mentioned in diaries and books of travel from 1817 to 1835 ; he had a house at Gurneh, just above tomb No. 52 ; not traced after 1837.

In 1836 he published *Researches and Discoveries in Upper Egypt made under the direction of Henry Salt Esq.*, which is mainly autobiographical ; *Hilmy*, i, 44 ; frequently mentioned under the name of Yanni in contemporary diaries and books of travel.

'AUAD (*c.* 1773–*c.* 1853)

A native of Gurneh who acted as guide and attendant to Lepsius at Thebes in 1844–5 and who was severely wounded in consequence of a family feud ; he was a faithful servant and had great knowledge of the district and of the antiquities ; Brugsch met him at Thebes in 1853, he being then about 80 years of age.

Lepsius, 271, 321 ; Brugsch, *Mein Leben*, 183.

AURÈS, Auguste (*fl.* 1860–1890)

French Mathematician of Nîmes ; wrote on Egyptian metrology. (*Mem. Acad. Nîmes*, Ser. 7, ii, 1–166 ; vii, 7–28).

Hilmy, i, 46.

AVELING, (*Rev.*) **Thomas William Baxter** (*d.* 1884)

Congregationalist minister ; travelled in Europe and the East ; pub. *Voices of Many Waters : Travels in the Lands of the Tibur, Jordan and Nile*, 1855, new ed. 1856 ; died 3 July, 1884.

DNB. 2, 274 ; *Hilmy*, i, 46.

AYRTON, Edward Russell (1882–1914)

Son of William Scrope Ayrton of the China Consular Service ; born Wuhu, China, 17 Dec. 1882 ; educ. St. Paul's School ; excavated at Abydos with Petrie, 1902–4 and at Dêr el-Bahri with Naville, 1904–5 ; with Theodore Davis in the Valley of the Kings, 1905–8 ; with E.E.F. at Abydos and Mahasna, 1908–9 ; accepted an appointment in the Arch. Survey of Ceylon, where he went in 1911 ; died in Ceylon in 1914, having been accidentally drowned while on a shooting expedition.

JEA. 2, 20 (Portr.).

BABINGTON, (*Rev.*) **Churchill** (1821–1889)

Scholar and naturalist; born Roecliffe, Co. Leicester, 11 Mar. 1821; private pupil of Charles Wycliffe Goodwin; St. John's Coll. Camb., 1839; B.A. 1843; M.A., 1846; D.D., 1879; elected Fellow and ordained, 1846; Vicar of Horningsea, 1848–61; Rector of Cockfield, Suffolk, 1861–89; Disney Professor of Archaeology, Cambridge, 1865–80; pub. *editio princeps* of the Hypereides papyri of Joseph Arden, A. C. Harris and Henry Stobart, 1850–58; a man of many interests which included archaeology and natural history, on which he published many works; died 12 Jan. 1889.

DNB. Suppl. 1, 92; *Proc. Linn. Soc.* 1888–90, 46; *BIBIB*. 12; *Goodwin*, 22, 61; *Journ. Bot.* 1889, 110.

BAGNOLD, Arthur Henry (1854–1943)

Colonel, R. Engineers; educ. Cheltenham and Woolwich Acad.; Lieut., 1873; Capt., 1884; Major, 1887; Lt.-Col., 1899; Col., 1903; retired, 1911; C.B., 1907; C.M.G., 1918 (for voluntary war-service); served in Egypt, 1884–7, and undertook the removal of the colossus of Ramesses II at Mît Rahîneh, a difficult operation described in detail in *PSBA*. 10, 452; died Dec. 1943.

R. Eng. Journ. 58, 131 (Portr.); *Budge N & T.* i, 103–4.

BAIKIE, (*Rev.*) **James** (1866–1931)

Scottish Free Church minister; born 25 Nov. 1866; educ. Edinburgh University; wrote many popular works on astronomy and archaeology; F.R.A.S.; Oxford University Extension Lecturer in Egyptology; his books on excavations and discoveries in the Near East did much to popularize Egyptology, particularly his *Century of Excavations* (1923) and *Egyptian Papyri* (1925); died 5 Feb. 1931.

WWW. iii, 50.

BAILEY, James (*c.* 1796–1864)

Classical scholar; T.C.C.; M.A., 1823; Member's Prizeman, 1815 and 1816; delivered an oration in Latin on the origin and nature of hieroglyphic writing, using the texts of the Flaminian Obelisk and the Rosetta Stone, pub. in *Classical Journ.* (Cambridge, 1816) 16, 313; travelled in Greece and Egypt, 1818–9; died 1864.

DNB. 2, 407; *Belzoni*, ii, 114; *Hilmy*, i, 48.

BAILLET, Auguste Théophile (1834–1923)

French archaeologist and Egyptologist; born Fouilloy-près-Corbie, 27 Nov. 1834; engaged in commercial life, but in his leisure made many contributions on French medieval antiquities; studied Egyptology under de Rougé, and wrote many papers thereon which were collected by Maspero in *Bibl. Égyptologique*, Vols. 15, 16 (1905), with a biographical notice by his son; died 6 Aug. 1923.

Bibl. Ég. 15, ut supra; *JEA*. 9, 223.

BAILLET, Jules (1864–1924)

French Egyptologist, son of Auguste Théophile B. ; born 1864 ; studied under his father and Maspero ; described the Eg. collections at Sens and Vannes and contributed a number of papers to *Rec. Trav.* and other journals ; attached to the Inst. Fr. d'Arch. Orient. at Cairo ; his most important work was the publication of the Greek graffiti in the Royal Tombs at Thebes (*Mémoires,* 42 (1920)) ; a paper on the same subject was contributed to *Rec. Champollion,* 103 (1922) ; died 1924.

BALDWIN, George (1743–1826)

Travelled in Egypt, 1773 and in 1775 established direct commerce from England to Egypt ; British Consul-General in Eg. 1785–1796 ; pub. reminiscences of conditions in Egypt and of the slave-trade and prevalent corruption ; died Earl's Court, Brompton, 19 Feb. 1826.

F.O. Records ; *DNB.* 3, 35 ; *Hilmy,* i, 50.

BALL, (*Rev.*) **Charles James** (1851–1924)

Hebraist and archaeologist ; e. s. Charles B. of Guildford, Surrey ; born 1851 ; Queen's Coll. Oxon. ; B.A., 1873 ; M.A., 1876 ; Litt. D. ; Classical Master and lecturer on Hebrew at Merchant Taylors' School ; Chaplain of King's Coll. London ; Rector of Bletchingdon, from 1899 ; an eminent Hebrew scholar and Biblical Critic ; contributed to *PSBA* and other journals on the origin of Phoenician and Hittite writings and their relation to Egyptian ; pub. *Light from the East,* a general introduction to biblical archaeology ; died 7 Feb. 1924.

Alumni Oxon. ; *Budge R & P.* 188.

BANCROFT, Edward Nathaniel (1772–1842)

Physician ; son of Edward B., F.R.S., born London 1772 ; St. John's Coll. Cantab. ; M.B., 1794 ; M.D., 1804 ; Physician to the Forces in various localities ; F.R.C.P., 1806 ; in Egypt in 1803 ; died Jamaica, 18 Sept. 1842 ; while in Egypt he collected antiquities and presented to B.M. in 1807 a pillar found at Abûkir inscribed in Greek to Serapis. [B.M. 99.]

DNB. 3, 106 ; Munk, *Roll Coll. Phys.* iii, 31.

BANIER, (*Abbé*) **Antoine** (1673–1741)

Published a number of communications on the mythology and cults of the Egyptians to the Acad. des Inscr. ; his *Mythologie et Fables,* 1st ed., 3 vols., 1738–40, 2nd ed., 8 vols., was translated into English and pub. in 4 vols., 1740 ; edited Paul Lucas's *Troisième Voyage,* 1719 and later editions.

Carré, i, 45 ; *Hilmy,* i, 51, 394.

BANKES, William John (*d.* 1855)

Scholar and traveller ; T.C.C., B.A. 1808 ; M.A., 1811 ; M.P., 1810–35 for various constituencies ; travelled in the East and acted for a time as secretary to Henry Salt, Consul-General in Egypt ;

travelled in Egypt, Nubia and Syria with Giovanni Finati and was a friend of Byron and Rogers, but very hostile to Champollion. In Egyptology Bankes's name is associated with the bilingual obelisk from Philae, discovered in 1815, brought to England, and erected in Bankes's park at Kingston Hall, Wimborne, Dorset, and with the table of kings in the B.M. discovered in 1818 in the temple of Ramesses II at Abydos : it had passed into the Mimaut collection ; died Venice, 15 Apl. 1855.

DNB. 3, 124 ; *Belzoni*, passim ; *Athanasi*, 41–5 ; *Salt*, i, 488 ; ii, 52, 118, 133, 139 ; *Hilmy*, i, 51, 232 ; *Life and Adventures of Giovanni Finati*, vol. ii, passim ; *Champollion*, i, 91, 251, 373, 422 ; ii, 78, 244, 278, 402.

BANVILLE, (*Vicomte de*) **Henri** (1837–1917)

A member of an ancient Norman family ; born Vire, 1837 ; on his marriage in 1864 he settled in the Château du Rosel in Fresnes (Orne) ; Conseilleur Générale de l'Orne and Maire de Fresnes ; accompanied de Rougé to Egypt, 1863–4, and made the photographs for the *Album Photographique* issued in 1865 ; as his services in this expedition were gratuitous, they were recognized by the award of the Croix de la Légion d'Honneur ; died 1917.

Bibl. Ég. 21, pp. lxv, cxvi–cxvii ; *Hilmy*, i, 177 ; *Inf. by H. de Banville* (grandson).

BARING, (*Sir*) **Evelyn, 1st Earl of Cromer** (1841–1917)

Statesman and diplomatist ; born Cromer, Norfolk, 26 Feb. 1841 ; educ. Ordnance School, Carshalton and Woolwich Acad. ; commissioned in R. Artillery, 1858 ; after various military appointments became Sec. to Viceroy of India, 1872 ; sent to Egypt as Commissioner of the Public Debt, 1877–9 ; after further Indian service, returned to Egypt as British Consul-General, 1883–1907 ; created Baron, 1892 ; Viscount, 1898 ; Earl, 1901 ; while in Egypt, Lord Cromer was one of the most influential and active administrators of his time ; although not an archaeologist himself, his long association with Egypt brought him into constant touch with Egyptologists, particularly in connection with the Arch. Survey of Nubia, which he did much to promote ; his book, *Modern Egypt*, 2 vols., 1908, gives a vivid picture of the social, political and economic conditions of the country ; after his retirement, he was elected President of the E.E.F., 1906–17 ; died 29 Jan. 1917.

WWW. ii, 246 ; *DNB*. Suppl. ; *JEA*. 4, 58.

BARKER, John (1771–1849)

Diplomatist ; born Smyrna, 9 Mar. 1771 ; educ. in England ; private secretary to John Spencer Smith, Ambassador to the Porte, 1797 ; pro-consul at Aleppo, 1799 ; consul for the Levant, 1803 ; fled from Aleppo owing to rupture between Britain and the Porte, 1807 ; remained in hiding and rendered great service to the East India Co. ; returned to Aleppo after the peace of 1809 and remained till 1825, when he was appointed British Consul in Alexandria and Consul-General in Egypt in 1829 which office he virtually held after the death of Salt in 1827 ; retired 1833 and resided in Syria, where he died 5 Oct. 1849 ; he visited England on leave in 1818 and 1844 ; while in Egypt, Barker made an important collection of antiquities which was sent to England and sold (anonymously) at Sotheby's, 15 and 16 March, 1833 (258 lots). The B.M. acquired many papyri, stelae, etc. at this sale.

Biography, by his son B. B. Barker, 2 vols. London, 1876 (Portr.) ; *B.M. Add. MS.* 25659, f. 19, 24, 25, 46.

BARNET, Charles John (1790–1856)

Lieut.-Colonel in the Army ; 3rd Regt. of Foot, Capt., 1812 ; Lieut.-Col. 1821 ; retired, 1830 ; fought at Waterloo ; British Consul-General in Egypt, May, 1841 to 1846 ; died Engelfield Green, 2 Aug. 1856.

F.O. Records ; *GM.* 1856, ii, 394 ; *Romer*, i, 87.

BARROCCO, Giovanni (1829–1914)

Founder of the Museo Barrocco, Rome : it consists chiefly of Greek and Roman art, but contains also Egyptian antiquities.

Wilbour, 256.

BARRY, (*Sir*) Charles (1795–1860)

Architect ; born 23 May, 1795 ; R.A. ; designed many important buildings in London, including the Houses of Parliament ; travelled in Europe and Egypt, 1817–20 ; his name, with date 1819, is carved on the Abu Sir Rock, 2nd Cataract ; he executed a fine series of plans, sections and drawings of temples, tombs, etc., in Egypt and Nubia which are now in the Griffith Inst., Oxford ; died 12 May, 1860 ; buried in Westminster Abbey.

DNB. 3, 210 ; Gr. Inst. *List of Records* (1947), 3.

BARSANTI, Alexandre (1858–1917)

Italian technician ; born Alexandria, 28 Aug. 1858 ; educ. Inst. des Beaux Arts, Florence ; came to Cairo in 1885 and was engaged by Maspero to succeed Floris in the Cairo Museum as restorer, technician and artist ; in 1891 he had the title of Conservateur-Restorateur ; he had great skill in repairing, restoring and mounting damaged articles ; in 1892 he went with de Morgan to Upper Egypt, and in 1894–5 assisted Daressy in the clearance of the Temple of Medinet Habu ; in 1895–6 he was in Nubia to superintend the consolidation and restoration of the temples, etc., affected by the barrage ; from 1899 to 1904, he worked in the pyramid-field at Sakkara, and restored and repaired many mastabas and later tombs, and 1911–13 he worked on the Theban temples ; died 24 Oct. 1917.

ASA. 17, 245–257 (Bibl. 258–60).

BARTHOLDI, Jacob Salomon (1779–1825)

Prussian diplomat ; born Berlin, 13 May, 1779 ; educ. Königsberg ; toured Greece with the artist Gropius ; in 1805 at Dresden renounced the Jewish faith and was baptized ; in 1809 joined the army as a volunteer and was wounded at the Battle of Ebersberg ; Consul-

General at Rome, 1816 till his death 26 July 1825 ; Bartholdi had a fine collection of Egyptian antiquities which was inspected by Champollion in 1825 and was acquired by the Berlin Museum.

Champollion, i, 189, 218, 407.

BATES, Oric (1883–1918)

American archaeologist ; born Boston, Mass., 8 Dec. 1883 ; educ. Harvard ; in 1906 appointed to Eg. Dept., Boston Museum of Fine Arts ; afterwards studied in Berlin and took part in two Nubian expeditions, those of the Khedival Govt., and Harvard-Boston ; in 1909 conducted an expedition in Tripoli ; in 1910 he was again exploring in Nubia and the Sudan ; in 1913, pub. *The Eastern Libyans* ; in 1914 appointed Curator of African Archaeology in the Peabody Museum, Harvard ; in 1917 he inaugurated the series of volumes *Harvard African Studies* ; when training for military service, he was taken ill, and died at Louisville, Kentucky, 8 Oct. 1918.

Memoir prefixed to *Harvard Af. Studies*, ii ; *JEA*. 6, 293.

BATISSIER, Louis (1783–1882)

Born Bourbon l'Archambault, 1783 ; French Consul at Suez ; wrote on ancient art, 1843–60 ; presented papyri to the Louvre (3174, 3176, 3177 etc.) ; died at Enghien 9 June, 1882.

Vapereau, 123 ; *Rev. Arch.* 8, 467 ; *Hilmy*, i, 56.

BEAMONT, (*Rev.*) **William John** (1828–1868)

Traveller and missionary ; born 16 Jan. 1828 ; T.C.C. ; B.A., 1850 ; M.A., 1853 ; Fellow, 1852 ; ordained, 1854 ; missionary in Palestine ; chaplain to British Army in the Crimea ; travelled in Egypt 1854 and 1860 ; pub. a diary and account of his travels ; died 9 Aug. 1868.

DNB. 4, 11 ; *Hilmy*, i, 57.

BÊATO, Antonio (*d.* 1903)

Italian professional photographer ; resident in Luxor from 1862 until his death ; made a large series of excellent photographs of the principal temples and monuments in Egypt in the 'sixties, 'seventies and 'eighties, many of which are extremely valuable records of the then state of monuments since defaced or destroyed ; sets of these photographs were sold to tourists and many were used as illustrations for books on Egypt ; in 1907, Maspero bought from his widow his negatives and stock of prints for the records of the Cairo Museum.

Maspero, *Rapports sur la marche du Serv. des Ant.* 1899–1910, Cairo, 1912, pp. xli, 250 ; *Wilbour*, 217, 236, 272, 463, 509 ; *Budge N & T*, ii, 326.

BEECHEY, Henry William (*d. c.* 1870)

Artist and traveller ; son of the portrait-painter Sir William Beechey, R.A. ; Secretary to Henry Salt, Brit. Consul-General in Egypt, 1815 ; resigned 1820 and returned to England ; sent by Salt in 1817–18 to supervise the operations of Belzoni and Athanasi ; in 1821–2, with his brother Frederick William, R.N., geographer, he explored and surveyed the N. African coast from Tripoli to Derna, the results being pub. in 1828; F.S.A., 1825; biographer of Sir Joshua Reynolds, 1835; in 1855 emigrated to New Zealand, where he died about 1870.

DNB. 4, 123; frequently mentioned in *Salt, Belzoni, Athanasi, Irby; Hilmy,* i, 58.

BELLERMANN, Johann Joachim (*d.* 1842)

German antiquary and theologian; particularly interested in antique gems and their symbols; pub. works on Abraxas-gems (1817–18) and on scarabs and their inscriptions; attempted to decipher hieroglyphic writing.

BIFAO. 5, 84; *Hilmy,* i, 60.

BELMORE, Earl of.—*See* LOWRY-CORRY

BELZONI, Giovanni Battista (1778–1823)

Italian explorer and adventurer; born Padua, 1778; came to England in 1803 and obtained a living by exhibiting himself in feats of strength (he was a very large and powerful man, 6 ft. 7 in. in height); it is usually said that he performed at Astley's Amphitheatre, but John Britton, who knew him, says that this is a mistake, and that Sadlers Wells was his theatre; travelled in Spain and Portugal impersonating Samson; invented a hydraulic machine and went to Egypt in 1815 to erect it for Mohammad Ali, but it was not successful; entered the service of Salt who employed him to remove a colossal head of Ramesses II for shipment to the B.M.; excavated for Salt at Thebes and in 1817 discovered the tomb of Sety I, generally known as Belzoni's Tomb; discovered the entrance to the Second Pyramid at Gizeh; travelled in Nubia and other parts of Egypt; returned to Europe in 1819 and exhibited a model of the Tomb of Sety I; in 1820 published his *Narrative,* three editions being called for up to 1822; in 1823, set out on a voyage to Timbuktu to trace the source of the Niger, but died of dysentery at Gato in Benin, 3 Dec. 1823; Belzoni was an able man, and whilst generally popular, he engaged in fierce quarrels with Salt and others.

DNB. 4, 205; Belzoni's *Narrative*; *Salt,* passim; *Athanasi,* passim; *Hilmy,* i, 61; *Champollion,* ii, 277 (Portr.); John Britton, *Autobiography* (1850), i, 112–115; *Bull. Inst. Ég.* 6, 27–42.

BELZONI, Sarah (1783–1870)

Wife of Giovanni B. Belzoni; married 1803; accompanied him on his travels to Nubia, and went alone to Palestine; contributed a chapter to the *Narrative*; after her husband's death she opened an exhibition in London of his drawings and models of the Tomb of Sety I, but it was a failure and was closed in May 1825; in 1828 she proposed to publish a series of lithographic plates and issued a prospectus, but this also was abortive; died 12 Jan. 1870.

The Times, 7 May 1825; *Sunday Times,* 20 Jan. 1828; Belzoni's *Narrative,* passim; *Champollion,* i, 70.

BENEDETTI, Vincent (1817–1900)

Corsican ; acting French Consul in Egypt 1844 ; Consul in Cairo, 1849 ; envoy at Turin, 1861 and Berlin, 1864 ; in retirement he returned to Corsica where he died, 1900.

French F.O. Records ; *Carré*, i, 285, 310 ; ii, 28.

BÉNÉDITE, Georges Aaron (1857–1926)

French Egyptologist ; born Nîmes 10 Aug. 1857 ; studied Semitic languages at Lycée St. Louis, Paris, 1871 ; studied art and drawing at École des Beaux Arts and in private studios, 1878–80 ; accompanied Chipiez to Egypt, 1880 ; studied Egyptology at École des Haute Études under Maspero, 1881–6 ; joined the Mission Archéologique 1887–8 and was mainly engaged in copying Theban tombs ; appointed to staff of the Louvre, 1888 ; Conservateur-Adjoint Ég. Dept., 1895 ; succeeded Pierret as Conservateur 1907 ; succeeded Maspero at the Collège de France, 1899–1914 ; Membre de l'Acad., 1924 ; visited Egypt 19 times and in 1925 explored Abyssinia ; contributed to many journals, 1888–1926 ; died at Luxor, 23 Mar. 1926.

Rev. de l'Ég. anc. i, 250–278 (Bibl. and Portr.).

BENSON, Margaret (1865–1916)

Daughter of Edward White Benson, Archbishop of Canterbury ; born 16 June, 1865 ; educ. Lady Margaret Hall ; visited Egypt 1894, 1895, 1896 and 1900 ; excavated the Temple of Mut at Thebes, 1895–6, with her friend Janet Gourlay, under the supervision of Newberry ; results pub. in *The Temple of Mut in Asher*, 1899 ; died 1916.

Life and Letters of Maggie Benson, by her brother, A. C. Benson, 1917 (Portr.) ; *Newberry Corresp.*

BEREND, William Berman Sedgwick (1855–1884)

American banker of New York ; took up the study of Egyptology and became a pupil of Maspero ; pub. an account of the Eg. stelae and sculptures in Florence (1882–4) and a French transl. of Lepsius's memoir on Egyptian metals (1879) ; sec. Congress of Orientalists, Lyons, 1878 ; died young, in Sweden, leaving a large fortune.

Maspero, *L'Égyptologie* (1915) 8, 9 ; *Wilbour*, 71, 309 ; *Hilmy*, i, 63.

BERENS, (*Rev.*) **Randolph Humphrey** (1844–1923)

Formerly McLaughlin ; born 11 Jan. 1844 ; assumed the surname Berens on his marriage in 1877 with Eleanor Frances, d. Henry Hulse Berens, J.P. ; T.C.D. ; B.A., 1866 ; M.A., 1869 ; ordained, 1867 ; Vicar of Sidcup, Kent, 1877–81 ; becoming wealthy on his marriage, he retired from clerical duty ; travelled in Egypt and collected coins and antiquities ; his collection of Eg. antiquities (155 lots) sold at Sotheby's 18 June 1923 ; a further collection belonging to his wife (who died in 1924) was sold 29 July 1923 (lots 299–313) and 31 July 1923 (114 lots) ; Berens died in 1923.

Inf. by P. E. Newberry ; Burke's Landed Gentry ; Clergy Lists.

BERGMANN, (*Ritter*) **Ernst von** (1844–1892)

Austrian Egyptologist ; studied at Göttingen under Brugsch and Ewald ; Keeper of Eg. antiquities in the Royal Museum of Vienna, 1862–92 ; visited Egypt 1877–8 ; published many texts and monuments, chiefly of the Vienna collection, in *Rec. Trav.*, *ZÄS.* and other journals.

ZÄS. 30, 126 ; Biogr. by Dedekind, *Des Ægyptologen Ernst von Bergmann's Leben und Wirken,* 2nd ed., 1906.

BETHELL, (*Hon.*) **Richard** (1883–1929)

Only son of 3rd Baron Westbury ; born 26 Apl. 1883 ; educ. Eton and Magdalen Coll. Oxon. ; Capt. Scots Guards ; made a collection of antiquities illustrating Egyptian art ; on Committee of E.E.S. 1920–6 ; assisted Howard Carter in the Tomb of Tutankhamun ; died 15 Nov. 1929.

WWW. iii, 106 ; *E.E.S. Annual Rep.* 1929, 8 ; *Newberry Corresp.*

BEUGNOT, (*Vicomte*) **Auguste Arthur** (1797–1865)

Historian and scholar ; collector of antiquities ; his collections were sold in Paris, 5 May 1840 ; the Catalogue, which includes many Egyptian items, was drawn up by J. de Witte.

BIOT, Jean Baptiste (1774–1862)

French physicist ; born Paris 21 Apl. 1774 ; Prof. of Mathematics at Beauvais and in 1800 Prof. of Physics at Coll. de France ; Membre de l'Acad. des Sciences, 1803 ; Légion d'Honneur, Chevalier, 1804, Commandeur 1849 ; F.M.R.S., 1815 ; Rumford Medallist, 1840 ; a prolific writer, his works covering a wide field of physical science ; was particularly interested in the astronomy of ancient Eg. and China and published several memoirs thereon ; died Paris, 3 Feb. 1862.

EB. ; *Bibl. Ég.* 18, p. lxxiv ; *Hilmy,* i, 70.

BIRCH, Samuel (1813–1885)

Egyptologist and Sinologist ; born 3 Nov. 1813 ; educ. Merchant Taylors' School, 1826–31 ; entered service of Commrs. of Public Records, 1834 ; transferred to B.M., 1836 ; Asst. Keeper, Dept. of Antiquities, 1844–61 ; established Champollion's system in England ; Keeper of Oriental, British and Medieval Antiquities, B.M., 1861–6, and of Oriental Ant. alone, 1866–85 ; LL.D., Aberdeen, 1862 ; LL.D. Cantab., 1875 ; D.C.L. Oxon., 1876 ; F.R.S.L. ; F.S.A. ; founder and first President of the Soc. of Biblical Archaeology, 1872 ; the list of his works is a long one, but specially to be mentioned is his Hieroglyphic Grammar and Dictionary, published as an appendix to Bunsen's *Egypt's Place* ; died in London, 27 Oct. 1885 ; buried Highgate Cemetery.

TSBA, 9, 1–43 (Bibl. and Portr.) ; *DNB.* Suppl. 1, 199 ; *Rev. Ég.* 4, 187–192 ; *Hilmy,* i, 70 ; ii, 378 ; also much interesting information in *Budge, N & T* and *R & P.*

BIRCHER, André (1838–1926)

Swiss merchant of Cairo, who later became a dealer in antiquities ; he formed a large and good collection which when advanced in years he began to dispose of ; Breasted purchased a considerable quantity for the Chicago collection ; some scarabs and other antiquities were pub. by Newberry.

Inf. by P. E. Newberry and L. Keimer.

BLACAS D'AULPES, (*Duc de*) **Pierre Louis Jean Casimir** (1771–1839)

Premier Gentilhomme de la Chambre du Roi to Louis XVIII and Charles X ; born 1771 ; a staunch friend to Champollion and used his influence to send him on his mission to Italy ; Champollion's reports were in the form of *Letters à M. le Duc de Blacas* ; collector of coins, antique gems and other antiquities, which were largely increased by his eldest son ; he (the son), Louis Charles Pierre Casimir was born in London in 1815 and died in Venice in 1868 ; by a special Treasury Grant of £48,000 the whole of the valuable Blacas collections were purchased by the B.M. in 1866 ; amongst the Egyptian items were two papyri (9947-8).

Champollion, i, passim ; *Rec. Champ.* 1–20 ; C. W. King, *Handbook of Engraved Gems*, 2nd ed. (1885), 164 ; Edwards, *Lives of the Founders of the B.M.*, 689.

BLACKDEN, Marcus Worsley (*fl.* 1890–1915)

Artist ; a volunteer member of the staff of the Archaeological Survey under Newberry at Beni Hasan, 1891–2, when he made coloured drawings of the wall-paintings, but his work was stopped by illness and was continued by Percy Buckman and Howard Carter ; many of Blackden's drawings were reproduced in colour in *Beni Hasan*, parts 1, 3, 4 ; assisted Newberry at El Bersheh, 1892, his drawings again being reproduced in *El Bersheh*, part 1 ; with G. Willoughby Fraser discovered and published the hieratic graffiti at Hat-Nub ; he later became a mystic and a member of the Societas Rosicruciana in Anglia, for which body he pub. *The Ritual and Mystery of the Judgment of the Soul*, 1915, based on the Papyrus of Ani.

Beni Hasan, i, pref. ; *JEA*. 2, 52 ; *Newberry Corresp.*

BLACKMAN, Winifred Susan (*d.* 1950)

Eldest daughter of Rev. J. H. Blackman and sister of Prof. Aylward M. Blackman ; visited Egypt many times and from 1920 was engaged in anthropological research on the modern Egyptians, with special reference to survivals from Pharaonic times ; took part in the Percy Sladen Expedition, 1922–6 ; Wellcome Medical Museum expedition, 1927 ; pub. *The Fellahin of Upper Egypt*, 1927 and numerous papers in *JEA* and other journals ; died 12 Dec. 1950.

The Times, 14 Dec. 1950.

BLANC, Alexandre Auguste Philippe Charles (1813–1882)

French writer on art ; contributed to many periodicals and pub. a work on the French Painters of the 19th cent., and an encyclopaedic history of painting in 14 vols. ; visited Egypt in 1869 and pub. *Voyage dans la Haute Égypte,* Paris, 1876 ; he was the first to describe the bas-reliefs in the Temple of Abydos explored by Mariette in 1864.

Carré, ii, 309 ; *Hilmy,* i, 76.

BLANCHARD, Ralph Harrup (*d.* 1936)

American dealer in antiquities at Cairo, his well-known shop was next to an entrance of Shepheard's Hotel ; in addition to his stock, he had a large private collection of scarabs, some of which were published by Newberry ; pub. *Handbook of Eg. Gods and Mummy-amulets,* Cairo, 1909 ; his collection was dispersed after his death.

Inf. by P. E. Newberry ; *Chron.* 12, 229.

BLAYDS, John (1754–1827)

Banker of Leeds ; born 1754 ; senior partner in the house of Blayds, Beckett & Co. of Leeds (the firm as Beckett & Co. continued until 1920, when it was absorbed by the Westminster Bank) ; D.L. ; twice Mayor of Leeds ; a public benefactor ; presented to the Leeds Philosophical Society a mummy of Dyn. 20 which was examined and described by William Osburn in a special publication, 1828 : this specimen is of importance in the history of the technique of mummification : it was lost by enemy action in 1941 ; Blayds died at Leeds, 21 Feb. 1827.

W. Osburn, *Account of an Egyptian Mummy,* Leeds, 1828 ; *G.M.* 1827, 285 ; 1828, 77.

BLUMENBACH, Johann Friedrich (1752–1840)

German Anthropologist ; born Gotha, 11 May 1752 ; educ. Jena and Göttingen ; M.D., 1775 ; Prof. of Medicine, Göttingen, from 1775 ; F.M.R.S., 1793 ; one of the founders of comparative anatomy and physical anthropology ; wrote on Egyptian mummies in *Phil. Trans.* 84, 177 and in *Beytrage zur Naturgeschichte,* ii, 45–144 ; died Göttingen, 22 Jan. 1840.

EB. ; Haddon, *Hist. Anthropology,* 13 ; *Mem. Inst. Ég.* 13, 8 ; *Hilmy,* i, 77.

BOESER, Pieter Adriaan Aart (1858–1935)

Dutch Egyptologist, born 26 July 1858 ; studied Egyptology at Berlin under Erman and Steindorf ; Doctor, Leiden Univ., 1889 ; Professor of Egyptology, Leiden, 1910–28 ; succeeded Pleyte as Director of the Eg. collections, Leiden Museum ; retired 1925 ; published many Coptic texts and antiquities in the Leiden collection ; died 25 Feb. 1935.

Chron. 10, 317.

BOKTY, Joseph (*fl.* 1817–1845)

Swedish Consul-General in Egypt before Anastasi ; his daughter was murdered during a revolt in Cairo ; resided in Salt's house in 1820 ; afterwards Prussian Consul in Egypt.

Belzoni, i, 14, 33 ; *Salt,* ii, 155 ; *Athanasi,* 17 ; *Lepsius,* 47.

BONNEFOY, — (*d.* 1859)

Assistant to Mariette in his Serapeum excavations, and afterwards his assistant in the museum of Bulak ; directed excavations at Dra Abu'l Neggah, 1858 ; was very loyal to Mariette and active in suppressing illicit digging ; nothing is known of his earlier history ; died early in 1859.

Rec. Trav. 12, 215.

BONOMI, Joseph (1796–1878)

Artist and traveller ; of Italian origin ; son of J. B. the elder (1739–1808), architect ; born London, 9 Oct. 1796 ; studied at R.A. schools under Nollekens and in 1823 continued his studies in Rome ; went to Egypt in 1824 to assist Robert Hay ; in 1828 assisted James Burton with his *Excerpta Hieroglyphica* ; in 1829 ascended the Nile as far as Dongola and accompanied Linant-Bey in his expedition to the Gold Mines ; again worked for Hay 1832–3, and travelled in Syria and Palestine, 1833–4 ; went to Rome to study the obelisks, 1838 ; worked at the B.M., 1839 ; prepared the illustrations for Wilkinson's *Manners and Customs* , went to Egypt with Lepsius's expedition, 1842–4 ; returned to England and married 1845 Jessie, d. of the painter John Martin ; set up the Eg. court at the Crystal Palace, 1853 ; made the hieroglyphic fount for Birch's *Dictionary*, pub. 1867 ; catalogued and illustrated many Egyptian collections, and lithographed the sarcophagus of Sety I and other monuments ; appointed curator of Sir John Soane's Museum in 1861 and was still in office when he died, 3 Mar. 1878 at Wimbledon.

DNB. 5, 364 ; *Diary* (transcript at Griffith Institute) ; *TSBA.* 6 (1879) ; *Hay Diary* ; *Hilmy,* i, 81 ; *Bull. Inst. Ég.* 32, 51.

BORCHARDT, Ludwig (1863–1938)

German Egyptologist ; born Berlin 5 Oct. 1863 ; educ. Berlin Univ. ; studied Egyptology under Erman ; visited Egypt first in 1895, and worked at Philae under Capt. Lyons ; conducted many excavations in Egypt in later years especially at Abusir and Amarna ; in conjunction with Maspero he inaugurated the great *Catalogue Général* of the Cairo Museum ; scientific attaché to the German Consulate at Cairo ; founded the German Inst. of Archaeology ; a bibliography of his many writings was issued in 1933 to celebrate his 70th birthday ; died Paris, 12 Aug. 1938.

ASA. 39, 43 (Portr.) ; *Chron.* 14, 141 ; *JEA.* 24, 248.

BORELLI, (*Bey*) **Octave** (*fl.* 1884–1900)

Lawyer of Cairo ; elected to Inst. Ég., 1884 and resigned in 1900 when he finally left Egypt ; made communications to the Inst. ; he had a fine collection of Egyptian, Greek and Roman antiquities which he disposed of to an unknown buyer ; the collection was sold again at Hôtel Drouot, Paris, 11–13 June 1913, and was described in the catalogue as " provenant de l'ancienne collection Borelli-Bey appartenant à M. *X*."

Inst. Ég. Records.

BOREUX, Charles (1874–1944)

French Egyptologist ; entered the Louvre 1903 ; attaché, 1913 ; conservateur-adjoint, 1919 ; conservateur, 1926, in succession to Drioton appointed to Cairo ; rearranged and catalogued the Louvre Egyptian collections ; in 1939, supervised the removal of the collection to places of safety during the war ; retired 1940 ; died 3 April, 1944.

Chron. 19, 259.

BOTTA, Paul Émile (1802–1870)

French naturalist and archaeologist of Italian origin ; born Turin, 1802 ; adopted French nationality ; mainly known as an Assyriologist, but went to Egypt in 1831 and visited Sakkara with Bonomi and Linant ; French Vice-Consul at Mosûl, 1842 ; carried out excavations at Kuyunjik and Khorsabad until 1845 when he brought back the fine Assyrian sculptures now in the Louvre ; died 1870.

Bonomi Diary, 16 Jan. 1831 ; *Budge R & P*, 67 ; R. Campbell Thompson, *A Century of Exploration at Nineveh*, 23 ff.

BOTTI, Giuseppe (*d.* 1903)

Italian archaeologist of Alexandria ; carried out excavations there and was the founder and first Director of the Graeco-Egyptian Museum at Alexandria ; the project was set on foot in 1891, the buildings erected in 1895, and additional galleries provided in 1896, 1899 and 1904.

Breccia, *Alexandrea ad Ægyptum*, 2nd ed. (1914), 143–145 ; *Sayce*, 274 ; *E.E.F. Arch. Report*, 1894–5, 1.

BOUGHTON, (*Sir*) William Edward Rouse (1788–1856)

Traveller and antiquary ; born 14 Sept. 1788 ; succeeded as 10th Bart. of Lawford and 2nd Bart. of Rouse Lench, 1821 ; F.R.S., 1814 ; F.S.A. ; travelled in Egypt with Dr. John Lee, 1810 ; pub. *Some remarks on Eg. Papyri and the Inscription of Rosetta* in *Archaeologia*, 18 (1815), 59 ; died 22 May 1856.

Hartleben, i, 369 ; Pettigrew, *Hist. Eg. Mummies*, 139 ; Hartwell Museum *Cat. Eg. Antiquities* (1858), 48.

BOURGUIGNON D'ANVILLE, Jean Baptiste (1697–1782)

French cartographer ; published 211 maps, including one of Egypt (1766) in which he used the results of the journeys of Sicard (q.v.) in 1722 ; this map was used in the works of Sonnini, Pococke and Norden ; Membre de l'Acad. ; Sec. to Duke of Orleans ; pub. *Mémoire sur l'Ég. ancienne et moderne*, 1766.

Carré, i, 73 ; *Hilmy*, i, 84.

BOURIANT, Urbain (1849–1903)

French Egyptologist ; his interest in Egypt originated in a visit to the Louvre in 1876, and he immediately joined Maspero's classes where he remained until the end of 1880 ; an original member of the Mission Archéologique, Jan. 1881–June, 1883 ; asst. conservator Bulak Museum, 1883–6 ; Director of Miss. Arch., 1886–1898, when his health failed and he returned to Europe ; many of his publications relate to Theban tombs and to Coptic texts ; contributed to *Mem. Miss. Arch.*, *Rec. de Trav.*, and other journals ; died of apoplexy, 19 June 1903.

Rec. Trav. 26, 29–32 (Bibl.) ; *BIFAO*, 3, 213 ; *Hilmy*, i, 85.

BOURVILLE—*See* WATTIER DE BOURVILLE

BRADBURY, Kate—*See* GRIFFITH, K.

BRADISH, Luther (1783–1863)

American lawyer ; born Cummington, Mass., 15 Sept. 1783 ; admitted to the Bar, 1804 ; sent to Europe on a special mission to the Turkish Govt. concerning American trade ; after leaving Constantinople he travelled in Egypt, Palestine and Syria and various European countries till 1826 ; while in Eg. in 1821 he happened to visit Dendera at the time when Lelorrain was removing the Circular Zodiac ; he carried the news to Cairo and thereby caused many difficulties and obstacles, which were, however, successfully overcome ; died Newport, R.I., 30 Aug. 1863.

Lelorrain, 44, 48 ; *Henniker*, 329 ; *DAB*.

BREASTED, James Henry (1865–1935)

American Egyptologist and orientalist ; born Rockford, Ill., 27 Aug. 1865 ; educ. Yale and Berlin, where he was a pupil of Erman ; collaborated in the Berlin *Worterbuch* and visited European museums collating texts for the same ; frequently visited Egypt and Nubia and other countries in the Near East and inaugurated many archaeological projects ; held many important lecturerships and academic honours in Europe and America ; Professor of Egyptology and Director of the Oriental Institute at Chicago since 1919 ; of his many publications, the most important are his *Ancient Records of Egypt*, 5 vols. (1906) ; *History of Eg.* (1905) ; *Development of Religion and Thought* (1912) ; *The Edwin Smith Surgical Papyrus* (1930) ; died Chicago, 2 Dec. 1935.

JEA. 21, 249 ; *JRAS.* 1936, 179 ; *WWW.* iii, 155.

BREMNER, David (*d.* 1873)

Scottish lawyer ; trustee and executor of A. H. Rhind, whose Eg. collections were bequeathed to the Nat. Museum of Antiquities, Edinburgh (now in the Royal Scottish Museum) ; for some reason three of the papyri were not deposited with the main collection, and Bremner sold them to the B.M., in 1865. These were the Mathematical Papyrus (B.M. 10057–8), the Mathematical leather roll (10250), and the magico-mythological text (10188). To this latter the name of Bremner has been quite unjustifiably attached.

Inf. by C. Aldred.

BRIGGS, Samuel (1767–1853)

Merchant and banker of Alexandria ; partner in the house of Briggs, Schutz and Walmas ; acted as Proconsul in Egypt during vacancies ; very helpful to travellers in Egypt ; joined with Salt in financing Caviglia's explorations at the Pyramids ; Belzoni's last letter, dated Benin, 2 Dec. 1822, was addressed to him ; died, unmarried in 1853.

Belzoni, i, 211, 213, 216, 401 ; ii, 18, 142 ; *Salt*, ii, 111, 114, 115, 120 ; *Westcar Diary* ; *Letters and Dispatches of Nelson*, vi, 336–7, 341 ; *Vyse*, i, 197 ; *Richardson*, i, 52, 130 ; ii, 174 ; W. R. Wilson, *Travels in Egypt*, 19, 245.

BRINE, Charles (*d.* 1821)

English manufacturer in the service of Mohammad Ali ; introduced the manufacture of sugar into Egypt ; went to Raramûn in 1817 where he superintended the equipment of a factory on the model of those in the West Indies ; it came into production in 1818 ; helpful to travellers in Egypt and received Belzoni at his house in 1817 and 1818, and Irby and Mangles in 1818 ; the discovery of the famous " Tomb of the Colossus " at El Bershah is probably due to him as Irby and Mangles, who first record it, were on a visit to him at the time ; collected antiquities for Salt ; Brine met his death in mysterious circumstances and was apparently murdered by his Sicilian servant in Cairo.

Belzoni, i, 224 ; ii, 1 ; *Irby*, 48, 52 ; *Henniker*, 198–9 ; *Madox*, i, 262 ; *Bonomi Diary*, 1831, June 23 ; Waddington and Hanbury, *Journal of a visit to Ethiopia*, pref. iv, 154 ; *Sherer*, 135 ; Wilkinson, *Modern Eg. and Thebes*, ii, 63 ; *Richardson*, i, 178 ; ii, 130 ; Baroness Minutoli, *Recollections of Eg.* 98–9.

BROCKLEHURST, Marianne (*d.* 1898)

Of Bagstone Grange, Swythamley, Staffs. ; visited Egypt 1882–3, 1890–1 and 1895–6 ; made a considerable collection of antiquities which went at her death to Macclesfield Museum ; two papyri are called by her name, (1) the hieratic funerary papyrus of Djedptah-efonkh, from the royal cache, (2) a Book of the Dead used by Naville (*Todtb.* Ax) ; the latter is now in Sudeley Castle, Winchcombe ; died 22 Oct. 1898.

Edwards, *Thousand Miles*, passim (where she is referred to as " M.B.") ; *Wilbour*, 235, 586 ; *JEA.* 33, 75.

BRODRICK, Mary (*d.* 1933)

A friend of Amelia Edwards ; studied Egyptology in Paris under Maspero, 1888, and in England under R. S. Poole and Renouf ; student at Univ. Coll. London, 1888–1906 ; translated Mariette's *Aperçu* as *Outlines of Ancient Eg. History*, 1890 ; revised edition of Brugsch, *Egypt under the Pharaohs*, 1891 ; edited Murray's *Handbook for Egypt*, 1895 ; collaborated with Alice A. Morton in *A Concise Dictionary of Eg. Archaeology*, 1902 ; in 1924 founded the Mary Brodrick Prize for Geography at Univ. Coll. ; bequeathed part of her library to College Hall (the hostel for women students at U.C.) ; died 13 July 1933.

Wilbour, 564 ; *JEA.* 33, 86 ; *U.C. Records.*

BROWN, (*Sir*) **Robert Hanbury** (1849–1926)

Irrigation engineer ; born Brixton, 13 Jan. 1849 ; educ. R. Mil. Acad., Woolwich ; entered R.E., 1870 ; served in the Afghan War,

1879–80 ; Irrigation Dept., Bengal, 1873 ; Egyptian Irrigation Dept., 1884–1903 ; K.C.M.G., 1902 ; retired Major, 1903 ; wrote technical works on irrigation and was interested in the history of Lake Moeris and the Exodus ; pub. *The Fayum and Lake Moeris*, 1892, and works on the chronology of the Exodus ; died Crawley, Sussex, 4 May 1926.

WWW. ii, 134.

BROWNE, Alexander Henry (1845–1898)

Of Callaby Castle, Northumberland ; born 10 May 1845 ; Major, Northb. L.I. ; nephew and heir of William Henry Forman (q.v.) whose property he inherited, including a large collection of antiquities ; the antiquities were sold after Browne's death at Sotheby's, 19–22 June 1899, and the Forman Library, 3 July 1899 ; a privately printed Catalogue of the Forman Collection was issued by Browne in 1892 ; died 11 Apl. 1898.

Private inf.

BROWNE, William George (1768–1813)

Oriental traveller ; born 25 July 1768 ; B.A., Oxon., 1789 ; went to Egypt, 1792 and to Darfur, 1793–4 ; returned to England in 1798 and pub. account of his travels which was translated into French and German ; travelled in Turkey and the Levant, 1800–2 ; set out for Tartary in 1812, but was murdered on his way in Persia in 1813 ; his MS. journal, 1791–8, is in the B.M. (Add. MS. 6132).

DNB. 7, 76 ; *Hilmy*, i, 91.

BRUCE, (*Sir*) **Frederick William Adolphus** (1814–1867)

Diplomatist ; y. s. Thomas Bruce, 7th Earl of Elgin ; attached to Mission to Washington, 1842 ; Colonial Sec. at Hong Kong, 1844 ; Lieut.-Governor of Newfoundland, 1846 ; Chargé d'Affaires, Bolivia, 1848, and Uruguay, 1851 ; Consul-General in Egypt, Aug. 8, 1853–57 ; in Embassy in China, 1857–62 ; Envoy to Washington, 1865 ; K.C.B., 1862 ; died at Boston, 1867.

F.O. Records ; *DNB*. 7, 97 ; Rhind, *Thebes, its Tombs*, &c. 79*n*.

BRUCE, James (1730–1794)

Scottish traveller ; son of David B. of Kinnaird ; born Kinnaird, 14 Dec. 1730 ; ed. Harrow ; entered a wine merchant's office in Portugal 1753, but after his wife's early death abandoned commerce and took to travelling ; studied oriental languages and travelled extensively in N. Africa, where in spite of many difficulties he carried out archaeological and geographical researches ; arrived in Eg. in July 1768 ; visited Luxor and Karnak and cleared the tomb of Ramesses III at Biban el-Moluk, which is still called " Bruce's Tomb "; proceeded to the exploration of Abyssinia, where he made a prolonged stay ; returned to Aswân in Nov. 1772 and reached Britain in 1773 ; published his *Travels* in 1790 (and later editions) ; his name is associated with the Bruce Papyrus, a Gnostic text in Coptic, now in the Bodleian (*Bruce MS*. 96) ; died 27 April 1794.

DNB. 7, 98 ; *Hilmy*, i, 91.

BRUGSCH, (*Pasha*) **Emile** (1842–1930)

Younger brother of Heinrich B. ; born 1842 ; in early life had an adventurous career in many capacities ; went to Egypt in 1870 as assistant to his brother when conducting his short-lived school of Egyptology in Cairo ; afterwards assistant to Mariette ; asst. conservator, Bulak and Cairo Museums, under Maspero in 1881 and so remained until his resignation after 45 years' service in 1914 ; was a skilful lithographer, and made the plates for Mariette's *Papyrus de Boulaq* ; was also an excellent photographer and made most of the plates for the *Cat. Gen.* of the Cairo Museum ; first entered the tomb of the Royal Mummies in 1881 in the absence of Maspero ; was made successively Bey and Pasha by the Khedive ; retired to Nice, where he died 14 Jan. 1930.

Cahiers, 3, pt. 1, 35 (Portr.) ; *JEA*. 33, 70 ; *Petrie*, index ; *Erman*, 213 ; H. Brugsch, *Mein Leben*, 225, 331.

BRUGSCH, (*Pasha*) **Karl Heinrich** (1827–1894)

German Egyptologist ; born Berlin 18 Feb. 1827 ; studied Egyptology at an early age ; after visiting the museums of Europe he was sent to Egypt by the Prussian Govt. in 1853 and formed a close friendship with Mariette ; sent to Persia on a special mission under Baron von Minutoli, 1860, and after M.'s death was acting ambassador ; German Consul in Cairo, 1864 ; after trying to find employment in Paris, was appointed Prof. of Egyptology at Göttingen, 1868 ; in 1870 was made Bey by the Khedive and directed the School of Egyptology in Cairo founded by the Khedive until its closure in 1879 ; Pasha, 1881 ; for the latter part of his life he remained chiefly in Germany, paying occasional visits to Egypt ; Brugsch's contributions to Egyptology are enormous : he was a pioneer in demotic and published a Demotic Grammar as early as 1855 ; his largest works were his hieroglyphic dictionary (7 vols., 1867–82), his geographical works (1857–1879) and his History of Egypt ; founded *ZÄS* in 1864 ; died 9 Sept. 1894.

Autobiogr. *Mein Leben und mein Wandern*, 1893 ; *ZÄS*. 32, 69–73 ; *JRAS*. 1895, 457 ; *Hilmy*, i, 93–100 ; ii, 383.

BRUNNER, (*Sir*) **John Tomlinson** (1842–1919)

Chemist ; born Everton, Liverpool, 8 Feb. 1842 ; with Dr. Ludwig Mond, F.R.S., founded the firm of Brunner, Mond & Co. Ltd. and the great chemical works at Northwich ; a benefactor of Liverpool University, in which he endowed three chairs, one of them being the Brunner Professorship of Egyptology of which the first holder was P. E. Newberry, appointed 1906 ; founded several public libraries and other institutions ; Hon. LL.D. ; created Baronet, 1895 ; died 1 July, 1919.

WWW. ii, 140.

BRUNTON, Guy (1878–1948)

Egyptologist and excavator ; his interest began as a boy and he afterwards frequented the Edwards Library at Univ. Coll. to consult books and study Egyptology seriously ; at the age of 18 he went to S. Africa for several years, where he married Miss Winifred Newbery, herself interested in archaeology, a skilful artist and his constant companion and collaborator in Egypt ; returned to London in 1911 and after two years of study at Univ. Coll. took part in Petrie's excavations at El Lahun, where he discovered the famous 12th Dyn. jewellery ; after military service, 1914–18, he worked again at El Lahun, 1919–21 and afterwards with Miss Caton Thompson at Kaw and Badari ; he wrote or contributed to several excavation memoirs and pub. many papers in *ASA* and other journals ; Asst. Keeper, Cairo Museum, 1931 ; retired in Mar. 1948 to S. Africa, where he died at White River, Transvaal, 17 Oct. 1948.

ASA. 49, 95 ; *E.E.S. Ann. Rep*. 1948, 6 ; *Petrie*, 232, 240, 242, 250, 254.

BRYCE, William Moir (1842–1919)

Scottish archivist ; born Edinburgh, 1842 ; on staff of Register House, Edinburgh ; joined a firm of professional record-searchers ; interested in Scottish history and wrote on local antiquities ; went to Egypt with Sayce, 1902–3 ; made a small collection of Egyptian antiquities which was sold after his death ; LL.D., Edinb. ; a hieratic tablet from his collection was pub. by Griffith, *PSBA*. 30, 272 ; died 2 Aug. 1919.

Sayce, 316, 461 ; *Inf. by C. Aldred*.

BUCKINGHAM, James Silk (1786–1855)

Author and traveller ; born 25 Aug. 1786 ; travelled in India and America, in Syria, Palestine and Egypt ; M.P. for Sheffield, 1832–7 ; published his travels in the East (1825) and various articles, and lectured on Egypt ; one of the founders of the Syro-Egyptian Society (1844), and contributed to its publications ; gave public lectures on Egyptian archaeology ; died 30 June 1855.

DNB. 7, 202 ; *Hilmy*, i, 103.

BUDGE, (*Sir*) Ernest Alfred Wallis (1857–1934)

Orientalist ; born 27 July, 1857 ; Christ's Coll. Cantab. ; Assyrian Scholar ; Hebrew Prizeman ; Tyrwhitt Hebrew Scholar ; M.A. ; Litt.D. ; D.Litt. ; D.Lit. ; F.S.A. ; Knight, 1920 ; Keeper of Egyptian and Assyrian Antiquities, B.M., 1893–1924 ; formerly assistant in the Dept. ; went to Egypt, the Sudan and Mesopotamia many times to obtain antiquities for the B.M. ; he had great success in his dealings with the natives and in overcoming official obstruction, and obtained for the B.M. many thousands of cuneiform tablets and other Assyrian and Babylonian antiquities, and countless Egyptian sculptures, papyri and smaller objects ; he also procured large numbers of Coptic, Syriac, Arabic, Ethiopic and other oriental MSS., as well as many highly important Greek papyri ; Budge's published output is the largest and most astonishing of any single orientalist : he edited Cuneiform, Hieroglyphic, Coptic, Syriac and Ethiopic MSS., many official publications of papyri and monuments, and a great number of popular or semi-popular works in all these fields ; he compiled an Egyptian Dictionary, a full edition of the Book of the Dead and other Egyptian texts ; in hieroglyphic scholarship his standard was not a high one, for he refused to keep abreast of modern philological development and obstinately adhered to obsolete methods : by his rapidity of working, many mistakes and inaccuracies occur in his published texts ; nevertheless, with all their faults, his numerous books have been of value to students, and above all he enormously enriched the B.M. collections ; Budge married in 1883, Dora Helen, d. Rev. Titus Emerson ; Lady Budge died in 1926, and in her memory he founded by his will an Egyptological studentship at University Coll. Oxon., and Christ's Coll. Cambridge, which bear her name ; he left his library to Christ's Coll. ; died 23 Nov. 1934.

JEA. 21, 68 (Portr.) ; *WWW*. iii, 185 (list of works) ; his book *By Nile and Tigris* (2 vols., 1920) is mainly autobiographical ; *DNB*. 1931–40, 121.

BUNSEN, (*Baron von*) **Christian Karl Josias** (1791–1860)

Prussian scholar and diplomatist ; born Korbach 25 Aug. 1791 ; educ. Marburg and Göttingen universities ; studied Hebrew and Arabic at Munich ; Prussian Ambassador in London, 1841–54 ; wrote much on philosophy and biblical subjects, provoking considerable controversy, but his name is known in Egyptology by his great work *Ægyptens Stelle in der Weltgeschichte*, 6 vols., 1844–57, translated into English as *Egypt's Place in Universal History*, 5 vols., 1844–57 ; the last volume was written almost entirely by Samuel Birch, and contains his Egyptian Grammar and Dictionary ; died 28 Nov. 1860.

E.B. ; *Hilmy*, i, 105 ; Brugsch, *Mein Leben*, 46.

BURCKHARDT, John Lewis (1784–1817)

Traveller ; born Lausanne, 24 Nov. 1784 ; of Swiss origin ; educ. Leipsic and Göttingen ; came to England 1806 and studied Arabic at Cambridge ; travelled extensively in the East ; in Egypt, 1814–17 ; full accounts of his travels have been published ; died Cairo 15 Oct. 1817 ; under his will 800 vols. of oriental MSS. were bequeathed to Cambridge University ; travelled under the name of Sheikh Ibrahim.

DNB. 7, 292 ; *EB*. ; *Salt*, i, 489 ; ii, 3, 39, 141 ; *Richardson*, i, 53, 161, 428 ; *Hilmy*, i, 105 ; *B.M. Add. MSS*. 30239, 30240A ; *Sherer*, 105, 175 ; Cailliaud, ed. Jomard, *Travels in the Oasis of Thebes*, 36.

BURGON, Thomas (1787–1858)

Smyrna Merchant ; born 1787 ; his son, John William, afterwards Dean of Chichester, was his clerk ; failed in business about 1841 ; after his failure, Burgon, who was an able numismatist, sought employment in the B.M., but his application was opposed by the Archbishop of Canterbury ; eventually, however, through the advocacy of Samuel Rogers and Lord Lyndhurst, he was made a supernumerary assistant in Department of Antiquities (which then included Coins and Medals, not yet a separate department) ; died 1858, and his library was sold at Sotheby's, 22 Dec. of that year ; a hieratic papyrus was acquired by the B.M. (10045).

P. W. Clayden, *Samuel Rogers and his Contemporaries*, ii, 240 ; Pettigrew, *Hist. Eg. Mummies*, 111.

BURTON, Harry (1879–1940)

American archaeologist and photographer; took part in the excavations of Theodore Davis at Thebes; in 1914 joined the Egyptian Expedition of the Metropolitan Museum of Art, New York, as photographer: made photographic records of the excavations and also of many of the private tombs at Thebes; in 1923 his services were lent to Lord Carnarvon and Howard Carter, and he took all the very numerous photographs of the contents of the Tomb of Tutankhamen; nearly 1,000 negatives are now in the Griffith Institute, Oxford; in April 1940, he was taken ill whilst working at Luxor and died in the American Hospital at Assiut, 27 June.

Bull. M.M.A. Jan. 1916, 13; May 1916, 102; Aug. 1940; *Chron.* 21, 207; *Newberry Corr.*

BURTON, James (1788–1862)

Traveller; son of James Haliburton, of Mabledon, Tonbridge, Kent, changed his name by licence to Burton; born 1788; T.C.C.; B.A., 1810; M.A., 1815; took part in the Geological Survey of Egypt made for Mohammad Ali in 1822; in 1824 joined Robert Hay and Wilkinson; went up the Nile with Edward William Lane in 1825; pub. *Excerpta Hieroglyphica,* 64 plates without letterpress, 1825–8, assisted by Bonomi; returned to England but in 1830–5 visited Egypt again; in 1838 he resumed the name of Haliburton, and after his final return to England devoted much time to genealogical research into his own family; when in Egypt, Burton made a large collection of valuable drawings and plans of monuments, copies of inscriptions and notes which were presented after his death to the B.M. by his younger brother, Decimus Burton, the architect; these are bound up in 63 volumes (Add. MSS. 25613–25675); he also made a large collection of antiquities which was sold at Sotheby's, 25–27 July, 1836 (420 lots), and many lots were bought by the B.M., including the well-known Papyrus of Nebseni (9900), the basis-text in Naville's *Todtenbuch*; Burton died 22 Feb. 1862 and was buried in West Dean Cemetery, Edinburgh, with the epitaph: " A zealous investigator in Egypt of its language and antiquities."

DNB. 24, 43; *Hay Diary*; *Bonomi Diary*; *Hilmy,* i, 108–111; *Proc. R. Geogr. Soc.* 4, 102.

BUTLER, (*Rev.*) **George** (1774–1853)

Schoolmaster and antiquary; born 1774; Sidney Sussex Coll. Cantab., B.A., 1794; M.A., 1797; D.D., 1805; headmaster of Harrow School, 1805–29; Chancellor, 1836, and Dean, 1842, of Peterborough; a friend of Thomas Young under whom he studied hieroglyphs and interested some of his pupils, at Harrow, amongst whom was (Sir) J. Gardner Wilkinson; died 1853.

DNB. 8, 49; Nichols, *Lit. Anecd.* ix, 223; *Dawson M.S.* 18, f. 132.

BUTLER, (*Rev.*) **Samuel** (1774–1839)

Schoolmaster and Bishop; born 30 Jan. 1774; educ. Rugby and St. John's Coll. Cantab.; B.A., 1796; Fellow, 1797; D.D., 1811; headmaster of Shrewsbury School, 1798–1836; Bishop of Lichfield,

1836–9 ; had a fine library and collection of Greek, Latin, Hebrew and other oriental MSS. ; the printed books were sold in two parts 23 Mar. and 1 June, 1840, but the MSS. were withdrawn and sold *en bloc* to the B.M. (Add. MSS. 11828–12117) ; among the MSS. were four papyri acquired at the Salt sale of 1835, the best known of which is the *Butler Papyrus*, containing the beginning of the Story of the Eloquent Peasant (B.M. 10274), the others being a Ramesside hieratic document (10333) and two demotic documents (10230, 10400) ; Butler died 4 Dec. 1839.

DNB. 8, 76 ; S. de Ricci, *English Collectors of Books and Manuscripts*, 114.

CADET, Jean Marc (1751–1835)

Usually called Cadet de Metz ; born Metz, 4 Sept. 1751 ; Délégué Général ; Inspector of Mines in Corsica ; his name is attached to the Papyrus Cadet which he owned and published : *Copie figurée d'un Rouleau de Papyrus trouvê á Thèbes dans un Tombeau des Rois, accompagnée d'une notice descriptive*, 18 plates, Paris, 1805 ; an essay on this papyrus was published by Alexandre Lenoir ; it is not from a royal tomb, but is a Ptolemaic Book of the Dead—the first to be published : it is now in the Bibliothèque Nationale (Cartons 1–19) ; Cadet died at Strasbourg, Sept. 1835.

CAILLIAUD, Frédéric (1787–1869)

French traveller and mineralogist ; born Nantes, 1787 ; studied mineralogy in Paris, 1809 ; travelled in Holland, Italy, Sicily, Greece and Asia Minor ; left Constantinople for Egypt, 1815, where he was employed by Mohammad Ali to find the emerald-mines described by the Arabic historians ; visited Upper Egypt and Nubia as far as Wady Halfa with Drovetti ; explored the routes to the Red Sea and discovered the quarries and the ruins of Coptos ; after returning to Paris, he revisited Egypt in 1819 and explored the Oases, and in 1821 ascended the Nile as far as Meroë ; returned to France in 1822 with a collection of more than 500 objects ; Croix de la Légion d'Honneur, 1824 ; pub. at the expense of the French Govt., *Voyage à l'Oasis de Thèbes*, 2 vols. 1822–4 ; *Voyage à l'Oasis du Syouah*, 1823, and *Voyage à Méroê*, 1823–7, text 4 vols., plates 3 vols. ; in the preparation of these works he was assisted by Jomard ; died 1869.

Carré, i, 221 ; Budge, *Eg. Sudan*, i, 38–54 ; *Journ. des Savants*, 1935, 176 ; *Belzoni*, i, 173, 385 ; ii, 7, 20–33, and often ; *Irby*, 5, 41 ; *Hilmy*, i, 113 ; *Athanasi*, 28–9, 33, 105–7 (there called " Calliot ").

CALICE, (*Graf von*) **Franz** (1875–1935)

Austrian diplomat and Egyptologist ; D.Jur., Vienna ; held various diplomatic appointments and at the time of his retirement was Ambassador at Budapest ; all his life Egyptology had been his principal interest and in his retirement he studied at Vienna, but before he could complete his thesis, he was killed in a motor accident ; he contributed articles, mainly grammatical, to *ZÄS* and *WZKM* ; died 1935.

Inf. by Dr. E. Komorzynski.

CALVERT, Henry Hunter (1816–1882)

British Vice-Consul at Alexandria, 1856–82; member of Inst. Égyptien; died 29 July 1882.

Lord Cromer, *Modern Egypt*, i, 142; *Bull. Inst. Ég.* 2nd Ser. iii, 77 (1883).

CAMPBELL (*Sir*) **Archibald Campbell** (afterwards Lord Blythswood) (1837–1908)

Army officer and astronomer; born 22 Feb. 1837; entered the Army and attained the rank of Colonel, Scots Guards; served in the Crimea and was wounded; created Baronet, 1880; Baron Blythswood, 1892; F.R.S.; F.R.A.S., LL.D., M.P. 1873–4, 1885–92; much interested in political and military questions, also a physicist and astronomer; visited Egypt in 1874 to observe the transit of Venus and recorded his results in the *Monthly Notes* of the R.A.S.; while in Egypt, bought the funerary papyrus of Pinodjem I, from the royal cache, for £400 (*see* Wardi, A.); died at his seat in Renfrewshire, 8 July 1908.

WWW. i, 72; Maspero, *Momies Royales,* 512; *Chabas,* 147.

CAMPBELL, (*Rev.*) **Colin** (1848–1931)

Scottish Minister; born Campbelltown, Argyllsh., 1848; educ. Glasgow Univ.; M.A.; D.D.; minister of Dundee from 1882; chaplain to Queen Victoria; published works on the Gospels; visited Egypt several times and pub. several popular works on the Theban tombs; translated Naville's Lectures on Eg. religion; formed a collection of Eg. antiquities, including many cones and ostraca, which are now in the Hunterian Museum, Glasgow, the Royal Scottish Museum, Edinburgh, and the Dundee Museum; in 1909 he described a sarcophagus belonging to the Duke of Hamilton, which is now in the Kelvingrove Museum, Glasgow; died 20 June 1931.

WWW. iii, 212.

CAMPBELL, Patrick (1779–1857)

Army officer and diplomatist; born Duntroon, 1779; entered the Army and attained the rank of Lieut.-Col., Royal Artillery, 1815; Secretary to the British Legation in Colombia; Consul-General in Egypt in succession to John Barker (q.v.) 1833; retired 1840; associated with Col. Howard-Vyse in the exploration of the Pyramids, 1837; his name is attached to Campbell's Tomb, a large hypogeum of Dyn. 26 at Gizeh, discovered by Howard-Vyse, and with one of the construction-chambers of the Great Pyramid.

F.O. Records; *Vyse,* passim; *Lindsay,* 22, 23, 39.

CAPART, Jean (1877–1947)

Belgian Egyptologist; born 1877; educ. Brussels University; studied Egyptology under Wiedemann at Bonn; entered the service of the Musées Royaux du Cinquantenaire, Brussels, in 1900 and rose to be Director; under his régime the organization of the museum was greatly improved and many important acquisitions made; frequently visited Egypt, his last excavations being at El Kab in

1937 ; a man of great energy and initiative, in addition to his scientific publications, he contributed largely to the popular press and gave public lectures which did much to create and stimulate interest in Egyptology not only in Belgium, but in the many other countries he visited, notably England and U.S.A. ; he specialized on Egyptian art and pub. many important works thereon ; in 1923 he conducted the Queen of the Belgians on a visit to Egypt and the Tomb of Tutankhamen, and so stimulated her interest that the Fondation Égyptologique Reine Elisabeth was at once established and has become an important centre of research, and under its auspices many important publications have appeared including the journal, *Chronique d'Égypte*, for which Capart secured continuity of publication even during the German occupation of Belgium ; in addition to the direction of the Museum, Capart was a Professor at the Univ. of Liége and a Vice-Pres. E.E.S. ; died at Brussels, 16 June 1947.

Chron. 22, 181–215 (Portr.) ; *JEA*. 33, 2.

CAPPER, James (1743–1825)

Colonel in H.E.I.C. Service ; born 15 Dec. 1743 ; traveller and meteorologist ; travelled from Egypt to India, 1779 ; pub. *Observations on the Passage to India through Egypt*, 1783, trans. into French and German ; died 13 Sept. 1825.

DNB. 9, 25 ; *Hilmy*, i, 119 ; *Valentia*, iii, 275.

CARAMAN, (*Comte de*) **Frédéric Adolphe de Riquet** (1800–1841+)

French traveller ; born Berlin, 1800 ; travelled in Italy, Ionian Islands, Asia Minor, Turkey and Greece, 1828–9 ; in Egypt and Nubia, as far as Abu Simbel, 1832–3 ; in Syria and Palestine, 1837–8 ; the MS. journals of these travels are in the B.M. (Add. MSS. 34197–9), 34198 being devoted to Egypt and Nubia ; it contains a number of plans of temples, etc., e.g. Kom Ombo (f. 41), El Kab (f. 44) and the Palace at Karnak (f. 49) ; not traced after 1841.

Bull. Soc. Géogr. Paris, Ser. 2, 13, 321 ; 15, 5 ; *Cat. Add. MSS.* B.M. 1888–93, 233.

CARMICHAEL, (*Sir*) **Thomas David Gibson, 1st Baron** (1859–1926)

Born Edinburgh 18 Mar. 1859 ; succeeded as 14th Bart., 1891 ; created Baron Carmichael of Skirling, 1912 ; St. John's Coll. Cantab. ; M.A. ; D.L. ; K.C.M.G. ; politician and statesman ; formed a collection of antiquities sold at Sotheby's, 8–10 June 1926, Eg. ant. lots 179–294, many of which came from the Hilton Price Collection ; died 16 Jan. 1926.

WWW. ii, 174 ; *Newberry Corresp.*

CARNARVON, Earl of—*See* HERBERT

CARNE, (*Rev.*) **John** (1789–1844)

Traveller and author ; born 18 June 1789 ; Queen's Coll. Cantab. ; ordained 1826 ; travelled in Greece, Egypt and Palestine ; pub. *Letters from the East*, 2 vols., 1826 and *Recollections of Travels in the East*, 2 vols., 1830 ; died 2 Feb. 1844.

DNB. 9, 135 ; *Hilmy*, i, 120.

CARTER, Howard (1873–1939)

Artist and Egyptologist ; son of Samuel John Carter, animal painter ; born Swaffham, Norfolk, 1873 ; educated privately ; on the recommendation of Lady Amherst, he joined the staff of the Arch. Survey under Newberry in 1891 ; excavated for Lord Amherst at Amarna under the supervision of Petrie, 1892, and was appointed draughtsman to the Arch. Survey ; for six years he worked under Naville at Deir el-Bahri and copied all the scenes and inscriptions of the temple which fill 6 folio volumes ; Inspector of Monuments of Upper Eg. under the Service des Antiquités, 1899 ; from 1902 supervised the excavations of Theodore Davis in the Valley of the Kings and made many important discoveries ; in 1907, Lord Carnarvon began his excavations in Egypt, and under Carter's supervision, they were very fruitful, and the results of the first five years' work were published in a sumptuous volume ; after the War, the winters of 1919 to 1922 were spent in the Valley of the Kings, culminating in the discovery of the tomb of Tutankhamen in Nov. 1922 ; this, the greatest archaeological discovery ever made in Egypt, produced objects of surpassing beauty and value which were made known by the press throughout the world, and described by Carter in 3 volumes ; the clearance of the tomb, the packing and removal of its contents, took Carter and a staff of expert helpers ten years to complete ; the records of this tomb together with all Carter's diaries and papers, are preserved in the Griffith Inst., Oxford ; during the last years of his life, Carter suffered much ill-health, and died in London, 2 Mar. 1939.

WWW. iii, 228 ; *JEA*. 25, 67 ; *ASA*. 39, 49 (Portr.) ; *Newberry Corresp.* ; *DNB*. 1931–40, 151.

CARTER, Owen Browne (1806–1859)

Architect, practising at Winchester ; visited Egypt 1830–1 when he was employed by Robert Hay to make drawings, plans and sections of Eg. temples ; pub. *Views taken at Cairo in* 1830, London, 1840 ; exhibited architectural drawings in R.A., 1847–9 ; died 30 Mar. 1859.

DNB. 9, 205 ; *Bonomi Diary*, 17 Aug. 1831.

CASTELLARI, Luigi (*fl.* 1840–1860)

Italian dealer in antiquities ; well-known in Luxor in the middle of the 19th cent., where he dwelt in a hut on the roof of the temple ; he had great power over the native diggers, many of whose finds he appropriated and sold to tourists ; many important objects passed through his hands, including the Hypereides Papyri which he sold to A. C. Harris and Joseph Arden, and the coffin of Princess Ahmose Hontempet.

Romer, i, 148, 280 ; *JEA*. 35, 162–3 ; *L.D., Text*, i, 222.

CASTIGLIONE, Carlo Ottavio (1784–1849)

Italian orientalist of Milan ; lived for many years in Cairo and Alexandria ; his Egyptian collections were acquired by the Russian Acad. of Sciences in 1826 and transferred to the Hermitage in 1862.

EB. ; Golenischeff, *Coll. Ég. Erm.* p. v.

CATHERWOOD, Frederic (*d.* 1856)

Traveller and artist ; visited Egypt with Henry Westcar, 1823–4 ; visited the Oasis with Hay and Hoskins, 1832 ; Syria and Palestine with Bonomi, 1833–4 ; made many drawings and notes, some of which are in the Hay MSS. ; made drawings of the Temple of Karnak from which a painting was made and exhibited in London in 1833 and a description of it pub. by Robert Burford ; his library was sold at Sotheby's, 1 Dec. 1856.

Westcar Diary ; Bonomi Diary ; *Madox*, ii, 28, 34 ; Hoskins, *Oasis*, 22 ; *Add. MSS.* 29831 ; 38094, f. 75–91 ; 95, 107, 184–6.

CATTAUI, (*Bey*) **Adolphe** (1865–1925)

Administrator and geographer ; born Cairo 1 Jan. 1865 ; educ. Paris, Lycée Condorcet and École des Hautes Études ; studied Egyptology under Revillout ; sent on a mission to Egypt, 1886 ; settled permanently in Egypt, 1888 ; an official in the financial administration ; reorganized the Soc. Roy. de Géographie d'Égypte of which he was secretary, 1918–25 ; published a few Egyptological papers ; three important papyri bear his name : (1) a long funerary text, now in the Louvre, (2) a Greek judicial papyrus ed. by Botti and by Grenfell and Hunt, now in Alexandria Museum, (3) a surgical text in Greek ; died Cairo, 11 June 1925.

Bull. Soc. Roy. Géogr. d'Ég. 13 (1925), (Portr.).

CAULFIELD, Algernon Thomas St. George (1869–1933)

Born 31 July 1869 ; educ. Eton and Cambridge ; prospected in Mashonaland, 1890–3 ; employed by Board of Agriculture, 1894 ; succeeded to his paternal estate in Donamon, Ireland, 1896 ; J.P. ; High Sheriff of Roscommon, 1900 ; D.L. ; went to Egypt, 1901–2 and worked for Petrie on the Temple of Abydos ; pub. report thereon, *The Temple of the Kings*, for the Eg. Research Account ; died 4 July 1933.

WWW. iii, 231 ; *Petrie*, 180.

CAVIGLIA, Giovanni Battista (1770–1845)

Genoese mariner, owner and master of a trading vessel in the Mediterranean ; his usual home-port being in Malta, he regarded himself as a British subject ; he was employed by Salt and others to excavate the Great Sphinx ; he also explored the Pyramids and neighbouring necropolis, 1816–19 ; on subsequent visits to Egypt he made further explorations of the Pyramids and worked for a time for Col. Howard-Vyse, but the arrangement terminated at the end of 1836 ; Caviglia was a man of energy and enterprise and an ingenious excavator ; he elicited new information concerning the interior of the Gt. Pyramid, he discovered the steps ascending the Sphinx and the pavement between its paws ; he also discovered the colossus of Ramesses II at Mît Rahîneh ; Salt sent him to Italy when Champollion was there to beg him to come to Egypt ; he was a deeply religious man, well versed in the Bible, which he constantly read and quoted ; he was also given to occultism and mysticism ; he retired to Paris early in 1837, and lived there as a protégé of

Lord Elgin ; died in the Faubourg St. Germain, Paris, 7 Sept. 1845. He presented a number of Eg. antiquities to the B.M., 1814–17.

QR. 19, 395 ; *Salt,* passim (see index) ; *Vyse,* i, passim ; ii, 152–176, 288–294 ; *Belzoni,* i, 213–7, 396 ; *Lindsay,* 40–46, 52 ; *Champollion,* i, 393 ; ii, 98, 101, 105, 114, 122 ; also frequently mentioned in contemporary diaries and books of travel.

CAYLUS, (*Comte de*) **Anne Claude Philippe de Tubières de Grimoard de Pestels de Lévis** (1692–1765)

French archaeologist and collector of antiquities ; born Paris, 31 Oct. 1692 ; a patron of art and a prominent figure in the social life of Paris ; travelled extensively in Italy, Greece, and the Near East ; formed a great collection of antiquities which was housed in large galleries in his mansion, and pub. in 7 vols., Paris, 1752–60, *Recueil d'Antiquités Égyptiennes, Etrusques, Grecques et Romaines* ; he was a Membre de l'Acad., to which he made many contributions ; died, Paris, 1765.

EB. ; Nisard, *Correspondance du Comte de Caylus,* 1877 ; *Mem. Inst. Ég.* 13, 12.

CECIL, Lady William—*See* AMHERST, Baroness

CHABAS, François Joseph (1817–1882)

French Egyptologist ; born 2 Jan. 1817 ; a wine-merchant by profession, he spent all his life at Chalon-sur-Saône engaged in his business, but devoted his leisure to study ; in 1852 he took up the study of Egyptology under the guidance of de Rougé and made rapid progress ; he corresponded regularly with Birch, Hincks, Goodwin, Mariette, Lepsius, Brugsch and other Egyptologists, and although working in a provincial town far from museums and libraries, his colleagues kept him well supplied with material ; he made many publications of great value in their day, notably his editions of the papyri *Harris Magical, Anastasi I* and *Sallier IV* ; he visited the museums of Italy, but never went to Egypt ; the list of his publications is a long one, and Maspero collected all his smaller works in 4 vols. in the *Bibl. Ég.* 9–12 ; died at Versailles in 1882 ; his valuable scientific correspondence is in the library of the Institut de France.

F. Chabas and P. Virey, *Notice Biogr. de François Joseph Chabas, Bibl. Ég.* 9 (also pub. separately, 1898) (Portr.) ; *Goodwin,* passim ; *Hilmy,* i. 122.

CHAMPOLLION, Jean François (1790–1832)

The Founder of Egyptology ; commonly called Champollion le Jeune ; born Figeac (Lot), 23 Dec. 1790 ; educ. by his brother and at the Lyceum, Grenoble ; at the age of 16 he read a paper before the Grenoble Acad. maintaining that Coptic was the ancient language of Egypt ; made rapid progress with the decipherment of hieroglyphic writing, and on 27 Sept. 1822 he read before the Acad. des Inscr. his celebrated *Lettre à M. Dacier relative à l'alphabet des Hiéroglyphes phonetiques,* which is the foundation-stone of Egyptian philology and archaeology ; was sent on a mission to visit the Museums of Turin, Leghorn, Rome and Naples, 1824 ; conducted a scientific expedition to Egypt with Rosellini, 1828–9; appointed to a chair of Egyptian archaeology at the Coll. de France, 1831; whilst still busily engaged in the study of hieroglyphic texts and in preparing for publication the results of his expedition, he was seized by a stroke, and died in Paris, 1832; he published a fuller statement on the decipherment of hieroglyphs in his *Précis du Système hiéroglyphique*, 1824 (2nd ed. 1828), but most of his works were posthumously published by his brother; although he had the support of many learned and influential men, Champollion had many opponents and detractors, and his life was embittered by the constant intrigues and obstacles with which he was faced.

The centenary of the publication of the *Lettre à M. Dacier* was marked by a celebration by the Univ. of Grenoble which was attended by Egyptologists from all countries, and a volume of studies with 45 contributors, was issued in 1922 to commemorate the event.

The rival claims of Thomas Young and his supporters have given rise to a vast literature.

Biographical notices of Champollion, of varying merit, are almost innumerable, but the authoritative work is H. Hartleben, *Champollion, sein Leben und sein Werke*, 2 vols., 1906, and *Lettres de Champollion*, edited by Hartleben, 2 vols., Paris, 1909 (*Bibl. Ég.* t. 21, 22); for a very complete bibliography of Champollion, see Seymour de Ricci, in *Rec. Champollion*, 763–784; and for the history of his decipherment, see Erman, *Die Entzifferung der Hieroglyphen*, in *Sitzungsb. Berlin Akad.*, 1922; J. Capart, *Le Centenaire du Déchiffrement des Hiéroglyphes par Champollion*, in *Bull. Acad. Roy. de Belgique*, No. 5, 1922; Renouf, *Young and Champollion*, *PSBA*. 19, 188–209; *JEA*. 37, 38–46.

CHAMPOLLION-FIGEAC, Aimé (1812–1894)

Son of J. J. Champollion-Figeac, and his assistant at the Bibliothèque Nationale; born Dec. 1812; author of historical works; he compiled a biographical and bibliographical study of his family in *Les Deux Champollion*, Grenoble, 1887; died 20 Mar. 1894.

CHAMPOLLION-FIGEAC, Jacques Joseph (1778–1867)

Elder brother of Jean François Ch.; born Figeac, 5 Oct. 1778; Professor of Greek and Librarian of Grenoble; afterwards Keeper of MSS. at the Bibliothèque Nat., Paris; was always his brother's mentor and guardian and edited his works after his death.

His life is so bound up with that of his brother, that to a great extent the life of one is the life of the other. See the references to J. F. Champollion.

CHASSINAT, Émile Gaston (1868–1948)

French Egyptologist; studied under Maspero and the Marquis de Rochemonteix whose work on the Temple of Edfu he continued and completed, Maspero having handed over the material to him after R.'s death; this great publication appeared in parts from 1892 to 1934, making 14 vols.; his publication on the Temple of Dendereh has reached 4 vols. (1934–5), but there is material for many more; succeeded Bouriant as Director of the Inst. Fr. d'Arch. Orientale in 1898 and held the post for 13 years, during which the activities of the Inst. were greatly extended, the printing-press being inaugurated in 1898, the *Bulletin* in 1900 and the *Bibl. d'Étude* in 1908 ; under his direction also the Inst. undertook excavations on a large scale, at Abu Roash, Meir, Assiut and other sites, and from 1906 in the Theban Necropolis ; contributed much to journals, etc. ; in Coptic his most important work was his edition of the Medical Papyrus of Mashaykh, 1921 ; died 26 May 1948.

Chron. 24, 95 ; *Bull. Soc. d'Arch. Copte,* 13, 197–203 (Bibl.) ; *Mél. Maspero,* p. xxiii.

CHERUBINI, Salvatore, (1797–1869)

Italian artist ; son of the famous composer Cherubini ; accompanied Rosellini and Champollion to Egypt, 1828 ; naturalized French ; he was brother-in-law of Rosellini who in 1827 married his sister Zenobia ; on his return from Egypt, he was appointed Inspecteur des Beaux Arts.

Bellaris, *Cherubini,* 1874 ; *Champollion,* ii, p. vi, 10.

CHESTER, (*Rev.*) **Greville John** (1831–1892)

Youngest son of William Chester, of Denton, Norfolk ; born 1831 ; Balliol Coll. Oxon. ; B.A. 1853 ; Perpetual Curate of St. Jude's, Moorfields, Sheffield, from 1858 ; owing to ill-health, Chester wintered abroad for many years, chiefly in Egypt, Syria and Palestine ; he collected many antiquities, including Coptic MSS. and Greek and Egyptian papyri, most of which were bought by the B.M. and the Bodleian ; he also collected for the South Kensington (now Victoria and Albert), Ashmolean, and other museums ; in 1865 he presented an altar inscribed with Meroitic to the B.M. (901) and in 1880 a fine stela of the Old Kingdom (1011) ; he was a skilful buyer of antiquities and was held in great respect by native dealers ; he obtained many finger-rings and gems for Sir Woolaston Franks ; contributed articles on Egyptology to the *Academy* and a catalogue of the Eg. collection of the Ashmolean Museum, 1881 ; died of angina pectoris 23 May 1892.

Budge N & T. i, 84 ; *Wilbour,* 215 ; *Petrie,* 22, 53, 77.

CHOISEUL-GOUFFIER, Marie Gabriel Florent Auguste (1752–1817)

French diplomatist and scholar ; born Paris 27 Sept. 1752 ; Ambassador at Constantinople ; travelled much in Greece and pub. *Voyages dans la Grèce* ; he formed a large collection of antiquities and made many communications to the Acad. des Inscriptions ; some of his MSS. are in the Bibliothèque Nationale (MSS. Fr. 7558) ; retired in ill-health to Aix-les-Bains, where he died 20 June, 1817 ; his large collection of antiquities, which contained many Egyptian, was sold in Paris in 1818, the catalogue being drawn up by L. J. J. Dubois.

Dacier, *Mem. Acad.* 1819.

CHOISY, Auguste (1841–1909)

Architect ; Professor at École Polytechnique and École des Ponts et Chaussées ; in addition to technical works he wrote a general history of architecture and also *L'Art de Batir chez les Égyptiéns*, Paris, 1904 ; died 18 Sept. 1909.

CIBRARIO, (*Comte*) **Luigi** (1802–1870)

Italian statesman, historian and antiquary ; born 23 Feb. 1802 ; died Oct. 1870 ; his collections of antiquities were sold in his lifetime (1859) and scattered over many museums ; some Eg. antiquities went to the Hermitage.

EB. ; Golenischeff, *Coll. Ég. Erm.* p. vi.

CIMBA, Maria (*fl.* 1820–1826)

Wife of Dr. Cimba, an Italian physician of Leghorn settled and practising in Cairo, and who was medical attendant to Henry Salt ; he, and all his family except his wife, died of plague in Cairo in 1824 ; she recovered and returned to Leghorn in 1825, taking with her a collection of Eg. antiquities which were sold in 1826 ; some of these were bought by the Leiden Museum, including reliefs from the Memphite tomb of Haremhab and the magical papyrus I. 345 of which another portion came to Leiden in 1828 with the Anastasi Collection (I. 343).

Salt, ii, 231 ; *JEA*. 7, 32.

CLARKE, (*Rev.*) **Edward Daniel** (1769–1822)

Mineralogist, antiquary and traveller ; born 5 June, 1769 ; Jesus Coll. Cantab., M.A., 1794 ; LL.D., 1803 ; Professor of Mineralogy, Cambridge, 1808 ; University Librarian, 1817 ; Rector of Yeldham, Essex, 1809–22 ; one of the founders of the Geological Soc. ; examined the sarcophagus of Sety I and pronounced it to be of aragonite ; his MSS. are in the Bodleian ; died 9 Mar. 1822.

DNB. 10, 421 ; *Belzoni*, i, 366 ; H. B. Woodward, *Hist. Geol. Soc.* 54.

CLARKE, Somers (1841–1926)

Architect and archaeologist ; born 22 July, 1841 ; entered the office of Sir Gilbert Scott and was mainly engaged in the restoration of churches ; Surveyor of the Fabric, St. Paul's Cathedral, 1897 ; Architect to Dean and Chapter of Chichester, 1900 ; F.S.A., 1881 ; retired from practice, 1902 ; frequently visited Egypt, and in 1893 joined J. J. Tylor in explorations at El Kab, and assisted Quibell in excavations at Hierakonpolis ; superintended the restoration of several temples and other buildings in Egypt ; made contributions to the publications of Soc. of Ant., to *JEA* and other journals and pub. *Christian Antiquities in the Nile Valley*, Oxford, 1912 ; on his retirement he built himself a house at Mehamid, near El Kab, where he died, 31 Aug. 1926.

JEA. 13, 80 ; *WWW*. ii, 202.

CLOT, (*Bey*) **Antoine Barthélmi** (1799–1867)

French medical practitioner ; born Grenoble, 7 Nov. 1799 ; studied at Hospice de la Charité, Marseilles and Montpellier ; practised as a surgeon in Marseilles until 1823, when he was appointed Surgeon-in-chief in Egypt by Mohammad Ali ; although he then knew no

Arabic, Clot accepted the appointment and with great energy and efficiency created a public health service and a centre of medical education, in spite of much opposition by the Moslems ; he overcame all difficulties, and with the help of a European staff trained many army surgeons for the Viceroy ; for his exertions during cholera epidemic, he was given the dignity of Bey ; in 1832 he returned to France, bringing with him some of his most promising pupils to complete their medical education ; visited England in 1837 and was entertained by Pettigrew ; he was soon recalled to Egypt, and in 1840 pub. his excellent *Aperçu génèrale sur l'Égypte,* 2 vols. ; in 1860 he finally retired and settled in Marseilles, where he died in 1867.

Clot-Bey formed a large collection of Eg. antiquities, and two large batches were acquired by the Louvre in 1852 and 1853, and in 1852 the B.M. purchased two papyri (9901, used by Naville (*Todtb.* Ag.), and 9995, " Book of Breathings ") ; the rest of his collection he sold for a nominal sum to the Municipality of Marseilles, and Maspero pub. a catalogue of it in 1889.

Carré, i, 282 &c. (Portr.) ; *Rev. de l'Art,* 43, 167 ; H. Thiers, *Le Docteur Clot-Bey, Rev. Pop.* 1869 ; *Hilmy,* i, 139 ; *Cahiers,* special number, 1949, 169–170 ; *Dawson MS.* 63, f. 106–7 ; Pückler-Muskau, *Travels and Adventures in Egypt,* Lond. 1847, i, 128, 159, 162, 223, 231–3 ; Brugsch, *Mein Leben,* 159.

COCHELET, Adrien Louis (1788–1852+)

Born Charleville, 29 April, 1788 ; French Consul-General in Egypt, 1939–41 ; was still living, 1852.

French F.O. Records ; *Carré,* ii, 28.

COHEN, Mendes Israel (*d.* 1847)

Jewish, of Portuguese origin, settled in Baltimore ; took part in the American War of 1812, with the rank of Colonel ; in 1832 made a voyage up the Nile ; he reached the Second Cataract, as his name, with the date, is carved on the Rock of Abu Sir ; he made many purchases from antiquity dealers and took nearly 700 objects back to America, to which considerable additions were made at the Salt sale, 1835 ; Cohen placed his collection at the disposal of George R. Gliddon in 1845 to illustrate his lectures ; after Cohen's death in 1847, the collection passed to his nephews by whom it was presented in 1884 to Johns Hopkins University.

Johns Hopkins Univ. Circulars, iv, No. 35, 21–3 (1884) ; N.Y. Hist. Soc. *Quarterly Bull.* iv, 5 (1920).

COLQUHOUN, (*Sir*) **Robert Gilmour** (*d.* 1870)

British Consul-General in Egypt, appointed 13 Dec. 1858 ; resigned 1865 ; K.C.B. ; succeeded by Sir Edward Stanton ; died, unmarried, 10 Nov. 1870.

F.O. Records ; Duff-Gordon, 373 ; *Khedives and Pashas,* 167, 213–4, 218.

COLTHURST, Emily Jane (1858–1916)

Student of Egyptology, d. Sir George Colthurst, 5th Bart. ; born London 4 Apl. 1858 ; studied Egyptology under Maspero in the

École des H.E., Paris, 1895–7, but apparently did not publish anything; died, unmarried, 30 May, 1916.

Annuaire, Éc. des H.E., 1897, 122; *Burke's Peerage*.

COMPTON, William George Spencer Scott, 5th Marquis of Northampton (1851–1913)

Born 23 April, 1851, 2nd son of the 4th Marquis; educ. Eton and T.C.C.; succeeded, 1897; in the diplomatic service; travelled in Egypt 1898–9 and financed excavations in the Theban Necropolis directed by Newberry and Wilhelm Spiegelberg, the results of which were published in a memoir in 1908; died 16 June, 1913.

WWW. i, 530; *Newberry Corresp*.

COOK, (*Rev.*) **Frederick Charles** (1810–1889)

Archaeologist and scholar; born 1810; educ. St. John's Coll. Cantab. 1824, B.A., 1831; M.A., 1844; studied oriental languages at Bonn; ordained 1839; Inspector of Church Schools; Chaplain-in-ord. to the Queen, 1857; Preacher at Lincoln's Inn, 1860–80; Canon Residentiary of Exeter, 1864; Precentor, 1872; general editor of *The Speaker's Commentary*, 1871–81; pub. *Origins of Religion and Language*, 1884; took up Egyptology at the suggestion of Renouf and translated the Hymn to the Nile and the Piankhi Stele in *Rec. of the Past*; is said to have known 52 languages; bequeathed his library to Exeter Cathedral; died Exeter, 22 June, 1889.

DNB. Suppl. ii, 54; *Hilmy*, i, 143; Letters to Renouf, *Dawson MS*. 18, f. 26–39.

COOK, (*Rev.*) **Joseph** (1791–1825)

Born Alnwick, 6 May, 1791; Fellow of Christ's Coll. Cantab.; M.A., 1816; travelled in Arabia and Egypt, 1824–5; reached the Second Cataract, where his name and the date, 1824, are carved on the rock of Abu Sir; died suddenly while riding a camel on his way to Sinai, March, 1825.

Alumni Cantab.; *Hay Diary*, 1825, Jan. 24, June 25; *Westcar Diary*, 280.

COOPER, (*Rev.*) **Basil Henry** (*fl.* 1860–1887)

Orientalist; F.R.S.L., 1878; Foundation member of Soc. Bibl. Arch.; much interested in Egyptology and Assyriology; a correspondent of Edward Hincks; published articles on the Exodus, the antiquity of metal-working in Egypt and on Mariette's discoveries; acted as reporter for *The Times* at the Congress of Orientalists in 1874.

Budge N & T. i, 10; *Budge R & P*. 271; *Hincks* (see index).

COOPER, Edward Joshua (1798–1863)

Astronomer; born Dublin, 1798; educ. Eton and Christ Church Oxon.; F.R.S., 1853; M.P., 1830–41, 1857–9; visited Egypt 1820–1 mainly to study the Zodiacs of Dendereh and Esneh; copied many inscriptions which are in a volume *Views in Egypt and Nubia*, privately printed, 1824–7 ; built an observatory on his estate at Markree, Sligo, and pub. astronomical works ; died 23 Apl. 1863.

Proc. R.S. 13 ; *DNB.* 12, 142 ; *Hilmy,* i, 143.

COOPER, William Ricketts (1843–1878)

Originally a carpet-designer ; introduced to Egyptology and Assyriology by Bonomi ; played an active part in founding and organizing the Soc. of Biblical Arch., and was its secretary from 1872 to 1878 ; he originated the "Archaic Classes" conducted by Sayce and Renouf, and the publication of *Records of the Past* and the *Archaic Classics* ; died, Ventnor, Nov. 1878.

DNB. 12, 115 ; *Budge N & T.* i, 7, 11 ; *Budge R & P.* 262 ; *Hilmy,* i, 143.

CORBAUX, Marie Françoise Catherine Doetta (1812–1883)

Commonly known as Fanny Corbaux ; daughter of an Englishman who resided much in France ; studied at the Nat. Gallery and Brit. Institution ; in 1830 was elected Hon. Member of the Soc. of Brit. Artists ; painted and drew portraits, landscapes and book-illustrations ; much interested in Biblical archaeology and contributed many articles thereon to the *Athenaeum* and *Journ. of Sacred Literature* (e.g. on Pap. Anastasi I, Jan. 1852) ; wrote the introduction to Dunbar Heath's *Exodus Papyri,* 1855 ; fell into ill-health in 1871 having for many years supported her family by her artistic and literary work ; granted a Civil List Pension, 1871 ; died at Brighton after a long illness, 1 Feb. 1883.

DNB. 12, 195 ; *Hilmy,* i, 145.

CORDERO DI SAN QUINTINO, Giulio dei Conti (1778–1851)

Italian archaeologist ; born Mondovi, 1778 ; studied ancient history and numismatics ; Keeper of the Egyptian Collections, Turin Museum ; pub. a number of works on Egyptian subjects ; he gave a friendly reception to Champollion whilst studying in the Turin Museum ; died 1851.

Champollion, i, 48, 67, 109, 168, 210, 412, 422, and often ; *Hilmy,* ii, 148.

COSTAZ, (*Baron*) **Louis** (1767–1842)

French savant and mathematician ; a member of Napoleon's Commission ; Membre de l'Inst. de France and of Inst. Égyptien ; led the expedition to Upper Egypt ; contributed to the *Description de l'Égypte* accounts of the Valley of the Kings and of El Kab.

Carré, i, 152 ; *Hilmy,* i, 146.

COSTER, Richard (*fl.* 1827–1854)

British Consular official at Alexandria from 1827 to 1854 ; private secretary to Consul Patrick Campbell, 1833–9 ; between 1833 and 1847 obtained many Eg. antiquities for Dr. Lee's Museum at Hartwell House ; when on leave in Aug. 1839, he visited Hartwell and made coloured drawings of some of the objects.

F.O. Records ; *Hartwell Museum Registers* (MS.) ; *Bonomi Diary,* 1831, June 16 and Nov. 15 ; *Barker,* ii, 68 ; *Letter to Lee, Dawson MS.* 18, f. 143.

COTTON, James Sutherland (1847–1918)

Barrister and archaeologist ; born in India, 17 July 1847 ; Scholar of T.C.O. ; Fellow and lecturer, Queen's Coll. Oxon ; wrote on Indian affairs ; called to the Bar, 1874 ; editor of *Academy* 1881 ; an early member of the Committee, E.E.F. ; Hon. Sec. 1896–1912 ; Asst. Editor, *JEA*, 1914–8 ; died 9 July, 1918.

WWW. ii, 232 ; *JEA*. 5, 140.

COUSINÉRY, Ésprit Marie (1747–1835)

Antiquary and numismatist of Marseilles ; born 8 June, 1747 ; contributed four letters on the Rosetta Stone to the *Mag. Encyclopédique*, 1807–8, reprinted separately, Paris, 1810 ; collected coins and antiquities ; the important stele Louvre, C.14 formerly belonged to him : he acquired it through Rollin at the Thédenat-Duvent sale in 1822 ; his rich collection of Roman coins was acquired by the Vienna Museum.

Champollion, i, 47, 170 ; *TSBA*. 5, 555 ; *Hilmy*, i, 149 ; *BIFAO*, 5, 84.

COVENTRY, Henry (*d.* 1752)

Scholar and author ; Magdalen Coll. Cantab. ; M.A., 1773 ; pub. a theological work *Philemon to Hydaspes* (1736–44), in which he discussed Egyptian hieroglyphics and was accused of plagiarizing Bishop Warburton's results, for which he afterwards published an *Apologetical Letter*, 1741.

Nichols, *Lit. Anecd.* v, 564 ; *DNB*. 12, 358.

COVINGTON, Lorenzo Dow (*fl.* 1902–10)

An independent American who made researches at the Pyramids of Gizeh, 1902–10 and excavations in the neighbouring mastabas ; explored Wady el-Kattar ; pub. reports in *ASA*, vols. 6, 9 and 10 ; he was assisted by J. E. Quibell.

Maspero, *Rapports sur la Marche du Serv. des Ant.* 101, 208, 234, 262, 292, 393.

COWPER, Henry Swainson (1865–1941)

Antiquary ; born 1865 ; educ. Harrow ; J.P., Lancs. ; F.S.A., 1889 ; had a choice collection of Eg. antiquities which was presented to the B.M. in 1943 ; died 7 Apl. 1941.

Ant. Journ. 21, 261, *Anc. Eg.* 1917, 146.

COXE, Eckley Brinton (1872–1916)

American ; born Philadelphia, 1872 ; frequently visited Egypt and in 1895 became a prominent member of the American branch of the E.E.F., of which he was Hon. Sec., 1913–6 ; gave substantial financial help to excavations in Egypt and Nubia ; in 1912, he discovered a large Predynastic settlement at Abydos, and in 1915 sent an expedition to explore the temple of Meneptah at Memphis ; died at Drifton, Pennsylvania, 20 Sept. 1916.

JEA. 4, 61.

CRADOCK (CARADOC), (*Hon.*) **John Hobart** (1799–1873)

Only s. of 1st Baron Howden ; born 16 Oct. 1799 ; an officer in the Army ; sent to Egypt on a secret mission, 1827–8 ; afterwards in the diplomatic service in S. America and Spain ; succeeded as 2nd Baron Howden, 1839 ; G.C.B. ; died at Bayonne, 1873.

DNB. 9, 29 ; *Barker*, ii, 73 ff. ; *JEA*. 35, 161 ; *B.M. Add. MS*. 25659, f. 21.

CROMER, Earl of—*See* BARING

CROMPTON, Winifred Mary (1870–1932)

Museum Curator ; born Old Trafford, Manchester, 10 July 1870 ; Manchester Univ. ; M.A. ; Asst. Keeper, Manchester Museum, 1912 ; for 20 years she was in charge of the Eg. collection and did much to promote Egyptology in Manchester, and took a prominent part in the Manchester Eg. and Oriental Society ; contributed to *JEA* and other journals ; died 8 Oct. 1932.

JEA. 18, 190 ; *JMEOS*. 18, 33–5.

CRUM, Walter Ewing (1865–1944)

Coptic scholar ; born 22 July, 1865 ; educ. Eton, 1879 and Balliol Coll. Oxon., B.A. 1888 ; while an undergraduate was interested in Egyptology and on leaving Oxford he studied first under Maspero in Paris, and afterwards under Erman at Berlin ; although generally grounded in hieroglyphics, he decided while at Berlin to confine himself to Coptic in which he became the foremost scholar of his generation ; from 1892 he began an intensive study of all the available materials, visiting British and foreign museums and libraries ; finding the dictionaries of Parthey, Tattam and Peyron inadequate to modern needs, he set about collecting materials for a Coptic dictionary and to this he devoted almost all the rest of his life ; the dictionary when ready for the printer comprised some 240,000 slips, it was produced by the Oxford Univ. Press in 6 parts, the first appearing in 1929 and the last in 1939, making a stout quarto volume of nearly 1,000 pages, closely printed in double columns ; in honour of this great achievement, Crum was elected F.B.A. in 1931 and D.Litt. Oxford, 1937 ; he pub. much else in addition to the dictionary, notably the Catalogues of the Coptic MSS. in the B.M. (1905) and the John Rylands Library (1909) ; the 2nd part of Vol. 25 of *JEA* was dedicated to him to celebrate the completion of the dictionary, and it contains a portrait and bibliography of all his writings ; died at Bath, 18 May, 1944. His correspondence is in the B.M. (Add. MSS. 45681–90) and his notebooks and papers in the Griffith Inst.

JEA. 30, 66 ; 25, 133 (Portr. and Bibl.).

CULLIMORE, Isaac (1791–1852)

Irish antiquary ; born 1791 ; took a great interest in the progress of Eg. decipherment ; pub. papers on Eg. chronology, lists of kings, etc., in *Trans. R.S.L.* ; for the Syro-Egyptian Soc., he pub. *Pharaoh and his Princes*, 1845 ; a friend of Dr. John Lee, and a frequent visitor at Hartwell ; died Clapham, 8 April, 1852.

DNB. 13, 282 ; *Hilmy*, i, 151.

CUMING, Henry Syer (1820–1902)

Archaeologist of Kennington, London ; born 1820 ; F.R.G.S. ; member of Brit. Arch. Assn., from 1844 and for many years V.P. ; F.S.A. Scot., 1867 ; Member of Soc. Bibl. Arch. 1875 ; contributed many papers to *Journ. Brit. Arch. Assn.* ; owned an Egyptian papyrus which was used by Naville (*Todtb*. Ay) ; died in London, 1902.

CURETON, Harry Osborn (1785–1858)

Dealer in coins and antiquities, of 81 Aldersgate, Barbican, London ; he had an excellent reputation and supplied many articles to the B.M. and other large museums, as well as private collectors such as Dr. John Lee ; he bought many Eg. antiquities at the sales of Barker, Burton, Lavoratori, Salt and Athanasi, and many coins and antiquities at the Strawberry Hill sale ; the demotic papyrus B.M. 10413 is called by his name.

CURTIS, George William (1824–1892)

American author ; born Providence, R.I., 24 Feb. 1824 ; spent some years in Europe and established himself in New York in 1850 as a journalist and author ; contributed to many newspapers and periodicals ; his connection with Egypt was the publication in 1851 of *Nile Notes of a Howadji*, of which a German ed. appeared in 1857 ; died 31 Aug. 1892.

Life, by Edward Cary, 1894 ; *Hilmy*, i, 151.

CURZON, Robert, 14th Baron Zouche (1810–1873)

Scholar and traveller ; born 16 Mar. 1810 ; educ. Charterhouse and Ch. Ch. Oxon. ; travelled in Egypt, Syria and Palestine, 1833–4, chiefly in search of manuscripts, of which he amassed a fine collection ; also collected Eg. antiquities ; his travels are described in his *Monasteries of the Levant* ; a privately-printed catalogue of the collection, limited to 50 copies, was issued in 1849, *Cat. of Materials for Writing : Early Writings on Tablets and Stones, Rolled and other Manuscripts and Oriental Manuscript Books, in the Library of the Hon. Robert Curzon at Parham in the County of Sussex* ; his own copy of this cat., with many notes and letters from Birch and others inserted, is in the Dept. of MSS., B.M. ; the collection of oriental MSS. was presented to the B.M. ; the Eg. antiquities remained in the family until they were sold at Sotheby's 2 Nov. 1922, lots 327–356 ; died 2 Aug. 1873.

DNB. 13, 354 ; *Hilmy*, i, 151.

CZARTORYSKI, Wladyslaus (1828–1894)

Polish nobleman, son of Prince Adam George C. (1770–1861) ; statesman and scholar ; had a museum in Cracow containing a large collection of Egyptian antiquities, as well as objets-d'art and a fine library ; visited Egypt 1889–90 ; a papyrus in his collection was used by Naville (*Todtb.* Pp.) ; died in Paris, 1894.

Wilbour, 546 ; B. Zaleski, *Life of Adam Czartoryski,* Paris, 1881.

CZERMAK, Johann (1828–1873)

Physiologist ; perfector of the laryngoscope ; made anatomical and microscopical researches on mummies, *Sitzungsb. Akad. Wien,* 9, 427–467 (1852).

DACIER, (*Baron*) **Bon Joseph** (1742–1833)

French savant ; elected to Acad. Fr. 1823 ; Secretaire-perpetuel de l'Acad. des Inscr., 1820 ; a firm friend to Champollion whose famous *Lettre* of 1822 is addressed to him ; died in Paris, 1833.

Hartleben, passim.

DALTON, Richard (1715–1791)

Draughtsman and engraver ; studied in Rome ; travelled in Greece and Egypt, 1749 ; pub. Views and Engravings in Greece and Egypt, 52 plates, and another collection with 79 plates, 1790–1, and other works ; F.S.A. ; an original member of the R.A.

DNB. Suppl. ii, 108 ; *Hilmy,* i, 154.

DALZIEL, (*Sir*) **Davison Alexander, 1st Baron Dalziel of Wooler** (1854–1928)

Born 5 Oct. 1854 ; created Bart., 1919 ; created Baron, 1927 ; collector of antiquities ; his collection sold at Sotheby's 31 July 1939 (Eg. ant. lots 17–25) ; died 18 April 1928.

DANINOS, (*Pasha*) **A.** (*c.* 1840–*c.* 1912)

Greek Egyptologist ; an assistant in the Louvre under Longpérier and Devéria ; studied hieroglyphics and went to Egypt in 1869 as assistant to Mariette ; took part in Mariette's excavations at Meidûm in 1871, and in the absence of his chief discovered the famous statues of Rahotpe and Nefert ; excavated at Feshn, Heliopolis, the Fayûm and Abukir, retired in 1897 and returned to Paris ; pub. *Les Monuments Funéraires,* Paris, 1899, with a preface by Maspero; pub. a Catalogue of the Tigrane Pasha Collection with 64 plates, 1911 ; he had a collection of antiquities which was sold at Hôtel Druot, Paris, 7 May, 1926 ; two stelae from this collection were published by Maspero, *Rec. Trav.* 15, 84.

Maspero, ubi supra ; *Rec. Trav.* 8, 69 ; 12, 209 ; *JEA.* 14, 175.

D'ARC, Gauthier (*d.* 1844)

French Consul-General in Egypt, 1842–3 ; from 1830 he had resided in Spain, and on his resignation from Egypt he returned there, and died of tuberculosis in 1844.

French F.O. Records ; *Carré,* i, 329 ; ii, 28 ; *Tresson,* 31.

DARESSY, Georges Émile Jules (1864–1938)

French Egyptologist ; born Sourdon (Somme), 1864 ; assistant keeper, Bulak Museum, 1887 ; carried out excavations under Maspero and Grébaut, when he cleared the great find of 21st Dyn. mummies in 1891 ; excavated at Medinet Habu ; arranged the Eg. collections on the removal of the museum to Gizeh in 1891 and on its return to Cairo in 1902 ; a voluminous contributor to journals and author of several volumes of the *Cat. Général* ; Sec., Serv. des Antiquités, 1914 ; retired, 1923 ; died 28 Feb. 1938.

Bull. Inst. Ég. 20, 259 ; *ASA*. 39, 11–17 (Bibl. 18–41).

DATTARI, Giovanni (*d.* 1923)

Collector of coins and antiquities ; resided in Cairo ; originally in the service of Thos. Cook & Son and afterwards a purveyor to the British Army in Egypt ; had a fine collection of antiquities, particularly of XVIII Dyn. glass ; some of his ant. pub. by Newberry, *PSBA*, 1901, 220 ; was well known as a numismatist and had a good collection of coins ; F.R.N.S. 1900 ; pub. *Num. Augg. Alexandrini*, 1901 ; died 1923.

Inf. by P. E. Newberry.

DAVIDSON, John (1797–1836)

Physician and traveller ; born 29 Dec. 1797 ; studied medicine at Edinburgh and St. George's Hospital, London ; in early life his health failed, and he gave up medical practice ; F.R.S., 1832 ; resided in Naples and travelled extensively in Africa and the Near East ; under the influence of Pettigrew, he took up Egyptology, and studied the history of mummification ; he unrolled and lectured upon two mummies at the Royal Institution, London, in 1833, and published a valuable account of them, entitled *An Address on Embalming generally*, London, 1833 ; he was murdered while exploring in the interior of Africa, 18 Dec. 1836.

DNB. 14, 127 ; *Mem. Inst. Ég.* 13, 13 ; *JEA*. 20, 171.

DAVIES, Norman de Garis (1865–1941)

Egyptologist ; born 14 Sept. 1865 ; Glasgow Univ., 1889 ; M.A. ; B.D. ; Marburg Univ. ; Congregational Minister at Ashton-under-Lyne where he became acquainted with Miss Kate Bradbury (afterwards Mrs. F. Ll. Griffith) who interested him in Egyptology, the study of which he forthwith began ; he next went as a Unitarian Minister in Melbourne until 1898, when he joined Petrie at Dendereh ; during the following years he copied many tombs for the Arch. Survey of the E.E.F. : Sheikh Said, 1901, Dêr el-Gebrawi 1902, and El Amarna, 1903–8 ; these, together with five tombs at Thebes were published in 10 vols. of the Arch. Survey Memoirs, both text and plates being executed by Davies ; the merit of this work was recognized by the award of the Leibniz Medal of the Prussian Acad. ; accompanied Breasted in his expedition to Nubia, and assisted Reisner at the Pyramids ; he married in 1907, Miss A. M. Cummings, herself an accomplished artist and a trained copyist ; thereafter he settled at Thebes and worked for many seasons copying tombs for the M.M.A., which were published in a series of sumptuous volumes ; in addition to these larger works, he made many contributions to

JEA and other journals ; Hon. Member of German Arch. Inst., 1928 ; Hon. M.A., Oxon ; died 5 Nov. 1941.

JEA. 28, 59 (Portr.) ; *Erman*, 220 ; *Newberry Corresp.*

DAVIS, Theodore M. (1837–1915)

A wealthy business man of New York, and Newport, R.I. ; first visited Egypt in 1899, and was introduced by Sayce to Newberry, who interested him in Egyptology ; he financed excavations carried out by Newberry and others and from 1903–12 had a permit to explore the Valley of the Kings under the supervision of the Service des Antiquités ; he bore the entire cost of the work, and also of the six sumptuous volumes in which the results were recorded ; the tombs discovered were those of Queen Hatshepsut, Tuthmosis IV, Siptah, Haremhab, Yuaa and Thuiu, as well as some minor ones ; all the objects discovered went to the Cairo Museum where they are exhibited in a special gallery known as Salle Théodore Davis ; his private collection is now in the Metrop. Museum, New York ; died in Florida, 23 Feb. 1915.

Sayce, 307, 322 ; *JEA*. 2, 251 ; *Newberry Corresp.*

DAVISON, Nathaniel (*fl.* 1765–1783)

Accompanied Edward Wortley Montague on his travels in the East ; arrived at Gizeh, 8 July, 1765, with Cousinéry, consul at Rosetta, and Meynard, a French merchant, to explore the Great Pyramid ; he discovered the first of the construction-chambers over the "King's Chamber," which is called by his name ; he was afterwards British Consul-General at Algiers, 1780–3 ; his journals and observations on the Pyramids and the Catacombs of Alexandria were published in 1818 by Walpole (q.v.).

F.O. Records ; Nichols, *Lit. Anecd.* iv, 637 ; Lauer, *Le Problême des Pyramides*, 40 ; *Walpole*, 350–387 ; *Lindsay*, 42, 155 ; Vyse, *Pyramids*, ii, 255.

DEDEKIND, Alexander (1856–1940)

Austrian Egyptologist ; born Wolfenbuettel, 5 Apr. 1856 ; Keeper of the Eg. collection in the Kunsthistorisches Museum, Vienna, 1892, in succession to E. von Bergmann, of whom he pub. a biography (2nd ed., 1906) ; pub. a history of the Vienna Collection, 1907 and contributions to various journals ; died in Vienna, 8 Nov. 1940.

Osterr. Volkszeitung, 29 Mar. 1936 (note on his 80th birthday) ; *Volkszeitung Wien*, 10 Nov. 1940.

DEFREMÊRY, Charles François (1822–1883)

French orientalist ; born Cambrai, 1822 ; pupil of the Arabist Caussin de Perceval ; in 1869 appointed by the Acad. to edit with De Slane, in succession to Laborde, the works of the Arabic historians of the Crusades ; in 1868 he succeeded Caussin de Perceval, to whom he had long been assistant, at the Collège de France, but soon had to retire through ill-health ; edited with B. R. Sanguinetti *Voyages d'Ibn Batoutah*, 4 vols., Paris, 1853–9 ; the vacancy in the Acad. caused by his death was filled by Maspero ; died 19 Aug. 1883.

Jour. Asiatique, Ser. 8, 4, 27–29 ; *JEA*. 33, 77 ; *Hilmy*, i, 8.

DELAPORTE, Pacifique Henri (1815–1877)

Born 25 Sept. 1815 ; French Consul in Cairo *c.* 1850–5 ; made a collection of Eg. antiquities which was acquired by the Louvre in 1864 ; died in Paris, 12 Oct. 1877.

French F.O. Records ; *Bibl. Ég.* 18, pp. xxxix, lii ; *Rev. de l'Art*, 43, 168.

DE MAILLET, Benoît (1656–1738)

French diplomatist ; born St. Mihiel, Lorraine, 1656 ; Consul-General for France in Egypt, 1692–1708 ; travelled and observed much in Egypt and sent to France a considerable number of antiquities which found their way into the cabinets of the King and of Counts Pontchartrain, De Caylus, and others ; he also obtained a considerable number of Coptic and Arabic MSS. ; retired to Marseilles and compiled an elaborate *Description de l'Égypte*, which was edited and pub. in his lifetime by the Abbé Le Mascrier, 1735 ; died Marseilles, 1738.

Carré, i, 56–65 (Portr.) ; *Hilmy*, i, 170.

DE MORGAN, Jacques Jean Marie (1857–1924)

French civil engineer, geologist and archaeologist ; born 1857 ; Director-General, Serv. des Antiquités, 1892–7, previously and subsequently explored the Caucasus, Persia and other sites in the Near East ; while in Egypt he discovered the royal tomb at Nakadeh, excavated the pyramids of Dashur and did much investigation into the predynastic antiquities of Egypt ; he inaugurated a scheme for cataloguing all the extant monuments in Egypt from the Sudan frontier ; several volumes were pub. but this was not continued by his successors ; his chief works were *Recherches sur les Origines de l'Égypte*, 2 vols., 1897 ; *Fouilles à Dahchour*, 1895 ; *Cat. des Monuments*, etc., 3 vols., 1894–1909 ; his great work, *La Préhistoire Orientale*, 3 vols., 1929 was posthumously published ; died 12 June 1924.

Syria, 5, 373 ; *Bull. Inst. Ég.* 7, 173 ; *Ant. Journ.* 5, 71.

DENON, (*Baron*) **Dominique Vivant** (1747–1825)

French antiquary and man of letters ; born Chalon-sur-Saône, 4 Jan. 1747 ; studied Law in Paris, but abandoned it for art and letters ; a favourite of Louis XV, who entrusted him with the arrangement of a collection of gems and medals for Madame Pompadour ; afterwards attached to the Embassy at St. Petersburg, then transferred to Sweden ; in 1775 was sent on a special mission to Switzerland and as chargé d'affaires at Naples till 1787 ; whilst travelling in Italy, he heard that his property had been confiscated by the revolutionaries and his name proscribed, but with great courage he returned to Paris and his life was spared ; became acquainted with Napoleon and joined the commission in Egypt ; travelled in Upper Eg. making a great collection of drawings and antiquities, which he published in his *Voyage dans la Basse et la Haute Égypte*, 1802, a work which passed through several editions and was translated into English and German ; in 1804 appointed

Director-General of Museums, a post he held until 1815 ; his extensive collections were sold in Paris in 1826, a considerable part of it was acquired by provincial museums, especially that of Boulogne ; died in Paris, 27 April 1825.

Carré, i, 117–141 (Portr.) ; *Bull. Inst. Ég.* v (1923), 163–193 ; *Hilmy*, i, 172.

DE ROUGÉ, (*Vicomte*) **Jacques** (1842–1923)

French Egyptologist ; eldest son of E. de Rougé ; born 1842 ; studied under his father in Paris, and accompanied him to Egypt, 1863–4 ; edited the inscriptions copied on this journey, 4 vols. 1877–9 ; pub. geographical texts from Edfu and other works ; at the age of 81 he attended the Champollion centenary celebrations in 1922 ; died 1923.

Chron. 13, 327 ; *Hilmy*, i, 177.

DE ROUGÉ, (*Vicomte*) **Olivier Charles Camille Emmanuel** (1811–1872)

French Egyptologist ; born 11 April 1811 ; educ. by Jesuits at Coll. de St. Acheul and afterwards attended lectures at the Coll. de France and the Sorbonne ; he was attracted to Egyptology by Letronne who succeeded to Champollion's chair in 1837 ; on perusing Champollion's *Grammaire*, he set himself to learn the language ; after prolonged study, he decided to make Egyptology his career, and on the retirement of Letronne, succeeded him ; under his instruction many French Egyptologists, notably Maspero, began their careers ; visited Egypt with his son Jacques in 1863–4 ; he published many works of high importance in their time ; his lesser writings were collected and publ in the *Bibl. Ég.* by Maspero in 6 vols. ; died 27 Dec. 1872.

Maspero, *Notice Biogr.* (*Bibl. Ég.* 21, Portr.) ; *Hilmy*, i, 177.

DESPIRRO, Antonio (*fl.* 1828–9)

Dealer in antiquities in Cairo with whom Champollion had dealings ; he carried on excavations in Egypt.

Champollion, ii, 411.

DEVAUD, Eugène Victor (1878–1929)

Swiss Egyptologist ; born Fribourg, 1878 ; studied under Loret at Lyons, and afterwards at Berlin ; lecturer at Fribourg University ; his first important work was a study of the Pap. Prisse and its variants ; his later published work was mainly concerned with Coptic, and he made important contributions on etymology in various journals, and in his *Études d'Étymologie Copte*, 1923 ; he also edited the Bohairic version of the Psalms ; in addition to Egyptian, Devaud studied other oriental languages, including Assyrian and Chinese ; his manuscripts are now in the Griffith Inst., Oxford ; died 1929.

JEA. 15, 273 ; *Kémi*, 3, 20 (Bibl.) ; Griffith Inst. *List of Records* (1947), 5.

DEVERELL, Robert (1760–1841)

Politician and scholar ; born 22 June 1777 ; Fellow of St. John's Coll. Cantab. ; M.A., 1784 ; M.P., Saltash, 1802 ; published a number of eccentric works on the learning of the ancients, including *Dis-*

coveries in Hieroglyphic and other Antiquities, 6 vols., London, 1813 ; this work he suppressed on publication, and it is very rare : there is a copy in the B.M. ; died 29 Nov. 1841.

DNB. 14, 424 ; *BIFAO*. 5, 85.

DEVÉRIA, Théodule (1831–1871)

French Egyptologist ; son of the painter Achille D. (*d.* 1857) ; born 1831 ; became interested in Egyptology under the influence of Prisse d'Avennes who was a friend of the family ; a visit to the Leiden Museum in 1846 intensified his interest ; studied Coptic under Charles Lenormant and Arabic at the École des Langues Orientales ; employed at the Bibliothèque Nat. 1851 ; his first published contribution to Egyptology was made in 1854 ; in 1855 he was employed in the Eg. Dept. of the Louvre, where the collections had been much enlarged by the discoveries of Mariette ; in 1858 he accompanied Mariette to Egypt as copyist and made three subsequent journeys ; the last ten years of his life were mainly devoted to examining and cataloguing the Eg. papyri in the Louvre, but he did not live to see his catalogue published ; his health was always frail and was greatly tried by the climate of Egypt ; he died at the early age of 40 in January 1871 ; Devéria was a brilliant scholar, but he published little ; his works were collected, together with a number of unpublished MSS., by Maspero in 2 vols. in 1896 (*Bibl. Ég.* IV, V ;) all Devéria's MSS. are now in the Louvre.

Biogr. notice by his brother, and Portr., *Bibl. Ég.* 4.

DEVILLIERS DU TERRAGE, (*Baron*) **René Edouard** (1780–1855)

French civil engineer ; member of Napoleon's Commission ; took a prominent part in the archaeological activities of the Commission and contributed to the *Descr. de l'Égypte* ; his journal was published in 1899.

Carré, i, 146 ; *Comptes Rendus*, 1900, 31 ; *Hilmy*, i, 186.

DIAMOND. Hugh Welch (1809–1886)

Physician and archaeologist ; born 1809 ; studied medicine at St. Bartholomew's Hospital and became assistant to Abernethy ; practised in Soho, and greatly distinguished himself in the cholera outbreak of 1832 ; specialized in mental disease and founded a home at Twickenham in 1858 in which he lived as resident physician till his death ; one of the pioneers of scientific photography ; F.S.A. ; published an account of a mummy purchased by him in 1843 (*Archaeologia*, 31, 408) ; this mummy is now in the Maidstone Museum, and some of its linen was given to Dr. Lee's Museum ; died 1886.

DNB. 15, 1 ; *Mem. Inst. Ég.* 13, 15 ; *Hilmy*, i, 187.

DIXON, James (1891–1915)

Egyptologist ; born 1891 ; educ. St. Paul's School ; in 1908 assisted Blackman in copying the Temple of Dendûr ; in 1909–10 worked for the E.E.F., with Naville, Peet and Legge at Abydos, and again 1910–11 ; in 1912 joined the Wellcome Sudan Expedition near

Senaar as excavator and draughtsman ; in addition to Egyptology, Dixon was interested in medieval history and heraldry ; he joined the Forces in 1914, a 2nd Lieut. in the 6th Battalion, Border Regt., and was killed in action at Suvla Bay, Gallipoli, 10 Aug. 1915.

JEA. 3, 48 (Portr.).

DIXON, Waynman (1844–1930)

Civil engineer ; born 1844 ; Assoc. Member Inst. Civil Engineers 1878 ; Member, 1882 ; resigned 1909 ; associated with his brother and Mr. (later Sir) Benjamin Baker in the removal of Cleopatra's Needle to London : Dixon moved it and enclosed it in an iron cylinder ; while in Egypt he made investigations at the Pyramids and discovered the air-passages from the " Queen's Chamber," 1872 ; died at Great Ayton, Yorks, 24 Jan. 1930.

Engineering, 31 Jan. 1930 ; *Proc. Inst. Civil Eng.* 61, 233 ; Edwards, *Pyramids*, 92.

DODGSON, Aquila (1829–1919)

Congregational Minister at Hull ; resigned in 1870 owing to failure of his voice and became a cotton-spinner at Ashton-under-Lyne ; much interested in Egyptology and arranged lectures by Amelia Edwards and Petrie, and raised funds for the promotion of Egyptology in Manchester ; retired 1891, and in the winter 1891–2 visited Egypt and spent some time with Petrie at Amarna ; later lived in Leeds and arranged the coins in the museum there ; was also interested in astronomy and built an observatory in his garden ; Dodgson's name is associated with an important demotic papyrus obtained in Egypt in 1881 by the Rev. Elkanah Armitage (q.v.) and pub. by Griffith, *PSBA* 31, 100, 289 ; it was presented by his family to the Ashmolean Museum in 1932 ; another Dodgson papyrus is in Melbourne.

PSBA, ubi supra ; *JEA*. 19, 97 ; *Inf. by Mrs. R. A. Talbot* (daughter).

DODWELL, Edward (1767–1832)

Traveller and archaeologist ; T.C.C. ; B.A., 1800 ; collected coins and vases, chiefly Greek and Roman ; settled in Rome, 1806 ; F.S.A. ; his collection of Egyptian, Greek, Roman and Etruscan antiquities was acquired after his death by the Munich Museum ; an Egyptian chalice was pub. by Newberry, *JEA*. 6, 154 ; his drawings and papers are in the B.M. in 4 volumes, the first of which is entirely devoted to Eg. antiquities (Add. MSS. 33958–61).

DNB. 15, 178 ; *Champollion*, i, 189, 204, 208.

DONALD, Donald—*See* OSMAN EFFENDI

DONALDSON, Thomas Leverton (1795–1885)

Architect ; born 19 Oct. 1795 ; Professor of Architecture, Univ. Coll. London, 1841–64 ; President, Institute of Architects, 1864 ; Membre de l'Inst. de France ; travelled in the East and wrote on the history of architecture, and on pyramids, obelisks, Mariette's excavations, etc. ; died 1 Aug. 1885.

DNB. 15, 214 ; H. H. Bellot, *Univ. Coll. London* (1929), 265–6 ; *Hilmy*, i, 190.

D'ORBINEY, (*Mrs.*) **Elizabeth** (*fl.* 1849–60)

An English lady, who purchased in Italy the famous papyrus that bears her name—the Story of the Two Brothers; she was in Paris in the winter of 1851–2, and whilst there she confided the papyrus to de Rougé who perceived its nature, and published an account of it in the *Athenaeum Français*, Oct. 30, 1852, followed by a translation in the *Rev. Arch.* ix, 385; in 1857 she sold the papyrus to the B.M. (10183) and a facsimile of it was pub. in *Select Papyri*, 2nd ser., 1860. This papyrus has been studied by almost every Egyptologist, and there are many editions of the text, and translations of varying merit.

Maspero, *Popular Stories* (London, 1915), 1; *Select Papyri*, ii, p. 7.

DRACH, Solomon Moses (1835–1879)

Jewish astronomer, mathematician and archaeologist; F.R.A.S., 1841; F.R.G.S.; an active member of the Soc. of Bibl. Arch. to the *Transactions* of which he contributed many papers, including two on the Great Pyramid; wrote on the Temple of Jerusalem; he wrote much on statistics, magic squares, etc.; contributed to *Records of the Past* and to the publications of the R.A.S.; died 8 Feb. 1879.

R.A.S. Records; *Hilmy*, i, 192.

DROVETTI, Bernardino (1775–1852)

Italian collector of antiquities; born Livourne, 1775; assumed French nationality, and served as Colonel in Napoleon's Egyptian campaign and saved the life of Murat; under the Empire until 1814 and again under the Restoration, 1820–9, he was French Consul-General in Egypt; he was an ardent collector of antiquities and employed many agents to excavate and buy from native diggers; his first collection, offered to and rejected by France, was bought by the King of Sardinia in 1824 and is the principal part of the great Egyptian collection at Turin; the second collection was bought by France by order of Charles X, for fcs. 250,000 and is now in the Louvre; the third collection was acquired for Berlin by Lepsius in 1836 for fcs. 30,000; Drovetti made a journey to the Oases in 1820 and his notes and geographical observations are embodied in Jomard's works of 1821 and 1823; he had great influence with Mohammad Ali and suggested many administrative reforms; Chevalier de la Légion d'Honneur, 1820; he was very hostile to other collectors and excavators in Egypt, and particularly to Salt and Champollion; his methods, and those of his agents, were often unscrupulous; towards the end of his life, his mind gave way, and he died in an asylum in Turin, 1852.

References to Drovetti are too numerous to specify: he is constantly mentioned in *Hartleben, Champollion*, and in *Salt, Belzoni, Athanasi, Carré*, and others.

DRUMMOND, (*Sir*) **William** (1770–1828)

Scholar and diplomatist; F.R.S., 1799; D.C.L. Oxon., 1810; P.C., 1801; Minister Plenipotentiary at Naples, 1801 and 1806; Ambassador to the Porte, 1803–6; interested in oriental history and archaeology ; pub. works on the Old Testament in which he explained many of the episodes as atronomical allegories ; pub. *Memoir on the Antiquity of the Zodiacs of Esneh and Dendera*, 1821; died in Rome, 29 Mar. 1828.

DNB. 16, 51 ; *Hilmy*, i, 193 ; *Champollion*, i, 194.

DUANE, Matthew (1707–1785)

Numismatist and antiquary ; a lawyer by profession, of Lincoln's Inn ; born 1707 ; F.R.S., 1763 ; F.S.A. ; Trustee of the B.M., 1766–85 ; a considerable donor to the B.M., 1764–77 ; he had a large collection of coins, chiefly purchased from well-known cabinets ; he had also a large collection of Greek, Roman and other antiquities and was one of the first in England to collect Egyptian antiquities, of which several were included in the sale of his coins and other collections, 3 May 1785 ; his library was sold in 1838 ; died in Bedford Row, 6 Feb. 1785 and buried in St. Nicholas, Newcastle-on-Tyne.

DNB. 16, 76 ; Nichols, *Lit. Anecd.* iii, 497.

DUBOIS, Léon Jean Joseph (1780–1846)

Draughtsman and lithographer ; born Paris, 1780 ; in 1807 became acquainted with Champollion and remained a staunch friend ; executed the drawings for the illustrations of Champollion's *Panthéon*, 1823, and other works ; made the drawings for the first fount of hieroglyphic type for the Imprimerie Nationale, 1840 ; conservator of the Eg. collections of the Louvre, 1832–46 ; he had some strange methods, one of which was to cut out from papyri the coloured vignettes of the gods to frame them and place them with the statues of divinities, regarding the texts themselves as indecipherable and useless ; drew up the sale-catalogues of many important collections of antiquities, including those of Choiseul-Gouffier, 1818 ; Léon Dufourney, 1819 ; Grivaud de la Vincelle, 1820 ; Thédenat-Duvent, 1822, and Mimaut, 1837 ; died in Paris, 2 Dec. 1846.

Rev. Arch. 3 (1846), 691 ; *Hartleben*, passim ; *Bibl. Ég.* 21, p. xviii ; *Rev. de l'Art*, 43, 166 ; *Hilmy*, i, 194.

DUEMICHEN, Johannes (1833–1894)

German Egyptologist ; born Grosslogau, 1833 ; studied theology and philology at Berlin and Breslau ; took up Egyptology and became a pupil of Lepsius and Brugsch ; Professor of Egyptology, Strassburg, 1872–94 ; frequently visited Egypt ; his principal publications are epigraphic and include *Bauurkunde des Tempels von Dendera*, 1865 ; *Geographische Inschriften*, 4 vols., 1865–85 ; *Kalenderinschriften*, 1886 ; *Tempelinschriften*, 2 vols., 1867–9 ; *Die Oasen*, 1878 ; *Geschichte des alten Ägyptens*, 1878–83 ; his publication of the great Theban Tomb of Pedamenopet (No. 33), *Der Grabpalast des Petuamenap* was left unfinished, only two of the projected seven parts having appeared, 1884–5 : some additions were made by Spiegelberg in 1894 ; a large mass of copies, squeezes, and other material was bequeathed by him to Strassburg University ; died 1894.

Rec. Trav. 16, 74 ; Ebers, *Richard Lepsius* (transl. Underhill), pp. i–v (1887) ; Brugsch, *Mein Leben*, 262, 285 ; *Hilmy*, i, 194.

DUFFERIN, (*Marquis of*)—*See* TEMPLE

DUFF-GORDON, (*Lady*) **Lucie** (1821–1869)

Only child of the jurist John Austin (1790–1859) ; born 24 June, 1821 ; married, 1840, Sir Alexander Duff-Gordon, Bt. (1811–1872) and was a prominent figure in literary society ; owing to ill-health, she resided at the Cape of Good Hope, 1860–3 and in Egypt, 1863–9, where she lived mainly at Luxor in the Maison de France vacated by Maunier ; apart from her literary works, her *Letters from Egypt* were pub. in 1865, *Last Letters from Egypt*, 1877, and a fuller edition with a preface by George Meredith, edited by her daughter, Mrs. Janet Ross, appeared in 1902 ; she died in Cairo, 14 July 1869.

DNB. 22, 220 ; *Hilmy*, i, 197 ; Edwards, *Thousand Miles*, 2nd ed. 451–5 ; Memoir prefixed to *Last Letters* (2nd ed. 1876) by her daughter (Portr.).

DUFOURNEY, Léon (1754–1818)

French architect ; born 1754 ; travelled in Italy, 1782 ; Professor at the École de l'Architecture, 1804 ; collector of works of art and of antiquities ; the sale-catalogue of his Greek and Eg. antiquities was drawn up by L. J. J. Dubois, in Paris, 1819.

DULAURIER, Jean Paul François Edouard (1807–1881)

French orientalist ; born Toulouse, 1807 ; elected to Acad. des Inscr., 1864 ; pub. accounts of the stelae in the Toulouse Museum and various Coptic texts, 1833–5 ; visited London in 1838 and copied the MS. *Pistis Sophia*, with a view to complete publication of the text, but he issued only a general account of it in 1847 ; he also pub. an examination of the doctrines of Champollion, 1847 ; died at Mendou, near Paris, 1881.

Hilmy, i, 198.

DUPUIS, Charles François (1742–1809)

French scientific writer and politician ; born 26 Oct. 1742 ; Professor at Lisieux ; studied law and became an advocate ; much interested in astronomy and the evolution of the calendar, and ascribed the origin of the Zodiac to Upper Egypt ; wrote many works on the origin of cults, etc., and on the Zodiac of Dendera ; died 29 Sept. 1809.

EB. ; *Hilmy*, i, 200.

DURAND, Paul (1806–1882)

French traveller and collector ; made three voyages to Egypt and made many drawings and copies of monuments which he gave to de Rougé ; he acquired in Italy the Egyptian collection of the Bishop of Nola, 1825–6 ; Durand's name is associated with a papyrus (3088) and other antiquities in the Louvre ; he was the son of J. B. L. Durand, author of *Voyage à Sénégal*, Paris, 1802, who was also a collector of antiquities which were sold in Paris in 1824 ; Paul Durand died in Paris, 27 Dec. 1882.

Champollion, i, 134, 245, 248, 249, 280, 295, 357.

DUTEIL, Camille (*fl.* 1830–50)

Assistant in charge of Egyptian antiquities in the Louvre under Longpérier ; wrote on the Zodiac of Dendera and on ancient weights and measures ; began to publish a *Dictionnaire des Hiéroglyphes* of which only one part appeared (1839) ; he was an opponent of Champollion.

Hartleben, ii, 556 ; *Bibl. Ég.* 21, pp. xviii–xix ; *Hilmy,* i, 201.

EAGLE, William (1788–1854)

Barrister ; of Lakenheath Hall, Suffolk ; educ. Charterhouse ; T.C.C. ; B.A., 1809 ; M.A., 1812 ; Called to the Bar, Middle Temple, 1817 ; Equity Draughtsman ; collector of antiquities ; his Egyptian, Babylonian and Etruscan gems, sold in London, 9 May 1859 ; died at Lakenheath, and buried there 27 July 1854.

Alumni Cantab. ii ; *Inf. Vicar of Lakenheath,* 1949.

EBERS, Georg Moritz (1837–1898)

German Egyptologist ; born Berlin, 1 Mar. 1837 ; studied law at Göttingen and oriental archaeology at Berlin under Lepsius ; Professor of Egyptology at Leipsic ; travelled much in Egypt ; wrote a descriptive work on Egypt, *Ægypten in Wort und Bild,* which enjoyed great popularity and was translated into French and English ; wrote many historical novels ; acquired from Edwin Smith at Luxor the famous medical papyrus which bears his name and of which he published a facsimile with an introduction and a glossary by Ludwig Stern, 2 vols., 1874 ; his works have been collected in 25 vols., *Gesammelte Werke,* Stuttgart, 1893–5 ; a festscrift in his honour was published in 1897 ; retired, 1889 ; died at Tutzing, Bavaria, 7 Aug. 1898 ; his library was acquired by the Cairo Museum.

Autobiogr. *Die Geshichte meines Lebens,* 1893 ; G. Gosche, *Georg Ebers,* 1887 ; *ZÄS.* 36, 140 ; *Academy,* 51, 284 ; *Hilmy,* i, 205.

EDGAR, Campbell Cowan (1870–1938)

Egyptologist and Greek Scholar ; born Tongland Manse, 26 Dec. 1870 ; educ. Ayr Acad. and Oriel Coll. Oxon. ; Craven Fellow, 1895 ; studied in Munich ; joined Brit. School in Athens, 1896–1900 ; went to Cairo on the Catalogue Commission, 1900 ; Inspector of Antiquities in the Delta, 1905–19 ; Asst. Conservator, Cairo Museum, 1919 ; Keeper and Secretary-General, 1925 ; retired 1927 ; died 10 May 1938, at Berkhamsted, Herts.

ASA. 39, 3 ; *JEA.* 24, 133.

EDMONSTONE, (*Sir*) **Archibald** (1795–1871)

Scottish traveller ; of Duntreath, Co. Stirling ; born 12 Mar. 1795 ; Ch. Ch. Oxon., B.A., 1816 ; travelled in Egypt, 1819 ; succeeded as 3rd Bart., 1821 ; pub. *Journey through the Two Oases of Upper Egypt,* 1822 ; brought back some antiquities from Egypt including a mummy which he gave to Dr. A. B. Granville, who published a very full account of it in *Phil. Trans.,* 1825, ii, 269 ; died 13 Mar. 1871.

DNB. 16, 398 ; *Hilmy,* i, 213.

EDWARDS, Amelia Blanford (1831–1892)

Author and Egyptologist; daughter of a military officer; born London 7 June 1831; showed as a child precocious talent for writing and drawing; a poem by her at the age of 7 was pub. in a weekly journal; took up journalism as a profession and contributed to *Chambers' Journal, Household Words, Sat. Review, Morning Post* and *Academy*; pub. 8 novels between 1855 and 1880; edited popular books on history and art; visited Syria and Egypt 1873–4 and thereupon Egyptology became her chief interest; took lessons in the language; pub. *A Thousand Miles up the Nile,* 1877, 2nd ed., 1889; considered scientific exploration the only remedy for the widespread destruction of monuments, and with the help of Reginald Stuart Poole and Sir Erasmus Wilson, founded the Egypt Exploration Fund in 1882; she acted as Secretary and gave up all other work; visited U.S.A. 1889–90 lecturing on Egypt; her lectures pub. as *Pharaohs, Fellahs and Explorers,* 1891; by her will she bequeathed her library and collections to Univ. Coll. London together with £2,400 to found a Chair in Egyptology, expressing a wish that Flinders Petrie should be appointed; he held the post for 40 years, retiring in 1933; died at Weston-super-Mare, 15 April 1892.

D.N.B. Suppl. ii, 176; *New England Mag.* (Boston, Mass.) N.S. 7, No. 5, 547–64; *Arena* (Boston), iv, No. 3, 299–310; *JEA*. 33, 66 (Portr.); *Hilmy,* i, 213; *Newberry Corresp.*

EISENLOHR, Auguste (1832–1902)

German Egyptologist; born Mannheim, 6 Oct. 1832; studied theology and natural science at Göttingen and Heidelberg; later took up Egyptology under Lepsius and joined the staff of Heidelberg Univ. 1869; Professor of Egyptology, 1872–1885; retired 1885, and made Honorary Professor, visited Egypt several times, and London in 1872, when he studied the Great Harris Papyrus and pub. a translation of it in collaboration with Samuel Birch; when in London also he secretly made tracings from Birch's facsimile of the Rhind Mathematical Papyrus and published them without authority; contributed to *ZÄS, PSBA* and other journals; died 24 Feb. 1902.

Sphinx, 6, 39; *JEA*. 35, 164; *Hilmy,* i, 220.

ENGELBACH, Reginald (1888–1946)

Engineer and Egyptologist; born Moreton Hampstead, Devon, 9 July 1888; trained as an engineer in the London Technical College, but his studies were interrupted by a long illness, and a visit to Egypt in convalescence in 1909–10 turned his attention to Egyptology; he studied Egyptian, Coptic and Arabic, and in 1911 went as assistant to Petrie and excavated at Heliopolis, Harageh and other sites; in 1914 he joined the Artists Rifles, and served in France and Gallipoli and was then sent by Allenby to report on the ancient sites in Syria and Palestine; after the war, he returned to Petrie at Lahun and Gurob, 1919, and in 1920 was appointed Chief Inspector in Upper Egypt for the Service des Antiquités; Asst. Keeper, Cairo Museum, 1924; Chief Keeper, 1931; retired 1941; contributed to excavation memoirs and to *ASA* and other journals; pub. two important works, on obelisks, 1922 and ancient Eg. masonry, 1930; died 26 Feb. 1946.

JEA. 32, 97 ; *ASA*. 48, 1 (Portr.).

ENGLISH, George Bethune (1787–1828)

American artillery officer ; born 7 Mar. 1787 ; in the service of the Egyptian army and accompanied the expedition of Ismail Pasha to Dongola and Senaar, 1820 ; pub. *A Narrative of the Expedition to Dongola and Senaar*, London, 1822 and Boston, Mass., 1823 ; died 20 Sept. 1828.

DAB. ; *Westcar Diary*, 12, 173, 179 ; *Hilmy*, i, 222.

ERMAN, Johann Peter Adolf (1854–1937)

German Egyptologist, of Swiss Protestant descent, born Berlin, 1854 ; educ. Berlin and Leipsic, where he was a pupil of Ebers ; director of Eg. Dept. of Berlin Museum and Professor of Egyptology, 1884–1923 ; his studies led to a completely new conception of the nature of the ancient Eg. language, which his own numerous works, and those of his pupils and successors, have established as the basis of all modern philological study ; he initiated, and for many years edited, the great *Worterbuch* which appeared in 5 vols., 1926–31 and for which the references are still mostly unpublished ; in addition to his many philological and technical works, he published popular works which have been translated into English as *Life in Ancient Egypt* (1895) ; *Egyptian Religion* (1907) and *Literature of the Ancient Egyptians*, 1927 ; Hon. F.B.A., 1933 ; died near Berlin, 26 June 1937.

Autobiogr. *Mein Werden und mein Wirken*, 1929 ; *JEA*. 23, 81 ; 24, 231 ; *ZÄS*. 73, *v*.

ESDAILE, James (1808–1859)

Surgeon ; born 6 Feb. 1808 ; M.D., Edinb., 1831 ; H.E.I.C. Med. Service, Bengal Presidency ; on furlough in Egypt and Europe, 1836–8 ; returned to India, 1838, in charge of Hoogly Hospital ; practised mesmerism as anaesthetic in surgical operations, for which he claimed high results, on which a Govt. report was pub. in Calcutta, 1846 ; pub. *Letters from the Red Sea, Egypt and the Continent*, Calcutta, 1839 ; died 1859.

DNB. 18, 1 ; D. G. Crawford, *Hist. Indian Med. Service*, ii, 153–6.

EUMORFOPOULOS, George (1863–1939)

Director of Ralli Bros. Ltd. ; born Liverpool, 1863 ; M.R.A.S., 1924 ; F.S.A. ; collector of antiquities, ceramics and objets-d'art ; a generous supporter of archaeological and other societies ; had one of the finest collections of ceramics ever made, a sumptuous catalogue of which, by R. L. Hobson, was privately printed in 6 vols., 1925–8 ; he was a benefactor of the E.E.S. ; travelled extensively in China and other parts of the East ; his Eg. antiquities sold at Sotheby's, 6 June 1940 (lots 146–160) ; died 19 Dec. 1939.

WWW. iii, 420 ; *Newberry Corresp*.

EVANS, (*Sir*) **John** (1823–1908)

Geologist and archaeologist ; born 17 Nov. 1823 ; educ. Market Bosworth School ; made geological investigations, especially into problems of water-supply ; formed large collections of fossils, stone and bronze implements, medieval antiquities and ancient British coins ; F.S.A., 1852 ; F.R.S., 1864 and Treas. 1878–98 ; President of many Societies : Brit. Assn., 1897–8 ; Geological Soc., 1874–6 ; R. Numismatic Soc., 1874–1908 ; Soc. of Antiquaries, 1885–92 ; Anthrop. Inst., 1877–9 ; Inst. of Chemical Industry, 1892–3 ; K.C.B., 1892 ; D.C.L. ; LL.D. ; Hon. Fellow of Brasenose Coll. ; his books include the standard works on the Coins of Ancient Britain and on Stone and Bronze Implements ; President, E.E.F., 1899–1906 ; died 31 May 1908.

WWW. i, 232 ; *DNB*. Suppl.

EVANS, John (*d*. 1903)

Military officer ; of Merles, Slinfold, Sussex ; Cornet Inniskilling Dragoons, 1854 ; Cornet, 9th Lancers, 1856, retired Colonel ; war service in the Crimea and Indian Mutiny ; with his regiment in Egypt, 1858–62 ; frequently visited Egypt and formed an important collection of antiquities ; exhibited at Burlington Fine Art Club, 1895 ; the collection sold at Sotheby's, 30 June and 1 July 1924 (356 lots) ; a demotic papyrus, not in the sale, was acquired by B.M. (10480) ; retired 1889 ; died 30 May 1903.

R.U.S.I. Records.

FELIX, Orlando (1790–1860)

Military officer and traveller ; born 1790 ; Rifle Brigade, Capt., 1824 ; retired Major-General ; served at Waterloo, wounded at Quatre Bras ; Waterloo Medal ; accompanied Lord Prudhoe (afterwards Duke of Northumberland, see PERCY, Algernon) in his travels to Egypt, Nubia and Sinai ; he met Champollion in Nubia in 1828 ; made many drawings and notes, some of which are at Alnwick, others in B.M. (Add. MSS. 25663, f. 42–107) ; in 1830 pub. a brochure with lithographic plates, *Notes on Hieroglyphics* ; his Waterloo medal was sold at Glendinings, 28 Jan. 1947, lot 20 ; died at Genoa, 5 Apl. 1860.

Dalton, *Waterloo Roll-Call*, 197 ; *Hay Diary* ; *Hartleben*, ii, 88, 207, 268, 275, 345 ; *Champollion*, ii, 207–8 ; *Add. MS*. 25658, f. 79–84 ; 25672, f. 29 ; *Hilmy*, i, 230.

FÉRET, Nicolas (1688–1749)

French Scholar ; attempted to decipher hieroglyphic writing ; pub. *Essai sur les Hiéroglyphes Scientifiques*, 1744, as a commentary on Warburton's work and other works dealing with ancient astronomy, weights and measures, etc.

BIFAO. 5, 82 ; *Hilmy*, i, 248.

FERLINI, Giuseppe (*c*. 1800–1876)

Italian physician of Bologna ; born about 1800 ; joined the service of the Egyptian army and appointed Surgeon-Major, 1830 ; served at Senaar and later at Khartûm ; excavated in the pyramid-field of Meroë, the expedition starting 10 Aug. 1834 ; the work was carried out in partnership with Antonio Stefani, an Albanian merchant settled in Khartûm ; Ferlini's finds were afterwards sold and acquired by the museums of Berlin and Munich ; an account of the excavations was published (in Italian), Bologna, 1837 and a French translation, Rome, 1838 ; both these publications contain a catalogue of the objects found ; died 1876.

Budge, *Eg. Sudan*, i, 285 (extracts from Ferlini's publication, trans. into English, 307 ff.–313 ff.) ; *Hilmy*, i, 230 ; *Lepsius*, 151, 197.

FERNANDEZ, Solomon (*fl.* 1830–60)

Jewish antiquity-dealer of Cairo ; exploited the necropolis of Sakkara and many important objects passed through his hands ; according to Prisse, the famous " Scribe accroupi " of the Louvre was not found by Mariette, but was bought by him from Fernandez for fcs. 120 ; Wilkinson examined his collection in 1830, and Lepsius in 1842.

Bibl. Ég. 18, pp. xxvii, xxx, xxxvi, lii ; W. Reil, *Ægypten als Winteraufenhalt*, 1859, 198 ; Prisse, *Petits mem. secrètes*, ed. Auriant, 1930, 40 ; *Carré*, i, 312 ; *Wilkinson MSS.* ; *L.D.*, *Text.* i, 14, 16, 222.

FINATI, Giovanni (1787–1829+)

Italian traveller ; born Ferrara, 1787 ; went as a young man to Alexandria and enlisted in the service of Mohammad Ali ; took part in the capture of Mecca and Medina and the Wahabi and Arabian campaigns ; afterwards acted as dragoman and interpreter to European travellers in the East ; went with W. J. Bankes to Upper Egypt, Nubia, Syria and Palestine, 1815–18 ; accompanied Sir Frederick Henniker to Abu Simbel, 1819–20 ; visited England for two years, and returned to Cairo with Lord Prudhoe and accompanied him in his travels in Egypt, Nubia and Syria, returning to Cairo in 1829 and is believed to have established a hotel there ; he dictated an account of his life and travels to Bankes, who translated and published it in 1830 ; not traced after 1829.

Life and Adventures of Giovanni Finati, ed. W. J. Bankes, 2 vols., London, 1830.

FIRTH, Cecil Mallaby (1878–1931)

Egyptologist ; born 1878 ; trained for the Bar and went to Cyprus to take up a judicial appointment, but went on to Egypt and entered the Service des Antiquités, in which he served for 30 years, except whilst on military service, 1914–18 ; associated with Reisner in the Arch. Survey of Nubia, 1907–10, and undertook the preparation of a long series of reports on the excavations ; Inspector of Antiquities at Sakkara, 1923, and carried out excavations in that area ; returned to England on leave in 1931 ; on arrival he was taken ill, and a few days later died of pneumonia in a London nursing-home, 25 July 1931.

JEA. 17, 255.

FLORIS, Mattéo (*d.* 1884)

A Corsican handyman employed by Mariette to make cases, pedestals and mounts for the first museum of Bulak ; he also made restorations and casts and was employed as an assistant conservator in the museum ; nothing is known of his previous history.

Maspero, *Bibl. Ég.* 18, p. xcii ; *Guide* (4th ed. 1915), pref. xiv ; *Rapports sur la Marche du Serv. des Antiquités*, 159 ; Devéria, *Mem. et Fragm.* i, 326.

FORBIN, (*Comte de*) **Philippe Auguste** (1777–1842)

French artist and traveller ; Gentilhomme de la Chambre du Roi ; Directeur-Général des Musées ; extended the Louvre and founded the Musée de Luxembourg ; travelled in the Near East, and visited Egypt 1818 and 1828 to acquire antiquities for the Louvre ; visited Upper Egypt and conducted excavations directed by J. J. Rifaud and came into conflict with the agents of Drovetti and Salt ; pub. *Voyage dans le Levant*, Paris, 1819 ; was hostile to Champollion.

Carré, i, 194 ; *Champollion*, i, passim ; *Belzoni*, i, 389, 392 ; *Hilmy*, i, 163.

FORMAN, William Henry (1793–1869)

Of Pipbrook House, Dorking, Surrey ; collector of antiquities and works of art ; born Doncaster, 1793 ; educ. Charterhouse ; his large collection of antiquities, including many Eg. items, together with his library and all his property, was bequeathed to his nephew, Major Alexander Henry Browne (q.v.) by whose executors they were sold at Sotheby's—the antiquities 19–22 June 1899 and the library, 3 July 1899 ; the collection was begun by Thomas Seaton Forman, his elder brother, who had travelled in the East, and who died at Pisa, 1850 ; W. H. Forman died unmarried, 29 Aug. 1869.

Inf. by the Browne family.

FOUCART, Georges (1865–1946)

French Egyptologist, son of the classical scholar Paul F. ; born Versailles 11 Dec. 1865 ; trained by his father, and attended classes at École des Hautes Études ; travelled in Greece with his father and in 1891 went to Egypt where he was appointed by De Morgan Inspector of Antiquities in Lower Egypt ; from 1892–4 he visited all the sites in his district, including Bubustis ; Professor of Ancient Hist., Univ. of Bordeaux, 1897, and of the History of Religions at Aix-en-Provence, 1903 ; D.Ph., 1910 ; Director of Inst. Fr. Arch. Orientale, 1915 ; retired 1928 ; pub. many important papers, particularly on the history of religions ; died at Zamalek, 18 May 1946.

Chron. 21, 81–7.

FOULD, Achille (1800–1867)

French statesman and art-collector ; born Paris, 1800 ; son of a Jewish banker and sénateur ; elected to Acad. des Beaux-Arts, 1857 ; Ministre des Finances, 1861–7 ; collected antiquities and bought many lots at the Anastasi Sale of 1857 ; his Eg. antiquities were acquired by the Louvre in 1860 ; died at Tarbes, 1867.

Rev. de l'Art, 43, 168.

FOUQUET, Daniel Marie (1850–1914)

French physician; born 16 Mar. 1850 at Doué-la-Fontaine, Saumur; studied medicine in Paris; made two journeys to S. America, then settled in Cairo in 1881; rendered important service in the cholera outbreak in 1883; Maspero enlisted his service to examine the royal mummies (*Momies Royales*, 773–82); published a memoir on embalming full of erroneous observations and inferences (*Bull. Inst. Ég.*, 1896, 89); made a fine collection of antiquities, particularly rich in bronzes, which was sold in Paris, June 12–14, 19–20, 1922 (608 lots); died in Cairo, Aug. 1914.

Bull. Inst. Ég. 5 ser. 8, 295; Daressy, *Les Antiquités de la Collection Fouquet*, 1922.

FOURIER, Jean Baptiste Joseph (1768–1830)

French mathematician; born Auxerre, 21 Mar. 1768; sec. Acad. des Sciences; a member of Napoleon's Commission; took an important part in the preparation of the *Description de l'Égypte*, and wrote the historical introduction and the account of the astronomical monuments; died, Paris, 16 May 1830.

EB.; *Carré*, i, 123, 140, etc.; *Hilmy*, i, 238.

FOURMONT, Claude Louis (1703–1780)

French scholar and archaeologist; born Cormeilles, 1703; pub. *Description . . . des plaines d'Hêliopolis et de Memphis*, 1755; accompanied his uncle Michel Fourmont on his travels; went to Egypt in 1746 with Lironcourt, newly appointed Consul in Cairo; interpreter to the Bibliothèque du Roi; his MSS. are in the Bibl. Nat.

NBG. 18, 370; *Larousse* 19e *cent.* 8, 680; *Carré*, i, 63; *Hilmy*, i, 238 (confusion with Etienne, F.).

FOURMONT, Étienne (1683–1745)

French orientalist; born Herbelay, St. Denis, 23 June 1683; Membre de l'Acad.; F.R.S., 1738; Professor of Arabic, Collège de France; travelled in the East; pub. *Reflexions . . . sur les Anciens Peuples*, 1735; elder brother of Michel F., Professor of Syriac, Coll. de France, and uncle of Claude Louis F.; his MSS. are partly in the Bibl. Nat., Paris, and partly at Munich; died 19 Dec. 1745.

NBG. 18, 354; *Carré*, i, 63; *Hilmy*, i, 238.

FOWLER, (*Sir*) John (1817–1899)

Civil engineer; born near Sheffield, 15 July 1817; Engineer-in-Chief, Forth Bridge, 1882–90; created Bart., 1890; in 1869 visited Egypt to advise the Khedive Ismail on railway development in which he had played a prominent part in England, and was chief engineering adviser in Egypt for 8 years from 1871; projected railway and irrigation works in Egypt and the Sudan; Pres. Inst. Civil Eng. 1865; K.C.M.G., 1885; although not an archaeologist his association with Egypt made him interested in Egyptology and he was elected Pres. E.E.F. in 1887, which he held until his death, which occurred at Bournemouth, 20 Nov. 1899.

EB.; *DNB.* Suppl. ii, 233; *WWW.* i, 256.

FOX, Robert (1798–1843)

Surgeon and antiquary ; M.R.C.S., 1819 ; practised in Huntingdon and later at Godmanchester ; founded the Literary and Scientific Inst. of Huntingdon, 1841 and lectured on natural history and archaeology ; F.S.A., 1831 ; pub. a leaflet describing a shawabti with cartouches, drawn by Bonomi ; a friend of Dr. Lee of Hartwell and Pettigrew ; died at Godmanchester, 8 June 1843 and bequeathed his collections to the Huntingdon Lit. and Sci. Inst.

DNB. 20, 132 ; *GM*. N.S. 20, 99.

FRANZ, (*Pasha*) **Julius** (*fl*. 1881–1912)

Hungarian Jew, Engineer to the Wakf Ministry and Architect to the Khedive Ismail ; founded the Museum of Arab Art in Cairo in 1881 and was Director of it until he left the Government service in 1887 ; inaugurated the Comité de Conservation des Monuments de l'Art Arabe ; pub. works on the architecture of Islam in Egypt and in Andalusia ; died in or soon after 1912.

Erman, 209, 276 ; *Inf. by Dr. P. E. Kahle.*

FRASER, George Willoughby (*fl*. 1889–1923)

Civil engineer ; assisted Petrie in his excavations in the Fayûm, 1889 ; attached to the E.E.F. Archaeological Survey under Newberry and drew plans, etc., at Beni Hasan and El Bersheh ; with M. W. Blackden copied and privately printed the hieratic graffiti at the quarries of Hat-nub ; in 1897 presented to B.M. a limestone door-socket dated the 30th year of Ammenemes II ; pub. papers in *PSBA* ; F.S.A. 1893–6, resigned, and re-elected 1904, again resigned, 1906 ; was still living in 1923.

Newberry Corresp. ; *Petrie*, 106, 107 ; Newberry, *El Bersheh*, ii, 55.

FREER, Charles Lang (1856–1915)

American manufacturer and art collector ; born Kingston, N.Y., 1856 ; educ. Ulster County, N.Y. ; Hon. A.M., Michigan Univ. ; formed a large and valuable art collection which he presented to the Smithsonian Inst., Washington, together with $1,000,000 for a building ; in Egyptology he is known for the valuable collection of Coptic manuscripts formed by him, which were pub. in 1923 by Prof. W. H. Worrell ; died 25 Sept. 1915.

WWWA. i, 425 ; Worrell, *The Coptic MSS. in the Freer Coll.*, N.Y. 1923.

GABET, —. (*fl*. 1859–1862)

Assistant to Mariette ; acted as inspector and superintendent of excavations, and as assistant conservator in the Bulak Museum ; he was appointed about 1859, but nothing is known of his previous history ; a long letter from him to Mariette, dated Gourneh, 16 Dec. 1862, reporting on his work in the Theban necropolis and temples, was pub. in *Rec. Trav.* 12, 215–8.

Bibl. Ég. 4, 326–7 ; 18, p. xci.

GAILLARD, Claude (1861–1945)

French naturalist ; born Villenbanne, Rhône, 1861 ; began life in commerce, but on the introduction of the anthropologist F. Chantre of the Lyons Museum, he joined the staff there as preparator ; under Loret's encouragement he studied at the Faculté des Sciences, and accompanied Loret to Egypt ; he studied particularly the ancient fauna of Egypt and collaborated with Lartet and Daressy in publications thereon in Cairo *Cat. Gen.*, and *Archives* of Lyons Museum ; succeeded Lartet as Director of the Museum and retired in 1939 after 53 years' service ; President, Soc. Linnéenne de Lyon, 1918 ; died 1945.

GALTIER, Joseph (1864–1908)

French orientalist ; studied at the Éc. des Hautes Études ; member of the Inst. Fr. d'Arch. Orient., Cairo ; succeeded Léon Barry as Librarian of the Cairo Museum ; died 2 April, 1908.

Maspero, *Rapports sur la Marche du Serv. des Antiq.* (1912), 279.

GANNAL, Jean Nicholas (1791–1852)

French surgeon ; served in the Medical Dept. of the French Army and afterwards took up chemical research ; made many improvements in technical and medical chemistry, and devoted much attention to the preservation of tissues for anatomy and to the embalming of the dead, for which he invented a new system which was largely adopted ; pub. *Hist. des Embaumements*, 1838, 2nd ed., Paris, 1841 in which he deals very fully with Eg. mummification.

Mem. Inst. Ég. 13 (1929), 16.

GAU, François Chrétien (1790–1853)

French architect ; of German origin, born Cologne 1790 ; naturalized French, 1826 ; studied in Paris ; in 1818–9 went to Egypt and made drawings of the monuments of Nubia between the first and second cataracts which were published in parts, 1821–7 ; this work, *Antiquités de la Nubie*, a large folio, was intended as a supplement to the *Description de l'Égypte*, Champollion criticised the accuracy of the drawings ; discovered at Kalabsheh the Greek inscription of Silko the Ethiopian ; Gau was afterwards a well known architect of public buildings in France.

Carré, i, 220, 232, 239 ; *Champollion*, ii, 176, 177, 211, 455 ; *Hilmy*, i, 254 ; *Edwards*, 376.

GAYER-ANDERSON, (*Pasha*) **Robert Grenville** (1881–1945)

Army surgeon ; M.R.C.S. ; L.R.C.P. ; joined R.A.M.C. 1904 and served with the Egyptian Army, 1907–17 ; served in Gallipoli and Egypt, 1914–8 ; retired Major, 1920 ; Oriental Secretary at the Residency, Cairo, 1922–3 ; resigned, 1923 ; revisited Egypt, 1942 ; made a considerable collection of Eg. antiquities which he presented to Fitzwilliam Museum, Cambridge, 1943 ; died at Little Hall, Lavenham, Suffolk, 16 June, 1945.

Lancet, 1945, ii, 62 ; *Newberry Corresp.* ; *Chron.* 21, 88.

GAYET, Albert Jean (1856–1916)

French Egyptologist ; studied under Maspero in Paris ; went to Egypt with the Mission Archéologique, 1881, and was first employed in copying the Temple of Luxor ; afterwards excavated for many years at Antinoë and undertook publications for the Musée Guimet.

Maspero, *l'Égyptologie* (1915), 10, 17, 29, 30 ; *Wilbour*, 357, 521, 525, 532, 547, 589 (Portr. facing p. 240) ; *Sayce*, 268.

GELL, (*Sir*) **William** (1777–1836)

Scholar and traveller ; born Hopton, Co. Derby, 1777 ; Jesus Coll. Cantab., B.A., 1798 ; M.A., 1804 ; Fellow of Emanuel Coll. ; studied art at R.A. Schools ; visited the Troad, 1801, and pub. *Topography of Troy*, 1804 ; sent on mission to Ionian Islands, 1803 ; Knighted, 1803 ; travelled in Greece for some years from 1804, and published a number of works on the topography and antiquities of Greece ; accompanied Princess (later Queen) Caroline to Italy, 1814 ; from 1820 until his death he lived in Rome and Naples ; was much interested in hieroglyphic decipherment and corresponded with Young, Wilkinson and others on the subject ; F.R.S. ; F.S.A. ; died Naples, 4 Feb. 1836 ; two note-books on hieroglyphics are now in the library of Sir Alan Gardiner.

DNB. 21, 115 ; *JEA*. 2, 76 ; *Hartleben*, passim ; *Champollion*, i, 204, 208, 376, 382 ; ii, 401.

GIERS, Nikolai Karlovich de (1820–1895)

Russian statesman ; born 21 May 1820 ; held many important posts in the Ministry of Foreign Affairs, particularly in the East ; in private life a collector of antiquities ; the Egyptian part of his collection was acquired by the Hermitage Museum in 1867 ; died 26 Jan. 1895.

EB. ; Golenischeff, *Erm*. pp. vi–vii.

GIPPS, (*Sir*) **George** (1791–1847)

Army officer ; entered R.E., 1809 ; wounded at Badajoz, 1812 ; Capt., 1814 ; discovered the Nilometer at Elephantine, 25 Mar. 1822 ; afterwards a Colonial Governor.

DNB. 21, 387 ; *Henniker*, 147, 345.

GLADSTONE, John Hall (1827–1902)

Chemist and physicist ; born London, 1827 ; ed. Univ. Coll., London and Giessen ; Ph.D. ; D.Sc. ; F.R.S. ; wrote on ancient metals from Egypt in *PSBA*, vols. 12–14 and in Petrie, *Dendereh* ; died 6 Oct. 1902.

WWW. i, 277 ; A. Lucas, *Anc. Eg. Materials*, 2nd ed., 147, 172, 184.

GLIDDON, George Robins (1809–1857)

American Egyptologist ; born Devonshire, 1809 ; s. John Gliddon, a merchant, who became U.S. Consul at Alexandria ; was taken to Egypt at an early age and later became U.S. Vice-Consul in Egypt ; in 1842 went to America and lectured on Eg. archaeology at Boston, 1842–3, and at the Lowell Institute, 1843–4 ; in the following years made lecture-tours as far West as St. Louis ; he pub. several works on Egypt, one of which had a very large sale ; he made a contribution to mummification in his *Otia Ægyptiaca*, 52–113, which though discursive, made some good points ; died at Panama, 1857.

N.Y. Hist. Soc. Q. Bull. iv, 1920, 6–8 ; *MMA. Bull.* 25, 1920, 88 ; *Mem. Inst. Eg.* 13, 1929, 17 ; *Hilmy*, i, 263.

GOLENISCHEFF, Vladimir Samionovich (1856–1947)

Russian Egyptologist ; son of a Grand Duke by a morganatic marriage ; born 1856 ; inherited his father's estates but not his titles ; he visited Egypt no less than sixty times and brought back a rich collection of antiquities which he ceded in 1911 to the Moscow Museum ; after the Revolution he never returned to Russia, but resided in Nice ; he was for some time employed in cataloguing the hieratic papyri in the Cairo Museum ; his first important publication was *Die Metternichstele*, 1877 ; Golenischeff's name is associated with many important papyri : the literary papyri and the Story of the Shipwrecked Sailor, now in the Hermitage Museum, and the Mathematical Papyrus, the Onomasticon, the Hymns to the Diadem, the Story of Wenamun, and other papyri at Moscow ; he died in 1947.

JEA. 33, 2 ; *Sayce*, 265, 415 ; *Hilmy*, i, 265.

GOODWIN, Charles Wycliffe (1817–1878)

Scholar and Egyptologist ; son of a lawyer of King's Lynn, Norfolk ; born 2 April, 1817 ; educated High Wycombe and St. Catherine's Hall, Cantab. ; M.A. ; Fellow ; Called to the Bar, Lincoln's Inn, 1843 ; practised as a barrister in London ; assistant Judge, China and Japan, 1865 ; judge, 1877 ; a fine Greek, Hebrew and Anglo-Saxon scholar ; his principal interest throughout life was Egyptology, begun in school days ; a brilliant decipherer of hieratic texts and made many philological discoveries ; his essay *Hieratic Papyri* in Cambridge Essays, 1858, marks an epoch in Egyptology ; visited Alexandria and Cairo on his way to the Far East, 1865 ; died, Shanghai, 17 Jan. 1878 ; Goodwin's Egyptological MSS. are in the B.M. (Add. MSS. 31268–98).

DNB. 22, 142 ; W. R. Dawson, *Charles Wycliffe Goodwin*, Oxf. 1934 (Portr. and Bibliogr.) ; Glanville, *Growth and Nature of Egyptology*, 1947, 6–9 ; *Dawson MSS*. 9, f. 86–126 ; 18, f. 41–79 ; *Hilmy*, i, 267.

GOODYEAR, William Henry (1846–1923)

American archaeologist ; born New Haven, Conn., 21 Apl. 1846 ; educ. Yale, Heidelberg and Berlin ; Curator Metrop. Museum of Art, N.Y., 1881–8 ; visited Egypt 1891–2 ; Curator, Brooklyn Inst. of Fine Arts, 1899–1923 ; founder of Amer. Anthropological Assn., 1902 ; wrote much on ancient art, his most important contribution to that of Egypt being his *Grammar of the Lotus*, 1891 ; died 19 Feb. 1923.

WWW. ii, 418 ; *Newberry Corresp*.

GORDON, Alexander (*c*. 1692–*c*. 1754)

Scottish author and traveller ; born about 1692 ; M.A., Aberdeen ; Sec. Soc. for Encouragement of Learning ; F.S.A., Sec. 1736–41 ; member of Spalding Soc. ; Sec. Egyptian Society, 1741 ; pub. many antiquarian works, and two large pamphlets, with good plates, on the mummies belonging to Dr. Richard Mead and Capt. Lethieullier, 1737, and by subscription, 25 plates, without letterpress, of Eg. antiquities and hieroglyphs, 1737–9 ; went to S. Carolina as sec. to Governor Glen, where he died about 1754.

DNB. 22, 164 ; Nichols, *Lit. Anecd.* 5, 329–337 ; *BIFAO,* 5, 82 ; *JEA.* 23, 259 ; *Hilmy,* i, 268.

GORDON, Robert James (*d.* 1823)

Naval officer and explorer ; Capt., R.N. ; set out to explore the interior of Africa for the African Association ; sailed from Malta to Egypt with John Madox (q.v.) Feb. 1822 ; climbed the Second Pyramid and copied the Arabic inscription on the apex ; Salt provided him with letters to various potentates and a firman from the Pasha ; ascended the Nile to Upper Nubia and died at Senaar, 1 July 1823.

Henniker, 213, 343 ; *Madox,* i, 98, 122, 263 ; *Salt,* ii, 205, 211.

GORRINGE, Henry Honeychurch (1841–1885)

American naval officer ; born 11 Aug. 1841 ; superintended the erection in the Central Park, New York, of the obelisk presented by the Khedive Ismail in 1877 ; it was brought from Egypt in 1880 and set up in 1881 ; pub. *Egyptian Obelisks,* N.Y., 1882 ; collected antiquities, which are described in *Anc. Eg.,* 1916, 49 ; retired Lieut.-Commander ; died 6 July 1885.

DAB. ; *Hilmy,* i, 270.

GOULIANOFF, Ivan Alexandrovich (1789–1841)

Russian Egyptologist ; born Moldavia, 1789 ; served in the Russian Ministry of Foreign Affairs in various places ; Member of Russian Acad., 1821 ; pub. *Discours sur l'étude fondamentale des langues,* 1822 ; *Essai sur les hiéroglyphes d'Horapollon,* 1827 ; *Zamiechania o Diendierskom zodiakie* [Remarks on the Dendereh Zodiac], Moscow, 1831 ; *Archéologie égyptienne,* Leipsic, 1839 ; died at Nice, 1841.

Inf. by Prof. J. Černý.

GOURDIN, François Philippe (1739–1825)

French Benedictine monk ; pub. in *Mag. Encyclopédique* a dissertation attempting to prove the identity of Egyptian hieroglyphic and Chinese writing.

BIFAO. 5, 85 ; *Hilmy,* i, 271.

GOURLAY, Janet A. (*d.* 1912)

Met Miss Margaret Benson (q.v.) in Egypt in 1895 and joined with her in the excavation of the Temple of Mut at Thebes and in the publication of it, *The Temple of Mut in Asher,* 1899, assisted by P. E. Newberry ; she spent several seasons in Egypt between 1895 and 1901 ; died, unmarried, in 1912.

A. C. Benson, *Life and Letters of Maggie Benson,* 152, 189, 420, and often (Portr. facing p. 376) ; *Newberry Corresp.*

GRAF, (*Ritter*) **Theodor** (*d. c.* 1920)

Dealer in antiquities in Cairo and Vienna ; sold the great find of papyri from Arsinoë made in 1877–8 to the Archduke Rainer of Vienna ; sold 160 Tell el-Amarna tablets to Berlin Museum, 1888 ; the Romano-Egyptian portrait-panels bequeathed by Dr. Ludwig Mond to the Nat. Gallery came from the Graf collection ; other objects from his collection often appear in sales ; held an exhibition in Paris, 1889, of portrait-panels and other antiquities from the Fayûm ; his collection of portrait-panels is now mainly in Berlin ; made Ritter, 1884 ; died about 1920.

J. Karabacen, *Die Theodor Graf'schen Funde in Ægypten*, Vienna, 1883 ; Maspero, *Ét. de Myth*, vi, 288 ; *Wilbour*, 469 ; *Hilmy*, i, 339 ; Paul Buberl, *Mumienbildnisse der Sammlung Th. Graf*, 1923 ; *Erman*, 224–5.

GRANT, (*Bey*) **James Andrew Sandilands** (1840–1896)

Son of a banker ; born Methlick, 1840 ; educ. Aberdeen Grammar School and University ; M.A., 1862 ; M.D., 1864 ; LL.D., 1882 ; went to Egypt to deal with a violent outbreak of cholera ; he was so successful he was given the Order of Medjidieh ; returned to Scotland as Superintendent of the Banff Asylum ; returned to Egypt, when he settled in Cairo, had a Government appointment, and was made Bey by the Khedive ; made a good collection of Eg. antiquities which he bequeathed to the Museum of Aberdeen University ; died, Bridge of Allan, 1896.

Aberdeen Mus. Records ; frequently mentioned in *Petrie* and *Wilbour* (see index).

GRANVILLE, Augustus Bozzi (1783–1872)

Physician of Italian origin, son of Carlo Bozzi, postmaster ; born Milan, 1783 ; studied medicine at Pavia under Spallanzani and Volta, but his studies were interrupted by political imprisonment ; on his release, he travelled in the East and settled in England assuming the name of Granville ; M.D., 1802 ; M.R.C.S., 1813 ; L.R.C.P., 1817 ; F.R.S., 1817 ; practised in Savile Row, London, specializing in the diseases of women and children ; left London in 1871 and settled in Dover, where he died, 3 Mar. 1872 ; much interested in Egyptology and published a valuable account of a mummy of the Persian period with uterine disease (*Phil. Trans.* 1825, 269–316, cf. *JEA.* 11, 76).

DNB. 22, 412 ; Munk, *Roll Coll. of Physicians*, iii, 174–7 (Bibliogr.) ; *Hilmy*, i, 272 ; *Mem. Inst. Eg.* 13, 17 (1929).

GRDSELOFF, Bernhard (1915–1950)

Polish Egyptologist ; born 1 July 1915 ; began his studies in the Berlin Museum and became a pupil of Sethe ; attached to the German Archaeological Institute in Cairo and worked there under Borchardt, who appointed him secretary ; editorial sec. of the Soc. des études juives en Égypte ; a brilliant scholar, by his early death he left much unfinished work, but during his last illness he prepared and dictated six articles which have been published posthumously, *in memoriam* ; died 8 Oct. 1950.

ASA. 51, 123–8 (Portr. & Bibl.), with 6 articles *ut supra*, 129–166.

GRÉBAUT, Eugène (1846–1915)

French Egyptologist ; son of a notary ; born 1846 ; educ. École des Hautes Études ; studied Arabic under Guyard and Egyptology under Maspero ; pub. the Cairo Hymn to Amun, 1872–5, a work that showed great promise ; lectured at École, 1876–8 and continued to study there till 1883 ; appointed to succeed Lefébure as Director of the Mission Archéol. at Cairo, 1884–6 ; succeeded Maspero as Director of the Serv. des Antiquités, 1886–92 ; he was by nature unsuited to this work and caused much ill-feeling both with Egyptologists and natives ; resigned 1892 and returned to Paris, becoming lecturer in Ancient History at the Sorbonne until his death, 8 Jan. 1915.

Maspero, *L'Égyptologie* (1915), 8, 13, 16 ; *Rev. Arch.* 4th Ser., 24, 333 ; numerous references to Grébaut will be found in the indexes of the following : *Budge N & T, Petrie, Sayce, Wilbour* ; *JEA*. 33, 80 ; *Hilmy*, i, 276.

GREEN, Frederick William (1869–1949)

Egyptologist and antiquary ; born London 21 Mar. 1869 ; Jesus Coll., Cantab. ; B.A., 1898 ; M.A., 1901 ; took an early interest in Egyptology which he studied under Sethe at Göttingen and later at Strasbourg ; excavated in Egypt with Petrie and Reisner ; in 1898 while working with Quibell for the Egyptian Research Account, he discovered the famous decorated tomb of Hierakonpolis ; Hon. Keeper of Antiquities, Fitzwilliam Museum, Cambridge, 1908–49 ; in charge of the Mond excavations at Arment, 1929–30 ; worked for Eg. Govt. Geological Survey, 1897–1900, and prepared maps for other surveys, 1905–14 ; died Great Shelford, Cambs., 20 Aug. 1949.

Inf. by Mrs. Green.

GREENE, John Baker (*c.* 1830–*c.* 1886)

Surgeon, barrister and archaeologist ; born about 1830 ; A.B., Dublin, M.D. and L.S.A., 1853 ; M.R.C.S., 1853 ; studied Egyptology under de Rougé ; excavated at Thebes in 1854–5 and pub. his results in a large folio vol. *Fouilles exécutées à Thèbes*, Paris, 1855 ; Asst. Surgeon, 1st Royal Scots in the Crimean War ; Barrister-at-Law, Middle Temple, 1858 ; LL.B. London, 1861 ; member of council, R. Hist. Soc., 1880–6 ; pub. *The Hebrew Migration from Egypt*, 1882, 2nd ed. 1883, contributions to *PEFQS* (1884, 230–7 ; 1885, 67) and other works ; died about 1886.

Med. Directory, 1885 ; *Chabas*, 14, 18 ; *Hilmy*, i, 276 ; ii, 418.

GREENFIELD, (*Mrs.*) **Edith Mary** (*d.* 1935)

Widow of H. B. Greenfield of Derby, a contractor who carried out harbour works at Alexandria in 1880 ; while in Egypt he bought the fine funerary papyrus of Princess Estnibasher ("Nesitanebtashru"), from the cache of royal mummies, the longest funerary papyrus known ; this papyrus was presented to the B.M. in May 1910 by Mrs. Greenfield, and it was published by the Trustees, *The Greenfield Papyrus*, 1912, ed. Budge ; Mrs. G. died at Morley Manor, Derby, 13 May 1935.

Cromer, *Modern Eg.* i, 171 ; *The Times*, 15 May, 1935.

GREENHILL, Thomas (1681–1740)

Physician and surgeon; born 1681; practised in King Street, Bloomsbury, and had a distinguished clientèle and a high reputation; he was not F.R.S., but he made two communications to *Phil. Trans.*; pub. ΝΕΚΡΟΚΗΔΕΙΑ, *or the Art of Embalming*, London, 1705, in which Eg. mummification enters largely; his father had been Sec. to General Monk; his mother had 39 children, all born living, in commemoration of which an augmentation was granted to the family arms; the grant is dated 1 Sept. 10 Wm. III (1698), and is made to Thomas Greenhill as the 39th child; died 1740.

DNB. 23, 80; *Mem. Inst. Eg.* 13 (1929), 18–20; *Hilmy*, i, 277.

GRENFELL, (*Mrs.*) **Alice** (*d.* 1917)

Collector and student of scarabs; widow of John Granville Grenfell, Master of Clifton College and mother of Bernard Pyne Grenfell; she had an important collection of scarabs, described in *Anc. Eg.* 1916, 22; contributed many learned articles to *Rec. Trav.* and other journals on the symbols etc. used in scarabs, and described the collection in Queen's Coll. Oxford (*JEA.* 2, 217); died 8 Aug. 1917.

JEA. 4, 280.

GRENFELL, Bernard Pyne (1869–1926)

Papyrologist; born Birmingham, 16 Dec. 1869; educ. Clifton Coll. and Queen's Coll. Oxon; Fellow, 1894; M.A.; D. Litt.; F.B.A.; hon. member of many foreign academies; Prof. of Papyrology, Oxford, 1916; went to Egypt in 1894 for training in excavation under Petrie and in 1895 and succeeding years explored the Fayûm sites for papyri for the E.E.F.; on the formation of the Graeco-Roman Branch of the E.E.F., he edited with Hunt many volumes of the *Oxyrhynchus Papyri* and other publications of that Branch, though his work was often interrupted by ill-health; he also collaborated with Hunt in the catalogues of the Amherst, John Rylands and Cairo collections; his first independent work was the *Revenue Laws of Ptolemy Philadelphus*, 1896, based on the important papyrus obtained by Petrie in 1894; died 17 April 1926.

WWW. ii, 436; *JEA.* 12, 285; *Aegyptus*, 8, 114; *Rev. Arch.* Ser. 5, 24, 76.

GRENFELL, Francis Wallace, 1st Baron (1841–1925)

Field Marshal; born 29 Apl. 1841; entered the Army, 1859; Colonel, 1882; General, 1904; Field Marshal, 1908; P.C.; G.C.B.; G.C.M.G.; LL.D.; F.S.A.; created Baron Grenfell of Kilvey, 1902; served in Egypt and Sudan, 1882–9; Commander-in-Chief, Egyptian Army; conducted excavations at Assuan and collected antiquities; a good friend to archaeologists in Egypt; his collections sold at Sotheby's, 12–14 Nov. 1917 (479 lots); died 27 Jan. 1925.

WWW. ii, 436; *Budge N & T.* i, 74, 81, 88; *Sayce*, 239; *Petrie*, 122, 135; *PSBA.* x, 4–40.

GRENVILLE, George Nugent, 1st Baron Nugent (1788–1850)

Younger son of 1st Marquis of Buckingham; born 1788; succeeded to his mother's Irish peerage, 1833; a Lord of the Treasury, 1830–2;

High Commissioner of the Ionian Islands, 1832–5 ; travelled in Egypt in 1844 and made a collection of antiquities, which passed first to his niece, Lady Boileau of Kettering Park, Norfolk, and then to Lord Vernon ; it was sold at Sotheby's, 12 Dec. 1926 ; some of the most interesting objects were pub. by Blackman, *JEA*. 4, 39 ; died 1850.

DNB. 23, 119.

GREY, (*Rev.*) **George Francis** (1794–1854)

Scholar and traveller ; of Backworth, Northumberland ; Univ. Coll. Oxon ; B.A., 1814 ; M.A., 1822 ; Fellow, 1814–53 ; travelled in Egypt in 1820 and accompanied Sir Frederick Henniker to Upper Egypt ; bought some papyri at Thebes which he submitted to Thomas Young ; pub. " Inscriptions from the Waady el-Makketeb copied in 1820," *Trans. R.S.L.* ii, 147 (1834) ; died 6 Oct. 1854.

Al. Oxon. ; *Henniker*, 75 ; *Syro-Eg. Soc. Inscr.*, 1852 ; Young, *Discoveries*, 38, 55, 76, 145 ; Pettigrew, *Hist. Eg. Mummies*, 150 ; *Champollion*, i, 91, 92 ; *Hilmy*, i, 277.

GRIFFITH, Agnes Sophia—*See* JOHNS

GRIFFITH, Francis Llewellyn (1862–1934)

Egyptologist ; born, Brighton, 1862 ; educ. Brighton Coll., Sedbergh, Highgate, Queen's Coll. Oxon ; M.A. ; D.Litt. ; F.B.A. ; F.S.A. ; excavated in Egypt with Petrie and Naville, 1884–8 ; Assistant, B.M., 1888–96 ; Asst. Prof., Univ. Coll., London, 1892–1901 ; Reader in Egyptology, Univ. of Oxford, 1901, and Professor, 1924, until 1932 ; Emeritus Professor, 1932 ; frequently visited and excavated in Egypt and Nubia and edited many publications for the E.E.F. and other bodies ; greatly advanced demotic studies and pub. many important works thereon ; he married first, 1896, Kate Bradbury of Ashton-under-Lyne, who had studied under Petrie, and died 1902 : and secondly Nora Macdonald, who survived him ; honorary member of numerous foreign societies and academies ; by his will he bequeathed his magnificent library and a large sum of money to build and maintain an Institute of Near-Eastern Archaeology at Oxford ; this took effect on the death of his wife in 1937, and the Griffith Institute, attached to the Ashmolean Museum, was built, equipped, and formally opened, 21 Jan. 1939 ; on Griffith's 70th birthday, a fine volume of *Studies* by his colleagues, pupils and friends, was presented to him ; died 14 Mar. 1934.

WWW. iii, 559 ; *JEA*. 20, 71 (Portr.) ; *Proc. Br. Acad.* 20 ; *Rev. d'Ég.* 2, 125 ; *Griffith Studies*, 485 (Bibl.) ; *Newberry Corresp.* ; *DNB*. 1931–40, 375.

GRIFFITH, Kate (*d.* 1902)

Née Bradbury ; d. C. T. Bradbury, of Ashton-under-Lyne ; first wife of F. Ll. Griffith ; a friend of Amelia Edwards, whom she accompanied to America in 1890 ; assisted in the early work of the E.E.F., and served for many years on the committee ; excavated in Egypt with Petrie ; in 1896 married, and a settlement made by her father enabled her husband to devote the whole of his time to Egyptology and provided the basis of the endowment which he bequeathed to the Univ. of Oxford ; she translated two of Wiedemann's books on Eg. religion into English (1896–7) and took an active part in her husband's scientific works and publications ; she died in March, 1902.

E.E.F. Arch. Report, 1901–2, 37 ; *Newberry Corresp.*

GRIFFITH, Nora Christina Cobban (1873–1937)

Née Macdonald, d. Surgeon-Major James M. of Aberdeen ; second wife of F. Ll. Griffith ; visited Egypt in 1906 and becoming interested in Egyptology, she became a pupil of Griffith at Oxford, and married him in 1909 ; assisted in his studies and in excavations in Egypt and Nubia, 1910–13, 1923, 1929, 1930 ; maintained his library, destined for Oxford Univ., and prepared his unfinished works for publication ; by her will she added her fortune to that of her husband for the building and endowment of the Griffith Institute at Oxford ; died 21 Oct. 1937.

JEA. 23, 262.

GRIVAUD DE LA VINCELLE, Claude Madeleine (1762–1819)

French virtuoso ; born Chalon-sur-Saône, 5 Sept. 1762 ; his name was originally Grivaud, but he added Vincelle after the death of his wife ; he had a fine collection of Greek and Egyptian antiquities which was sold in Paris in 1820, the catalogue being drawn up by L. J. J. Dubois.

GROFF, William N. (1857–1901)

Born in America, 1857 ; studied Egyptology in Paris under Maspero, 1878 ; in Cairo, 1891–9 and Athens, 1899 ; was particularly interested in the relation of Egypt to Old Testament history ; pub. many papers in *Bull. Inst. Eg.* and other journals ; his works were collected and edited by Maspero, with a biographical notice by his sister, Florence Groff, and a portrait.

Bibl. Ég., Oeuvres de W. N. Groff, 1908, pp. i–iv.

GRUEBER, Herbert Appold (1846–1927)

Numismatist and antiquary ; born 1846 ; entered B.M., 1866 ; Keeper of Coins and Medals, 1893–1906 ; one of the founders of the Eg. Expl. Fund, of which he was Treas., 1883–1912 ; pub. many numismatic works ; his library sold at Sotheby's, 14 Nov. 1912 (lots 99–148) ; died 21 Nov. 1927.

WWW. ii, 442 ; *Newberry Corresp.*

GUIEYSSE, Paul (1841–1914)

French Egyptologist ; studied Egyptology under de Rougé and Maspero ; pub. a study of Book of the Dead LXIV (1876) and some minor works ; although he remained attached to the École des Hautes Études as Maître de Conférances from 1880 till his death, he had long before virtually abandoned Egyptology for politics.

Maspero, *L'Égyptologie* (1915), 6, 7 ; *Bull. Soc. d'Ethnogr.* N.S. 4, 73 ; *Hilmy,* i, 279.

GUIGNES, Charles Joseph de (1721–1800)

Professor of Syriac at the Collège de France ; communicated a memoir to the Acad. des Inscr. attempting to prove that Egyptian is derived from Chinese writing, and that China was an Egyptian colony.

BIFAO, 5, 83 ; *Hilmy*, i, 164.

GUIMET, Émile Étienne (1836–1918)

Founder of the Musée Guimet ; son of Jean Baptiste Guimet, French industrial chemist (1795–1871) ; succeeded his father in the direction of the factory at Fleurien-sur-Saône ; founded the archaeological and anthropological museum at Lyons, 1879 ; it was handed over to the French Government and transferred to Paris, 1885 ; the Musée Guimet contains a fine collection of antiquities from the Far East, also Greek, Roman and Egyptian antiquities ; a fine series of publications has been issued by the Museum, many of them Egyptological ; Guimet died at Fleurien, 12 Oct. 1918.

Musée Guimet Records ; *Hilmy*, i, 280 ; *Vapereau*, 740.

GUNN, Battiscombe George (1883–1950)

Egyptologist ; born London, 30 June, 1883 ; educ. Westminster and Bedale's Schools ; began the study of Egyptology at an early age ; pub. *The Instruction of Ptah-hotep*, 1906 ; excavated with Engelbach at Harageh, 1913–14 ; after military service assistant to Dr. (now Sir) Alan Gardiner ; excavated at Amarna for E.E.S. 1921–2, and at Sakkara for Serv. des Antiquités, 1924–7 ; Asst. Curator, Cairo Museum, 1928–31 ; Curator of Eg. antiquities, Philadelphia Univ. Museum, 1931–4 ; Prof. of Egyptology, Oxford, 1934–50 ; Fellow of Queen's Coll., 1934 ; M.A. ; F.B.A., 1943 ; his principal work is *Studies in Eg. Syntax*, 1924, but made many contributions to journals and other publications ; editor of *JEA*, 1934–40 ; died 27 Feb. 1950.

Nature, 165, 549 ; *JEA*. 36, 104 (Portr.) ; *ASA*. 50, 421 (Portr. Bibl.) ; *Proc. Br. Acad.* (Bibl.).

HAGGARD, (*Sir*) **Henry Rider** (1856–1925)

Administrator and novelist ; born 22 June 1856 ; held many important official appointments in South Africa ; on retirement settled at Ditchingham Hall, Norfolk ; K.B.E., 1919 ; J.P. ; did much to promote agriculture ; his novels were extremely popular, and several of them are based on ancient Egyptian themes ; had a small but choice collection of Egyptian antiquities, described by Blackman ; died 14 May 1925.

WWW. ii, 449 ; *JEA*. 4, 43.

HAIGH, Daniel Henry (1819–1879)

Antiquary ; born near Chorley, Lancs., 7 Aug. 1819 ; after some time in commerce in Leeds, attached himself to St. Saviour's Church there ; in 1847 joined the Roman Church and entered St. Mary's Coll., Oscott ; endowed St. Augustine's Church, Birmingham and resided there till 1876, when he returned to Oscott ; much interested in Anglo-Saxon, Assyrian, Egyptian and biblical archaeology generally, and was the chief authority in England on Runic inscriptions; pub. many works and contributed to many archaeological journals, and wrote on Egyptian and Assyrian chronology, etc., in *ZÄS.*; died at Oscott, 10 May 1879.

DNB. 23, 440; *Hilmy*, i, 283; B.M. *Egerton MS.* 2856, f. 373, 379.

HALL, Harry Reginald Holland (1873–1930)

Historian and Egyptologist; born London, 30 Sept. 1873; educ. Merchant Taylors' School, and St. John's Coll. Oxon.; B.A., 1895; M.A., 1897; D.Litt., 1920; entered B.M. 1896; Asst. Keeper, Dept. of Eg. and Assyr. Ant., 1919; Keeper, 1924–30; assisted in excavations at Deir el-Bahri and Abydos for E.E.F. 1903–10, 1925; directed B.M. excavations in Babylonia (Ur, etc.), 1919; F.S.A.; F.B.A.; travelled in Greece and Near East; pub. a number of works on Aegean and Near Eastern archaeology and history; contributed to E.E.F. memoirs and official publications of the B.M.; died 13 Oct. 1930.

WWW. iii, 579; *JEA.* 17, 111 (Portr.).

HAMILTON, William Richard (1777–1859)

Antiquary and diplomatist; son of Anthony H., Archdeacon of Colchester; born London, 9 Jan. 1777; educ. Harrow, Oxford and Cambridge; entered Diplomatic Service and appointed Sec. to Lord Elgin, Ambassador at Constantinople, 1799; sent by Lord Elgin on a mission to Egypt, 1801 on the evacuation of the French; discovered that the Rosetta Stone had been secretly shipped by the French, and with a military escort, he recovered possession of it; superintended the shipment of the Elgin Marbles and the recovery of those lost at sea; Under-Sec. for Foreign Affairs, 1809–22; Brit. Minister in Naples, 1822–5; Trustee of B.M., 1838–58; in 1809, pub. *Ægyptiaca*, which contains much valuable information together with a transcript and translation of the Greek text of the Rosetta Stone; died in London, 11 July 1859.

DNB. 24, 234; *Legh*, 34, 47; *Hilmy*, i, 285.

HAMMER-PURGSTALL, (*Freiherr*) **Josef von** (1774–1856)

Austrian orientalist; born Gratz, 9 June 1774; educ. Vienna; entered diplomatic service, 1796; attached to Austrian embassy at Constantinople, 1799–1807; inherited Purgstall estates in Styria, 1835; President, Vienna Acad., 1847; pub. numerous texts and translations of Arabic, Persian and Turkish MSS.; a work on Eg. hieroglyphics from an Arabic MS. (1806), an Eg. papyrus, *Copie figurée d'un rouleau de Papyrus*, 1822, and a memoir on the Mysteries of Isis (1815); died at Vienna, 23 Nov. 1856.

Biogr. by Schlottmann, Zurich, 1857; *Champollion*, i, 9, 137, 241; *Hilmy*, i, 285.

HAMY, Ernest Théodore (1842–1908)

French anthropologist; wrote on the Stone Age in Egypt and on the races of man depicted on the monuments; collaborated with

Quatrefages, Longpérier and F. Lenormant in craniological and historical works.

Haddon, *Hist. Anthropology*, 24 ; *Hilmy*, i, 41, 286.

HANBURY, (*Rev.*) **Barnard** (1793–1833)

Born Halstead, Essex, 1793 ; educ. Hertford School and Jesus Coll. Cantab. ; B.A., 1816 ; M.A., 1822 ; admitted to T.C.C., 1822 ; ordained 1817 ; Vicar of Bures, Suffolk, 1824–8 ; Rector of Chignall, Essex, 1832–3 ; Chaplain to the Duke of Sussex ; travelled in Egypt and Nubia in 1821 with Rev. George Waddington (q.v.) ; died 23 Jan. 1833.

Alumni Cantab. ; *Hilmy*, ii, 314.

HARLÉ, Auguste (1806–1876)

Hebrew scholar and orientalist ; attended de Rougé's Eg. classes at the Coll. de France, but did not take up the study seriously and published nothing thereon ; he had a valuable Egyptological library, a catalogue of which was printed in 1872 and to which Devéria was much indebted in his early studies ; Harlé's name is associated with the valuable stela, Louvre C.201, which he presented in 1872.

Devéria, *Mem. et Fragm.* 1, p. vii ; *Revue de l'Art*, 43, 169 ; *Hilmy*, i, 287.

HARRIS, Anthony Charles (1790–1869)

British merchant and commissariat official in Alexandria, but not Consul, as usually stated ; a collector of, and dealer in, Eg. antiquities ; formed an important and valuable collection of antiquities, including many classic papyri—the Great Harris Pap., the Harris Magical, Harris Homer, the Tomb-Robbery Papyri, etc. ; the collection, bequeathed to his daughter, was acquired from her by the B.M. in 1872 ; pub. his Hypereides Papyrus, 1848 and a work on Nome-Standards, 1852 ; President, Eg. Soc. of Cairo, 1836 ; died in Alexandria, Nov. 1869.

JEA. 35, 161–166 ; Brugsch, *Mein Leben*, 121, 136 ; *Hilmy*, i, 289.

HARRIS, Selima (*c.* 1830–1895)

Adopted daughter of A. C. Harris ; a negress ; educated in England ; she was her father's constant companion and on his death inherited his rich collection of Eg. antiquities which she brought to England in 1872 and sold to the B.M. ; Lady Member of Soc. Bibl. Arch. 1872 ; died in Alexandria about 1895.

JEA. 35, 164 ; Brugsch, *Mein Leben*, 122 ; *Newberry Corresp.* ; *Wilbour*, 6, 7.

HARTLEBEN, Hermine (1846–1918)

Biographer of Champollion ; born Semkenthal, Harz Mts., 1846 ; related to the poet Otto Erich Hartleben ; educ. Hanover and Paris ; lived for some years in Constantinople where she held a scholastic appointment ; spent about six years in Egypt ; after a later visit to Egypt in 1891, she became interested in Champollion, and in 1893 began systematic investigations into his career ; visited Paris and Grenoble to inspect documents in public collections and in the hands of Champollion's family ; in 1906, pub. *Champollion, sein Leben und sein Werke,* 2 vols., and in 1909, *Lettres et Journaux de Champollion,* 2 vols. ; these works constitute one of the most important contributions to the history of Egyptology ; she retired to Templin, Brandenberg, where she died in 1918.

JEA. 8, 285.

HARTMANN, Robert (1832–1893)

German zoologist and anatomist ; born Blakenburg am Hertz, 8 Oct. 1832 ; Professor and Prosector of Anatomy, Berlin, 1868 ; travelled in Africa, 1859–60 ; pub. zoological and anatomical works ; studied the animals of ancient Egypt (*ZÄS*. 2, 7, 19) ; died 1893.

Hilmy, i, 290.

HAWORTH, Jesse (1835–1921)

Manufacturer of Lancashire ; born 1835 ; about 1880 his interest in Egyptian archaeology was awakened by a tour in Egypt and he became acquainted with Amelia Edwards, who stimulated it ; in 1887 he provided funds for Petrie's excavations and continued to do so for many years ; he also supported the Egypt Expl. Fund ; in 1912 he gave a large donation for the extension of Manchester Museum and presented to it all the antiquities he had received from Petrie's excavations ; he made a further gift of £10,000 to the Museum in 1919, and £30,000 under his will ; he was also a generous donor to the B.M., Ashmolean and other museums ; Hon. LL.D., Manchester, 1913 ; first president of the Manchester Egyptian and Oriental Society ; died 1921.

JEA. 7, 109 ; *JMEOS*, 4, 49 (Portr.) ; *Petrie*, 22, 79, 157.

HAY, Robert (1799–1863)

Traveller and collector of antiquities ; 4th son of Robert Hay of Drumelzier ; born 1799 ; inherited the estate of Linplum from his brother ; began life in the Navy as a midshipman, but in 1824 left his ship at Malta, and met there Catherwood and Parke, who had recently returned from Egypt, where they went up the Nile with Westcar and Scoles ; the information and drawings they showed him inspired a desire to visit Egypt, and in Nov. 1824 he landed at Alexandria for the first time, revisiting the country on several occasions up to 1838 ; he was accompanied at different times by Arundale, Bonomi, Catherwood and Lane ; pub. *Illustrations of Cairo,* 1840, lithographed from drawings by Owen B. Carpenter ; he made a large collection of drawings, plans, copies of inscriptions, etc., of great value in view of subsequent damage to the monuments ; his papers and drawings are in 58 vols. in the B.M. (Add. MSS. 29812–29860 ; diary, 31054 ; letters, 38510) ; he was an accurate copyist and a good draughtsman, and he employed Bonomi and other artists ; he formed a large collection of antiquities ; these were sold in 1865, the B.M. acquiring most of the papyri and smaller objects, and the Boston Museum of Fine Art the other monuments ; died at Armsfield, East Lothian, 4 Nov. 1863.

DNB. 25, 275 ; Hoskins, *Ethiopia,* 2 ; *Oasis,* 16, 22, 183 etc. ; *Bonomi Diary,* passim ; *Hilmy,* i, 292.

HAYES, Charles (1780–1803)

Captain, Royal Engineers ; born 1780 ; educ. Woolwich Acad., 1794 ; served in W. Indies, 1796, in Holland, 1799, and in Egypt under Abercrombie, 1800 ; surveyed the Delta and inspected Upper Egypt ; was retained in Egypt to assist Col. Misset, the Consul-General, to supervise British interests ; executed the plates for Hamilton's *Ægyptiaca* (pub. 1809) ; died of disease in Egypt, 26 July 1803.

Hamilton, pref. vi–x ; *Light*, 113 ; *Hilmy*, i, 285, 294.

HAYTER, Angelo George Kirby (1863–1927)

Schoolmaster and excavator ; born 1863 ; educ. Highgate School and Queens' Coll. Cantab. ; M.A. ; F.S.A., 1916 ; a schoolmaster by profession ; in 1901 attended classes in Egyptology at Univ. Coll., London ; assisted in excavations of Petrie at Hawara and Memphis, 1910–11 ; of Quibell at Sakkara, 1912–14 ; of E.E.S. at Amarna, 1921–2, and of Michigan Univ. in the Fayûm, 1925–6 ; died 15 Oct. 1927.

JEA. 14, 323 ; *Petrie*, 221.

HEARST, (*Mrs.*) **Phoebe Apperson** (1842–1919)

Patron of archaeology ; née Apperson ; born 3 Dec. 1842 ; for many years she financed the scientific expeditions of the University of California in Peru, North America and Egypt ; she bore the cost of the publications of the Hearst Expedition in Egypt under Prof. G. A. Reisner ; the Hearst Medical Papyrus obtained by Reisner in 1901 was published by him and named in honour of Mrs. Hearst ; she died 13 Apl. 1919.

Inf. by Dr. Dows Dunham.

HEARST, William Randolph (1863–1951)

American journalist and newspaper proprietor ; born San Francisco, 1863 ; collector of antiquities ; a large collection of Egyptian, Babylonian, Greek, Roman and other antiquities sold at Sotheby's, 11–12 July, 1939 (403 lots ; Eg. 11–189) ; many of the Eg. antiquities came from the Hilton Price and Meux collections ; died 14 Aug. 1951.

HEATH, (*Rev.*) **Dunbar Isodore** (1816–1888)

Scholar and clergyman ; born 1816 ; T.C.C. ; B.A., 1838 ; M.A., 1841 ; Fellow ; Vicar of Brading, Isle of Wight ; preached in 1859 and published in 1860 a sermon considered heterodox, and action was taken in the Court of Arches ; his sentence was deprivation of his benefice, which took place in 1862, and was upheld on appeal ; he then lived in retirement at Esher, Surrey, for the rest of his life ; took up the study of Egyptology, and especially that of hieratic papyri ; he was a good decipherer, but his ' translations ' are fantastic ; his copy of *Select Papyri*, full of valuable notes, is now in the possession of Sir Alan Gardiner ; he pub. *The Exodus Papyri*, 1855, in which he believed to have found references to biblical history in the Sallier and Anastasi Papyri, and *A Record of the*

Patriarchal Age or the Proverbs of Aphobis, 1858, based on the Prisse Papyrus ; *Phoenician Inscriptions,* 1873 ; died Esher, 27 May 1888.

DNB. 25, 341 ; *Goodwin,* 58, 67, 75 ; *Add. MS.* 31295, f. 52 ; *Hilmy,* i, 295.

HENDERSON, Benjamin Clifton (1788–1881)

Surgeon in H.E.I. Co.'s service ; born 14 Aug. 1788 ; M.R.C.S., 1810 ; Asst. Surgeon, Bombay Establishment, 1811 ; transferred to Prince of Wales Island Estab., 1818 ; Surgeon, 1825 ; retired, 1830 ; in retirement he remained for some years in India, later at Southampton, and finally Paris ; visited Egypt in 1820, and brought from Thebes two mummies, both of which are historic ; they were sold in 1831 by D. Harwood, a dealer of Houndsditch—one was bought by John Davidson (q.v.) and unrolled at the Royal Institution, the other by the R. Coll. Surgeons and unrolled by Pettigrew : it was destroyed by enemy action in 1940 ; Henderson died in Paris, 1881.

India Office Med. Records ; R.C.S. Records ; JEA. 20, 171–4 ; *Salt,* ii, 158 ; Pettigrew, *Hist. Eg. Mummies,* p. xviii.

HENNIKER, (*Sir*) **Frederick** (1793–1825)

Traveller ; born 1 Nov. 1793 ; educ. Eton, St. John's Coll. Cantab., B.A., 1815 ; succeeded as 2nd Bart., 1816 ; travelled in Egypt and Palestine in 1820, and accompanied George Francis Grey to Upper Egypt ; was the first to climb to the apex of the Second Pyramid, a difficult task owing to the smooth casing-stones being still in situ ; pub. *Notes during a visit to Egypt, Nubia, the Oasis, Sinai and Jerusalem,* 1823 ; presented the mummy of Soter to the B.M. (6705) ; died, unmarried, 6 Aug. 1825.

DNB. 25, 425 ; *Salt,* ii, 164 ; *Westcar Diary,* 12, 246 ; *Hilmy,* i, 298.

HERBERT, George Edward Stanhope Molyneux, 5th Earl of Carnarvon (1866–1923)

Excavator and collector of antiquities ; born 26 June 1866 ; educ. Eton and T.C.C. ; succeeded 1890 ; excavated at Thebes from 1906 and made many important discoveries with the aid of Howard Carter, culminating in the Tomb of Tutankhamen in Nov. 1922, but he did not live to see the clearance completed, for he died in Egypt, 6 Apl. 1923 ; his previous excavations were pub. in a sumptuous volume, *Five Years Explorations at Thebes,* 1912 ; he had a very choice and valuable collection of Egyptian antiquities which was acquired in 1927 by the Metropolitan Mus. of Art, N.Y.

WWW. ii, 175 ; *JEA.* 9, 114 ; Memoir by his sister prefixed to Vol. i of Howard Carter's *Tomb of Tutankhamen,* 1–40 (Portr.) ; *Newberry Corresp.*

HERTZ, Bram (*fl.* 1843–1865)

Collector of antiquities and objets-d'art ; his pictures and articles of vertu were sold in a four days' sale in 1843 ; had a valuable collection of engraved gems and in 1839 bought many from the famous Poniatowsky Coll. ; his main collection of gems was sold in 1859 and some further gems and antiquities in 1861 ; had an extensive coll. of antiquities, of which a cat. was pub. in 1851 : *The Coll. of Assyrian, Babylonian, Egyptian, Greek, Roman, Indian and Mexican Antiquities formed by B. Hertz* ; the coll. was sold in 1857 and bought by Joseph Mayer of Liverpool, who resold what he did not require at Sotheby's in 1859.

Inf. by Liverpool Museum ; C. W. King, *Handb. of Engraved Gems*, 1885, 196 ; *Hilmy*, i, 300.

HERZ, (*Pasha*) **Max** (*d.* 1919)

Hungarian Jew ; went to Egypt in 1882 and worked under his countryman Julius Franz in the service for the preservation of Arab monuments ; succeeded Franz as Director of the Museum of Arab Art, Cairo, in 1887, where he remained until June 1914, when with all the Germans, Austrians, etc., he left Egypt ; on leaving Egypt he settled in Switzerland where he died in 1919 ; Membre de l'Inst. Ég. ; pub. many works on Arab art and architecture.

Al-Hilah, 27 (1919), 921–8 (Memoir and Bibl. in Arabic, by Tewfik Askaros).

HESS von WYSS, Jean Jacques (1866–1949)

Swiss Egyptologist ; educ. University of Freiburg ; Ph.D. ; studied Egyptology under Brugsch ; Professor at Freiburg 1889 ; travelled in N.W. Arabia, 1910 ; Professor Extraordinary of Oriental Languages, Zürich, 1918 ; retired 1936 with title of Honorary Professor ; pub. an edition of the London-Leiden Demotic Papyrus, 1892 and the demotic stories of Khamuas ; in his later years he paid particular attention to Arabic ; his notebooks and papers are in the Griffith Institute, Oxford ; died 1949.

Kürschner, *Deutscher Gelehrten Kalender*, 1931 ; Univ. Zürich *Jahresbericht*, 1948–9.

HILZHEIMER, Max (1877–1946)

German zoologist ; born Kehnert, Kreis Wolmirstedt, Saxony, 15 Nov. 1877 ; Privatdozent at the Tieraerztliche Hochschule, Stuttgart, 1907–14 and at Berlin, 1928 ; Director of the Natural Science Dept. of the Märkisches Museum, Berlin ; published many works, chiefly on the history and evolution of domestic animals ; contributed a chapter to Borchardt's *Das Grabdenkmal des Königs Sahure*, 1910 ; died 10 Jan. 1946.

Kürschner, 1931 and 1950.

HINCKS, (*Rev.*) **Edward** (1792–1866)

Scholar and clergyman ; son of Thomas Dix Hincks, LL.D. ; born Cork, 19 Aug. 1792 ; T.C.D., 1807 ; M.A., 1811 ; Rector of Killyleagh, Co. Down, 1825–1866 ; established a high reputation as a cuneiform and hieroglyphic decipherer, and made valuable contributions to both ; of special value are his papers in *Trans. R.I. Acad.* and *Trans. R.S.L.*, and his *Cat. Eg. Papyri* in the Library of T.C.D., 1843 ; died, Killyleagh, 3 Dec. 1866 ; his correspondence is in the Griffith Inst., Oxford.

E. F. Davidson, *Edward Hincks*, Oxford, 1933 (Portr.) ; *Budge, R & P.* see index (Portr.) ; *Dawson* MS. 18, f. 80–90 ; *Hilmy*, i, 304.

HODGES, (*Sir*) **George Lloyd** (1790–1862)

Army officer ; born Old Abbey, Limerick, 1790 ; 13th Regt. Light Dragoons, Lieut., 1808 ; served at Waterloo ; retired, Colonel, 1833 ; C.B. ; K.C.B., 1860 ; British Consul-General in Egypt, 1833–41 ; afterwards Chargé d'Affaires, Hanse Towns ; died Brighton, 14 Dec. 1862.

F.O. Records ; *GM.* 1863, i, 517.

HOFFMANN, Jean Henri (1823–1897)

French collector and dealer in antiquities, of Rue Benouville, Paris ; born, Hamburg, 1823 ; came to Paris at an early age to assist his father who was a mineralogist and conchologist ; took up the study of antiquities and visited the principal museums of Europe ; from 1862–4 he edited *Le Numismate* ; in 1894, G. Legrain pub. *Collection H. Hoffmann : Cat. des Antiquités Ég.* ; the objects came from many well-known collections—Stier, Sabatier, Castellani, Menascé, Posno, Fournier, etc. ; part of the coll. acquired by the Louvre in 1886 and further objects in 1895 ; some objects from the Hoffmann Coll. are in the Palais des Beaux Arts, Paris ; in 1898 his fine collection of Roman coins was sold in Paris, and there was a further sale of antiquities, 14 May 1899 ; died in Paris, 30 Apl. 1897.

Rev. de Numismatique, 1897, 226 ; *Rev. de l'Art,* 43, 171, 284 ; *Cat. Sommaire des Collections Dutuit,* Paris, 1925.

HOGG, Edward (1783–1848)

Physician and traveller ; born 1783 ; M.D., Glasgow, 1824 ; practised in Hendon and later in Naples ; travelled extensively in the Near East in 1832–3 and ascended the Nile as far as Wady Halfa, his name being carved on the rock of Abu Sir ; pub. *Visit to Alexandria, Damascus and Jerusalem,* etc. 2 vols., London, 1835 ; died at Chester, 12 Mar. 1848.

Med. Times, 8 Apl. 1848 ; *Hilmy,* i, 306.

HOLT, (*Rev.*) **Robert Fowler** (1792–1870)

Son of Robert Holt, of Finmore, Oxfordsh. ; born 1792 ; educ. Eton and Brasenose Coll. Oxon. ; B.A., 1813 ; M.A., 1816 ; Chaplain to the Earl of Belmore whom he accompanied in his travels in Egypt, Nubia, Syria and Palestine, 1816–8 ; his name is carved on the rock of Abu Sir, 2nd Cataract ; Chaplain to Slough Union, 1836–70 ; died 27 Jan. 1870.

Al. Oxon. ; *Richardson,* i, 365 ; ii, 233.

HOOD, (*Rev.*) **William Frankland** (*d.* 1864)

Collector of antiquities ; son of John Hood of Nettleham Hall, near Lincoln ; M.A. ; visited Egypt several times between 1851 and 1861 and made a valuable collection of antiquities, on one of these journeys, he travelled with A. H. Rhind ; the *Hood Papyrus* (onomasticon) he sold to the B.M. in 1872 ; the rest of the collection remained at Nettleham Hall until it was sold at Sotheby's, 11 Nov. 1924 (172 lots) ; died 21 Mar. 1864.

Burke's Landed Gentry ; *Preface (by Newberry) to Sale Cat.* ; Rhind, *Thebes, its Tombs and their Tenants,* 166.

HOPE, Henry Philip (*c.* 1771–1839)

Virtuoso and art patron ; born about 1771 ; travelled in the East ; interested in art and antiquities ; collected Dutch and Flemish paintings, and precious stones and gems ; among the latter were some fine Egyptian specimens ; the collection, valued at £50,000, was catalogued by Bram Hertz (q.v.) ; a generous patron of the arts, and although wealthy, lived in a very simple style ; died Cranbrook, Kent, 5 Dec. 1839.

DNB. 27, 329.

HORNER, (*Rev.*) **George** (1849–1930)

Coptic scholar ; born 10 June 1849 ; educ. Eton and Balliol Coll. Oxon. ; Curate of Cirencester, 1874–5 ; Rector of Selwood Mells, 1875–91 ; in 1891 withdrew from parochial work and devoted himself to Coptic, which he studied under Steindorff at Berlin, but he was mainly self-taught, as he was also in Arabic and Ethiopic ; pub. a critical text of the New Testament, Bohairic in 4 vols., and Sahidic in 7 vols., a task that occupied him for 26 years ; pub. also *Coptic Consecrations*, 1902, *Ethiopic Statutes of the Apostles*, 1904, and a translation of *Pistis Sophia*, 1924 ; died 10 Aug. 1930.

JEA. 16, 258.

HORRACK, Philippe Jacques Ferdinand de (1820–1902)

French Egyptologist, of Austrian origin ; born Frankfurt, 7 Sept. 1820 ; trained for a commercial career and in 1843 entered the banking-house of Greene & Cie., Paris ; in 1851 joined the firm of Tiffany & Co., of New York, London and Paris, in which he remained till his death ; cultivated a taste for archaeology and in 1858 became a life-long correspondent and friend of Chabas, under whose guidance he studied Egyptian ; having begun his studies with the false doctrines of Seyffarth and Uhlemann, after becoming acquainted with Chabas, he said, " j'ai perdu presque une année dans des études stériles "; although he had little leisure for study, he worked methodically and accurately and became a good copyist of texts ; the plates of his publications of the Lamentations of Isis and the Book of Breathings from papyri in the Louvre and Berlin, were beautifully lithographed by himself ; he was acquainted with Devéria, Birch and Lepsius and studied in the Louvre and the British and Berlin Museums ; his works were collected by Maspero in the Bibl. Ég., 1907 ; his books and papers were presented by his widow to the Musée Guimet ; died, 1902.

Virey, *Notice Biogr.* (*Bibl. Ég.* 17), 68 pp.

HOSKINS, George Alexander (1802–1863)

Traveller and antiquary ; 2nd s. George H., of Higham near Cockermouth ; born 1802 ; travelled in Egypt and Nubia, 1832–3 and 1860–1 ; pub. *Travels in Ethiopia*, 1835 ; *Visit to the Great Oasis*, 1837 ; three large volumes of drawings made on these journeys were acquired by Sir Alan Gardiner, and deposited in the Griffith Institute, Oxford ; Sec. and Treas. of the White Nile Assn., 1839 ; he married in 1843, Mary Thornton, who died in 1858, and Hoskins, much prostrated, made another journey to Egypt to recover his health ; pub. *A Winter in Upper and Lower Egypt,* 1863 ; he died in Rome, 21 Nov. 1863.

Burke's L.G. 1894 ; *GM.* 1864, i, 130 ; Budge, *Eg. Sudan,* i, 56–61 ; *B.M. Add. MS.* 25652, f. 4, 8, 14 ; *Hilmy,* i, 310.

HOUGHTON, (*Rev.*) **William** (1829–1895)

Naturalist and archaeologist ; born Liverpool, 1829 ; M.A., Oxon., 1853 ; Head master of Solihull School, 1858 ; Rector of Preston, Wellington, Salop, 1860 ; F.L.S., 1859 ; author of many popular books on Nat. Hist. ; made a special study of the Nat. Hist. of the ancients, on which he pub. a general work in 1879, embodying the results of many special studies (e.g. *TSBA.* 5, 33, 319 ; 6, 454 ; *PSBA.* 12, 81, etc.) ; died at Tenby, 3 Sept. 1895.

Proc. Linn. Soc. 1895–6, 37.

HOWARD-VYSE, Richard William (1784–1853)

Army officer ; son of General Richard Vyse (1784–1853) and his wife Anne, d. Field Marshal Sir George Howard ; born 1784 ; in 1812 by royal licence, assumed the additional name and arms of Howard ; entered the Army, 1800 ; Lieut., 1801 ; Capt., 1802 ; Major, 1813 ; Colonel, 1837 ; Major-General, 1846, in 2nd Life Guards ; Hon. D.C.L. Oxon., 1810 ; M.P., 1807, 1812–18 ; visited Egypt in 1835 ; carried out excavations at the Pyramids of Gizeh with Caviglia ; having secured the assistance of John Shea Perring in Jan. 1837, he returned to England leaving Perring to complete the work at his expense ; pub. *Narrative of Operations carried on at the Pyramids of Gizeh,* 2 vols., 1840, with a third vol. on Perring's work at Abu Roash, 1842 ; presented antiquities and 4 papyri to B.M. 1838 ; died at his seat, Stoke Poges, Bucks, 8 June 1853, and buried at Great Bookham, Surrey ; monument and hatchment at Stoke Poges.

DNB. 58, 398 ; *Lindsay,* 39, 78, 85, 97, 155 ; *Hilmy,* ii, 313.

HULL, John Fowler (1801–1825)

Orientalist ; visited Egypt on his way to India, 1824, and explored Thebes with Madox ; though very young he had a great genius for oriental languages and owned a valuable collection of Indian, Chinese, Persian and Arabic MSS., which he bequeathed to the B.M. ; died suddenly when about to leave Egypt.

Madox, i, 417 ff. ; ii, 379 ; *Athanasi,* 62, 126 ; *Westcar Diary,* 196, 201, 209, 241, 260.

HULTSCH, Friedrich (1833–1906)

German mathematician ; born Dresden, 22 July 1833 ; devoted special study to the mathematics of the ancients and published important papers on Eg. metrology and mathematics in *Abh. Sächs Ges. der Wiss.*, *Bibl. Mathematica*, *ZÄS.*, and other journals ; died Dresden, 6 Apl. 1906.

Peet, *Rhind Math. Pap.*, passim ; *Hilmy,* i, 312 ; ii, 422.

HUNT, Arthur Surridge (1871–1934)

Papyrologist ; born Romford, 1 Mar. 1871 ; educ. Cranbrook School, Eastbourne Coll., Queen's Coll. Oxon. ; M.A. ; D.Litt. ; F.B.A. ; hon. member of many foreign academies ; Professor of Papyrology, Oxford, 1913–34 ; frequently excavated in Egypt, 1895–1907, chiefly for papyri at Oxyrhynchus and other Fayûm sites ; edited singly or jointly with B. P. Grenfell many volumes of the *Oxyrhynchus Papyri,* and catalogues of many important collections, such as Amherst, John Rylands and Cairo and many separate editions of particular papyri or groups of papyri, including two volumes in the Loeb Classical Series ; died 18 June 1934.

WWW. iii, 678 ; *JEA*. 20, 204 (Portr.) ; *Aegyptus,* 14, 499 ; *Chron*. 9, 335.

HUSSON, Hyacinthe (*fl*. 1868–1878)

A pupil of Maspero at the Coll. de France ; author of " Mythes et Monuments Comparés " in *Rev. Gen. de l'Architecture,* 1868, *La chaîne traditionelle, Contes et Legendes au point de vue mythique,* Paris, 1874.

Maspero, *L'Égyptologie* (1915), 7 ; *Hilmy,* i, 313.

HUYOT, Jean Nicolas (1780–1840)

French architect ; born Paris, 1780 ; a friend of Champollion ; he travelled in Egypt and the Near East and brought back a large collection of drawings which he placed at the disposal of Champollion and which were of great service to him in correcting the errors in the plates of the *Description de l'Égypte* ; architect of the Arc de Triomphe, Paris ; died in Paris, 1840.

Champollion, i, 175, 359.

HYVERNAT, (*Abbé*) **Henri Eugène Xavier Louis** (1858–1941)

French orientalist ; born St. Julien-en-Jarret (Loire), 30 June 1858 ; educ. Séminaire de St. Jean, Lyons, and Lyons Univ. ; studied theology in Paris, 1882 and was appointed Doctor of Theology at the Pontifical Univ., Rome, 1882–5 ; acting Prof. of Assyriology and Egyptology at Rome, 1885–9 ; sent by French Govt. on a scientific mission to Armenia, 1888–9 ; Prof. Oriental Archaeology and Languages at the Catholic Univ. of Washington, 1889 ; Hon. Ph.D., Michigan, 1919 ; pub. many works of which the most important is *Album de Palaeographie Copte,* 1888 ; died 20 May 1941.

Chron. 37, 153–7 ; *Catholic World,* 1941, 653–6 ; *Cath. Univ. Bull*. 8 (1941) (Portr.).

IBSCHER, Hugo (1874–1943)

Technician and restorer of manuscripts and papyri ; born 28 Sept. 1874 ; trained as a bookbinder, he entered the service of the Berlin Museum in 1891, and was entrusted with the mounting and restoring of the papyri there, in which he displayed remarkable ability and skill ; he served at first under Ludwig Abel, but from 1894 was in sole charge ; although on the staff of the museum, he was permitted to undertake work elsewhere and many important papyri have been restored and mounted by him in the collections of Turin, London, Oxford, Brussels, Paris, Prague, Copenhagen, Cairo, Rome, and many others ; for his work on the restoration of parchments and other MSS. in the Vatican, he was awarded the Order of St. Gregory ; he was Hon. Dr. of Strasbourg, and received the Leibniz Medal of the Prussian Acad., and the medal of the Bavarian Acad. ; died 26 May 1943 ; his son, Dr. Rolf Ibscher, carried on his work at Berlin.

Forschungen und Fortschritte, 24, 245 (Bibl.) ; *Gnomon*, 1943, 286–7.

IDELER, Julius Ludwig (1809–1842)

German scholar ; son of the astronomer and chronologist Christian Ludwig Ideler whom he predeceased ; pub. *Hermapion sive Rudimenta Hieroglyphicae vetum Ægyptiorum Literaturae*, 2 parts, Leipsic, 1836–41, and other writings on Egypt.

Brugsch, *Mein Leben*, 45 ; *Hilmy*, i, 318.

INSINGER, Jan Herman (1854–1918)

Dutch resident in Luxor where he lived for many years on account of being afflicted with tuberculosis ; born 12 May, 1854, carried on a private business of money-lending and dealt in antiquities ; he was closely associated with Maspero *c.* 1880–6 and took many photographs for him ; he often acted as intermediary for the purchase of antiquities for the Dutch museums ; the famous demotic papyrus that bears his name he obtained from the French Consular Agent at Akhmîm in 1895 for fcs. 4,000 ; died Cairo, 27 Oct. 1918.

Sayce, 453, 457 ; *Budge N & T*. ii, 364 ; Pleyte and Boeser, *Le Livre Royal : Le Papyrus Démotique Insinger*, 3 ; Maspero, *ASA*. 2, 148 ; *Wilbour*, passim (Portr. facing p. 240) ; *Dutch Consular Records*.

IRBY, (*Hon.*) **Charles Leonard** (1789–1845)

Naval officer and explorer ; y. s. 2nd Lord Boston ; born 9 Oct. 1789 ; entered the Navy, 1801 ; saw much service, and retired Captain ; with Capt. James Mangles he travelled up the Nile to the 2nd cataract and in Syria and Palestine ; with Mangles printed privately in 1821 *Travels in Egypt, Nubia, Syria and Asia Minor in 1817 and 1818*, of which a popular edition was published in 1844 ; the first to mention the " Tomb of the Colossus " at El-Bersheh, but the discovery is probably due to Charles Brine (q.v.) ; died 3 Dec. 1845.

DNB. 29, 28 ; O'Byrne, *Naval Biogr*. 545 ; *Salt*, ii, 72 ; *Richardson*, ii, 294 ; *Belzoni*, i, 314–6, 332, 342 ; *Athanasi*, 11, 25 ; *Hilmy*, i, 325.

JAMES, (*Sir*) **Henry** (1803–1877)

Colonel, Royal Engineers ; Director-General of the Ordnance Survey ; entered R.E., 1826 ; Colonel, 1857 ; F.R.S., 1848 ; published standards of length of various countries and a work on the measurements and standards of the Great Pyramid.

DNB. 29, 210 ; *Hilmy*, i, 330.

JAYE, William Robert (1874–1949)

London merchant ; had travelled much and made a collection of antiquities, sold at Sotheby's, 18 July 1949, lots 84–97, the most important piece being the quartzite head of a statue, said to be Ramesses II ; retired in 1920 to the Old House, Ryde, Isle of Wight, where he died 22 Mar. 1949 and was buried at Binstead, near Ryde.

JÉQUIER, Gustave (1868–1946)

Swiss Egyptologist ; studied at Paris under Maspero ; excavated at Sakkara and other sites in Egypt ; studied the architectural history of Egyptian temples and pub. a series of monographs thereon and numerous other contributions to the literature of Egyptology ; his collections have been acquired by the University of Basel.

E.E.S. Ann. Rep. 1946, 4 ; *Chron.* 21, 207.

JOHNS, Agnes Sophia (1859–1949)

Née Griffith, sister of Francis Llewellyn G. ; born 27 Dec. 1859 ; married at Oxford, 9 Mar. 1910, the Rev. Claude Hermann Walter Johns (*d.* 1920), the well known Assyriologist and Master of St. Catharine's Coll., Cantab. ; pub. *Catalogue of Eg. Ant. Manchester Museum,* 1910 ; translated into English the works of Capart, Erman, Maspero and Koldewey under the respective titles : *Primitive Art in Egypt,* 1905 ; *Handbook of Eg. Religion,* 1907 ; *Egyptian Archaeology* (6th ed.) 1914 ; *Popular Stories of Ancient Egypt* (4th ed.), 1915 ; *The Excavations at Babylon,* 1914 ; died at Brighton, Sussex, 18 Nov. 1949.

Inf. by Griffith family.

JOHNSTONE, James L'Estrange (1865–1906)

Military officer ; born Alva, Scotland, 8 Aug. 1865 ; educ. Eton, R. Military Acad., Woolwich, and School of Military Engineering, Chatham ; R. Engineers, Lieut., 1884 ; Asst. Engineer, Works Dept. of India at Aden, 1888–9 ; Inspecting Engineer, R.E., Malta, 1890–1 ; employed in the preservation of the Temple of Abu Simbel for the Egyptian Public Works Dept., 1892 ; Inspector of Structures and Railways, War Office, 1895–9 ; M.V.O., 1904 ; died, a Major, 10 Oct. 1906.

WWW. i, 383 ; Maspero, *Ruines et Paysages,* 403.

JOMARD, Edmé François (1777–1862)

French engineer, geographer and archaeologist ; born Versailles, 17 Nov. 1777 ; took a prominent part in the foundation of the École Polytechnique, Paris ; a member of Napoleon's Commission in Egypt ; on leaving Egypt, he travelled in Greece and other European countries and returned to Paris in 1803 ; he took a large share in the editing of the *Description de l'Égypte* to which he made many contributions ; edited the works of Cailliaud ; elected to Acad. des Inscr., 1818 ; conservateur, Bibliothèque Nationale, 1828 ; was very hostile to Champollion and obstructed his advancement in every possible way ; wrote much on education ; died 23 Sept. 1862 ; his library and collections (Egyptian, lots 1–42) were sold in Paris in 1863.

Larousse, 19 *Cent.* 9, 1008 ; *Carré,* passim, see index (Portr.) ; *Bull. Inst. Ég.* No. 8, 1864 ; *Hartleben,* passim ; *Hilmy,* i, 333.

JONAS, Mary Charlton (1875–1950)

Secretary of the Egypt Exploration Society, 1919–39 ; formerly secretary to Prof. C. G. Seligman ; died 3 April 1950.

Newberry Corresp.; E.E.S. *Ann. Rep.* 1950, 4.

JONES, Harold (*d.* 1911)

Excavator and artist ; excavated at Kom el-Ahmar and other sites in Upper Egypt with Prof. J. Garstang ; made many water-colour drawings of antiquities for Lord Carnarvon, Theodore M. Davis and others, some of which have been reproduced as coloured plates ; he died while working at Biban el-Molûk, 10 Mar. 1911, and was buried at Luxor.

Newberry Corresp.

JONES, Owen (1809–1874)

Architect and designer ; visited Egypt, Greece and Turkey, 1833 ; superintendent of the Great Exhibition, 1851 ; pub. with Bonomi and Sharpe a *Handbook to the Egyptian Court,* 1854 ; decorated the Khedive's palace at Cairo ; pub. *Scenery of the Nile,* 1840, and *Views on the Nile from Cairo to the Second Cataract,* with notes by Samuel Birch, 1843.

DNB. 30, 150 ; *Hilmy,* i, 336.

JORET, Charles (1829–1914)

Philologist and historian ; born Formigny, Calvados, 1829 ; Hon. Professor of Foreign Literature at Aix ; Membre Acad. des Inscr., 1902 ; pub. *Les Plantes dans l'Antiquité et au Moyen Age*, Paris, 1897, which called forth an important article by Maspero, *Journ. des Savants,* 1897, 477–486 ; died in Paris, 1914.

JOUGUET, Pierre (1869–1949)

French Hellenist and Egyptologist ; born Bessèges, 14 May, 1869 ; after his education in Paris was appointed to the École d'Athènes ; at the request of De Morgan, he went to Egypt in 1894 to study Graeco-Roman sites and antiquities, especially papyri ; he went again to Eg. 1897–8 and in 1901 when he excavated in the Fayûm and returned to Europe with a rich store of papyri to the Inst. of Papyrology then founded at Lille, where he began a long series of publications of papyri ; remained at Lille till 1919, having in 1914 explored the Kôm of Edfu ; lectured at the Sorbonne, Paris, 1919–28 ; succeeded G. Foucart as Director of the Inst. of Oriental Arch. at Cairo, which brought him into active contact with all branches of Egyptology, 1928–39 ; Pres. of Soc. de Papyrologie founded under the auspices of Fuad I, 1930–49 ; organized the Inst. of Hellenic Research, Alexandria, 1947 ; returned to France, 1949 and died 9 July of that year.

Bull. Inst. Ég. 32, 325–47.

JOWETT, (*Rev.*) **William** (1787–1855)

Missionary and traveller ; born 1787 ; St. John's Coll. Cantab. ; M.A. 1813 and Fellow ; Missionary in Mediterranean countries and

Palestine, 1815–24 ; in Egypt, 1818 ; visited Upper Egypt and returned to Cairo, which he left for Syria, May 1819 ; was in Alexandria, April 1820 ; pub. works on his travels and missionary labours, 1822 and 1825 ; Sec. Church Miss. Soc., 1832–40 ; Vicar of St. John's Church, Clapham, 1851 ; died 1855.

DNB. 30, 215 ; *Salt*, ii, 109, 110, 124, 154*n*.

JUMEL, Louis Alexis (1785–1823)

French industrialist ; born Breuil-le-Sec (Oise), 1785 ; went to Egypt in the service of Mohammad Ali, 1818 ; introduced and organized the cotton industry in Egypt, 1820 ; was a friend of Linant de Bellefonds (who was his executor), Drovetti and Piccinini ; spent much money in collecting antiquities and also undertook excavations, his most important find being the great tomb of Bakenrenef at Sakkara, which Champollion visited in 1828 and called " le tombeau Jumel "; his " cabinet d'objets d'antiquités " was sold after his death ; died in Cairo, 27 June 1823.

Bull. Inst. Ég. 22 (1940), 49–97 ; *Champollion*, ii, 117.

KENNARD, Henry Martin (1833–1911)

Patron of archaeology ; of Falkirk and Crumlin Hall, Newport, Mon., and Lowndes Sq., London ; born 17 Feb. 1833 ; J.P. ; D.L. ; a generous supporter of the excavations of the E.E.F., and of Petrie, Garstang and others ; presented antiquities to B.M., Ashmolean, Manchester and other museums ; his own extensive collection of ant. was sold at Sotheby's, 16–19 July, 1912 (743 lots) and realized £5,220 ; his portrait by W. W. Ouless was exhibited at R.A., 1891 ; died 1911 ; his name is associated with an important Coptic papyrus which he presented to the B.M. (*Or*. 7561).

Petrie, 79, 83, 89, 110, 137 ; *Private information*.

KINGLAKE, Alexander William (1809–1891)

Historian and traveller ; born Taunton, 5 Aug. 1809 ; educ. Eton and T.C.C. ; called to the Bar, Lincoln's Inn, 1837 ; travelled in the East, 1835 and described his journey in *Eothen*, 1844, which has become an English classic ; visited Crimea, 1854, and pub. history of the campaign in 8 vols., 1863–87 ; died 2 Jan. 1891.

DNB. 31, 171 ; *Hilmy*, i, 342.

KITCHENER, Horatio Herbert, 1st Earl (1850–1916)

Military officer ; born 24 June 1850 ; K.G. ; G.C.M.G. ; P.C. ; Field Marshal ; Sidar of the Egyptian Army, 1890 ; created Baron, 1898 ; Viscount, 1902 ; Earl Kitchener of Khartoum, 1914 ; lost with H.M.S. *Hampshire*, 5 June 1916 ; during his long connection with Egypt he did much to encourage archaeology ; collected antiquities and ceramics ; his collection sold at Sotheby's, 16–17 Nov. 1938.

WWW. ii, 591 ; *Budge N & T*. i, 110 ; ii, 152, 289, 356 ; *Sayce*, passim.

KLAPROTH, Heinrich Julius (1783–1835)

German orientalist and traveller ; born Berlin, 11 Oct. 1783 ; son of the chemist Martin Heinrich K. (1743–1817) ; studied Asiatic languages ; held an appointment at St. Petersburg Acad. ; member of Count Golovkin's embassy to China, 1805 ; explored Caucasus, 1807–8 ; moved to Berlin, 1812 ; settled in Paris, 1815 ; obtained title and salary of Professor of Asiatic Languages, Berlin, with leave to remain in Paris and publish his works ; besides a number of works on his Asiatic travels and languages he pub. an elaborate but worthless *Examen Critique des Travaux de feù M. Champollion sur les Hiéroglyphes,* Paris, 1832 which was in turn criticised by de Saulcy in *Rev. Arch.* 1846, i, 12, 65 ; in 1829 he pub. in Paris a collection of Plates of Eg. antiquities collected by Palin and Passalacqua, with a criticism of Champollion prefixed ; died Paris, 28 Aug. 1835.

ADB. ; *Hilmy,* i, 344 ; *Champollion,* i, 127, 171.

KLEBS, Luise (1865–1931)

German Egyptologist ; née Sigwart ; born Tübingen, 13 June 1865 ; educ. Heidelberg University ; pub. *Reliefs des Alten Reiches,* 1914 ; *Reliefs und Malereien des Mittleren Reiches,* 1921 ; a similar work for the New Kingdom was in preparation but left unfinished ; died 24 May 1931.

ZÄS. 66, 75 ; *JEA.* 17, 255.

KOCH, Johann Georg (*fl.* 1780–90)

Dutch theologian ; attempted to decipher hieroglyphic writing in three works pub. at St. Petersberg, 1788–9.

BIFAO. 5, 86 ; *Hilmy,* i, 346.

KOLLER, (*Baron*) **Franz von** (1767–1826)

General in the Austrian army ; born Munchengraetz, 1767 ; after his retirement he resided in Italy and formed a notable collection of Greek and Roman coins, and many antiquities, including Egyptian ; his coins were sold in London in 1846 ; the Eg. antiquities were acquired by the Berlin Museum ; most of his collections he obtained in Italy but he made purchases in Egypt in 1824 ; his name is attached to a papyrus (Berlin 3043) pub. by Gardiner, *Late Eg. Misc.,* 116 ; died in Naples, 1826.

Larousse, 19th cent. 9, 1245.

KRALL, Jakob (1857–1905)

Austrian Egyptologist ; born Voloska, Istria, 27 June 1857 ; educ. Trieste, Athens (1875–8), Univ. of Vienna, 1879–80 ; studied Egyptology at the Coll. de France and the Louvre, 1880 ; Professor Extraordinary, Vienna Univ., 1890, Ordinary, 1897, full Professor, 1890 ; Corresp. Member, Vienna Acad., 1890 ; made many important contributions to Egyptological literature, especially in chronology, Coptic and demotic, notable amongst which is his edition of the Petubastis Story ; died in Vienna, 26 April 1905.

WZKM. 19, 251–62 (bibl.) ; *ZÄS.* 42, 86 ; *Rec. Trav.* 28, 131.

LACOUR, Pierre (1779–1858)

Painter and archaeologist of Bordeaux ; pub. *Essai sur les Hiéroglyphes,* 1821, with 14 plates, followed by a larger work on the same subject ; he attempted to prove the identity of Egyptian and Hebrew etymology.

BIFAO, 5, 86 ; *Hilmy*, i, 352.

LAMACRAFT, Charles Tandy (1879–1945)

Restorer and mounter of manuscripts ; he was a skilful craftsman and was for many years attached to the Dept. of MSS., B.M., but he also undertook much outside work ; in addition to his work on vellum and paper MSS., he unrolled and mounted many of the Egyptian, Coptic and Greek papyri in the B.M., and many papyri in other collections, such as those of Chester-Beatty and Lord Amherst.

Private information ; *Newberry Corresp.*

LANE, Edward William (1801–1876)

Arabic scholar ; born Hereford 17 Sept. 1801 ; educ. Grammar Schools of Bath and Hereford ; joined his brother in London as an engraver, but abandoned that career owing to ill-health ; learned Arabic and went to Egypt, 1825 ; made voyages up the Nile in 1826 and 1827 and has left in MS. a voluminous description and a large number of drawings (B.M. Add. MSS. 34080–8 ; others in the Griffith Inst., Oxford) ; spoke Arabic fluently and in 1836 pub. *Manners and Customs of the Modern Egyptians* ; translated *Thousand and One Nights*, 1838–40 ; again in Egypt, 1842–9 when he compiled his great Arabic dictionary, for which funds were provided by the Duke of Northumberland, which appeared in parts from 1863 ; Lane was the leading Arabic scholar of Europe, and although his works are concerned with the modern Egyptians, they are a great value to Egyptologists as he was closely associated with Hay and Wilkinson ; his coll. of antiquities acquired by B.M. in 1842 ; died at Worthing, 10 Aug. 1876.

DNB. 32, 71 ; *Hilmy*, i, 355.

LANGE, Hans Ostenfeldt (1863–1943)

Danish Egyptologist ; born 1863 ; studied Egyptology under Valdemar Schmidt, Copenhagen Univ., 1881 ; Assistant Librarian, Royal Library, 1886 ; Chief Librarian, 1901 ; did much to promote Egyptology in Denmark ; he contributed to *ZÄS* and other journals and described the Middle Kingdom Stelae in the Cairo *Cat. Gen.* ; in collaboration with Erman, he edited the Lansing Papyrus ; died 15 Jan. 1943.

Chron. 19, 259.

LANSING, (*Rev.*) **Gulian** (1825–1892)

American missionary of Dutch origin ; born Lishaskill, Albany County, N.Y., 1 Feb. 1825 ; graduated Union Coll., 1847 ; joined the Associated Reformed Church ; ordained 1850 and went as missionary to the Jews at Damascus ; in 1856 went to Egypt where he remained for the rest of his life ; a good Hebrew and Arabic scholar ; pub. *Egypt's Princes : a Narrative of Missionary Labour in the Valley of the Nile*, N.Y., 1865 ; in 1886 his health failed and he spent much time in England and America, but returned to Cairo ;

Lansing's name is associated with a fine literary papyrus, acquired from him by the B.M. in 1886 (9994); in the following year, on the recommendation of Renouf, the B.M. purchased from him a large number of Coptic papyri (10128–42, 10453–62); died in Cairo, 12 Sept. 1892.

DAB.; *Sayce*, 337; *Budge N & T.* i, 411.

LANZONE, Rudolfo Vittorio (1834–1907)

Italian Egyptologist; on the staff of Turin Museum, 1872–95; his principal publications are: *Dizionario di Mitologia Egizia* (autographed), 2 vols., 1881–5; *La Domicile des Esprits*, 1879; *Les Papyrus du Lac Moeris*, 1896.

LARREY, (*Baron*) **Dominique Jean** (1766–1842)

Surgeon-in-chief, French army; a member of Napoleon's Commission in Egypt; Membre Inst. Ég.; contributed to the *Description de l'Égypte* and pub. medical works; his treatise on military surgery was translated into English by J. Waller, 1815; brought back a collection of antiquities, some of which are in the Louvre.

P. Triaire, *Napoléon et Larrey*, 1902; *Carré*, i, 143, 147; *Rev. de l'Art*, 43, 280; *Hilmy*, i, 358.

LAURIN, (*Ritter von*) **Anton** (*fl.* 1835–1850)

Austrian Consul-General in Egypt, afterwards Consul at Bucharest; he was succeeded in Egypt by von Huber; presented a sarcophagus to Vienna Museum.

Rec. Trav. 6, 131; *Vyse*, i, 148, 228; ii, 152.

LAUTH, Frans Joseph (1822–*c.* 1890)

German Egyptologist; born Anzheim, 1822; studied at Munich and became a professor in the University; member of Munich Acad., 1866; resigned 1882; he made many contributions to the literature of Egyptology, and although he had the makings of a brilliant scholar, he was too fond of forming hypotheses on insecure bases and was acute, enterprising, but unsound; died about 1890.

Dawson MS. 18, f. 91; *Chabas*, 49; *Hilmy*, i, 359; ii, 429.

LAVALETTE, (*Marquis de*) **Charles Jean Marie Felix** (*c.* 1810–1881)

Born about 1810; French Consul-General in Egypt in 1844; afterwards attached to the French Embassy in London, from which he was recalled in 1870; died 10 May 1881.

French F.O. Records; *Carré*, ii, 28.

LAVISON, Édouard (*fl.* 1828–1840)

A native of Marseilles; Chancellor and dragoman to the Russian Consulate in Egypt; acting Consul-General for Russia from Feb. 1831 to Sept. 1832; received Champollion in Egypt in 1828; in 1840 he presented a papyrus to the Hermitage Museum (1113).

R. Cattaui, *La Règne de Mohamed Aly*, passim; *Champollion*, ii, 25, 199.

LAVORATORI, Maria (*d.* 1832)

Wife of an Italian merchant of Trieste who was in Egypt 1818–22 and acted as deputy for Salt during his absence from Cairo; he formed a collection of antiquities ; after his death in Cairo, it was sent to Leghorn, and was privately owned by his wife in Florence, 1822–32 ; on her death it was sent to London and sold at Sotheby's, 13–15 May 1833, 373 lots ; some items were bought by B.M. (including the papyrus 9941) and many by Dr. Lee ; his copy of the sale catalogue is now in the Griffith Institute and contains a note on which the above is partly based.

Madox, i, 107 ; *Sale Cat.* ubi supra ; *Champollion*, i, 245.

LAYCOCK, James Akenhead (*d.* 1890)

Of Worcester Coll. Oxon. ; matric. 1864 ; B.A., 1869 ; M.A., 1871 ; died 1890 ; by her will, dated 22 Aug. 1890, his widow, Mrs. R. A. Laycock, founded an Egyptological Studentship at Worcester College in memory of her husband ; this became effective in 1900, after her death, when the first Laycock student, Dr. D. Randall MacIver, was appointed.

E.E.F. Arch. Rep. 1900–1, 53 ; *Inf. by Bursar of Worcester Coll.*

LEBAS, Jean Baptiste Apollinaire (1797–1873)

French engineer ; born 1797 ; educ. École Polytechnique, Paris ; joined the Corps of Marine Engineers, 1818 ; lowered and transported to Paris in 1831 the Luxor Obelisk now in the Place de la Concorde, Paris ; of this operation he pub. a detailed account with 15 plates, *L'Obelisque de Luxor : histoire de sa translation à Paris*, etc. Paris 1839 ; Keeper of the Marine Museum of the Louvre, 1836–52 ; died 1873.

B. Dibner, *Moving the Obelisks*, (1950), 56 ; *Bonomi Diary*, 1831 ; *NBG.* 30, 69 ; *DBF.* 20, 285 ; *Hilmy*, i, 361.

LEBOLO, Antonio (*d.* 1823)

Piedmontese traveller in Egypt ; excavated at Thebes for Drovetti and on his own account ; he found a number of Ptolemaic mummies in a pit-tomb at Gurneh ; the best of these went to Drovetti, two to Minutoli (which were, however, lost at sea), one to Cailliaud, another to Anastasi, and he kept one for himself ; an account of these mummies was written by Quintino di San Giulio, *Lezioni archeologiche*, Turin, 1824, 25 ; the paper was read in the Acad. of Turin in the presence of Champollion ; Lebolo was very hostile to Belzoni, who was working for Salt, and in company with Rosignani (another employee of Drovetti), made a violent assault upon him at Karnak, and afterwards endeavoured by a trick to secure some antiquities at Philae belonging to Belzoni ; died at Trieste, 1823.

Salt, ii, 23 ; *Belzoni*, i, 235, 237, 239 ; ii, 107 ; *Athanasi*, 51.

LEDRAIN, (*Abbé*) **Eugène** (1844–1910)

French archaeologist ; born 1844 ; studied Egyptology under Maspero at Coll. de France ; contributed articles on Egyptological subjects to *Gazette archéologique*, *Le Contemporaire* and other journals ; pub. the Luynes Papyrus, *Rec. Trav.* i, 89, and contributed to *Rev. d'Assyriologie*, and compiled a *Dict. de la Langue de l'ancienne Chaldée*, 1908 ; died 10 Feb. 1910.

Rev. Arch. 4th ser. 16, 152 ; *Budge R & P.* 214 ; *Hilmy*, i, 362.

LEE, John (1783–1866)

Archaeologist and patron of science ; born 1783 ; St. John's Coll. Cantab. ; M.A., 1809 ; LL.D., 1816 ; his father's name was Fiott, but he changed it by royal licence on inheriting from the Rev. Sir George Lee, Bart., in 1815, the estate of Hartwell, Bucks, and other estates ; studied law, and admitted to Coll. of Advocates, of which he was Librarian and Treasurer ; practised in the Ecclesiastical Courts ; at the age of 80 he was admitted Barrister, Gray's Inn, and became Bencher and Q.C. in the following year ; all his life he took great interest in the promotion of science, literature and archaeology of which he was a generous patron ; at his seat at Hartwell he formed an extensive library and museum ; he had a rich collection of Eg. antiquities many of which he bought at the Barker, Lavoratori, Burton and Athanasi sales ; others he acquired during a journey to Egypt in 1807–10 ; a printed catalogue of the Egyptian collection, by Bonomi, was issued in 1858 ; after his death, the entire Eg. collection was bought by Lord Amherst ; foundation member R. Astron. Soc., 1820, president, 1862 ; F.R.S., 1831 ; F.S.A., 1828 ; scientific meetings were held at his house and out of these grew the Meteorological Soc., the Syro-Egyptian Soc., the Anglo-Biblical Soc., the Palestine Arch. Assn., and the Chronological Institute ; the last four were dissolved in 1872 and merged in the Soc. of Biblical Arch. ; Lee's name is associated with a judicial papyrus which passed into Lord Amherst's coll. and is now in the Pierpont Morgan Library, N.Y. ; Lee died at Hartwell, without issue, 25 Feb., 1866 ; his library and MSS. were sold at Sotheby's, 1876, and collections of deeds, etc., 8 Mar. 1939 ; some of the geological specimens are now in the Aylesbury Museum, others in B.M. ; the MS. registers of Lee's Museum in 4 vols., folio, are also at Aylesbury Museum.

DNB. 32, 362 ; W. H. Smythe, *Ædes Hartwellianae,* 1851.

LEE, Peter (*d.* 1825)

British Consul at Alexandria ; he was very helpful to British travellers in Egypt ; he died suddenly in Alexandria in the autumn of 1825, leaving a wife and children ; Mrs. Lee died in London, July 1845.

Salt, ii, 226, 232, 234, 235 ; *Barker,* ii, 1 ; *Henniker,* 6, 115 ; *Sherer,* 197, 203 ; *Westcar Diary,* 6, 12, 13–18, 78 ; *Light,* 4, 11 ; *Madox,* i, 99, 101, 125, 127, 239, 241 ; ii, 50.

LEEMANS, Conrad (1809–1893)

Dutch Egyptologist ; born Zalt-Boemal 28 Apl. 1809 ; studied at Leiden first for the Church, but on the advice of Reuvens, took up archaeology ; after performing military service, 1830–1, he joined the staff of the Leiden Museum ; in 1835 he succeeded Reuvens as Conservator and became Director in 1839 ; pub. Horapollo, *Hieroglyphica,* 1835 ; *Papyri Graeci,* 1843 ; in 1839 he began the great official publication of the monuments and papyri in the Leiden Collection, which appeared in parts until 1882 ; in 1885 a festschrift was published in his honour to celebrate his connection of fifty years with the Leiden Museum ; died 1893.

Hilmy, i, 363.

LEFÉBURE, Eugène Jean-Baptiste Louis Joseph (1838–1908)

French Egyptologist ; born Prunay, 11 Nov. 1838 ; married young, and the early death of his wife caused him to take up Egyptology as a diversion ; he came under the notice of Chabas and studied under his direction ; was employed in the French Postal Service until 1879, when he was appointed lecturer on Egyptology at Lyons ; in 1880 joined the Mission Arch. au Caire, and became director of it in 1881 ; his great work in Egypt was the publication of the Tombs of the Kings, those of Ramesses IV and Sety I being copied in extenso ; he was not physically fitted for field-work, and the frequent leave of absence for which he applied led to his recall in 1884 ; he resumed his work at Lyons for a short time, and then succeeded Grébaut at the Coll. de France ; he began work there in 1885, but was soon replaced by Guieysse, and went to the École de Lettres at Algiers, where he remained until his death ; Lefébure was an able man, and made valuable contributions to Egyptology, but he was by nature a poet and a mystic, and a tendency to mysticism is observable even in his Egyptological works ; he was an intimate friend of the poet Stéphane Mallarmé ; his shorter works were collected by Maspero in the *Bibl. Ég.* Vols. 34–36 ; died 9 April 1908.

Notice Biographique, by P. Virey, *Bibl. Ég.* 34 ; *Sphinx*, 12, 1, 105 ; *Hilmy*, i, 364 ; *La Table Ronde*, No. 38 (1951), 68–95 (Corresp. with Mallarmé).

LEGGE, George Francis (*d.* 1922)

A barrister by profession ; much interested in Egyptology, and especially in Gnosticism and magic ; began his contributions in 1897 and pub. many papers in *PSBA*, *JRAS*, and other journals ; was also a contributor to the *Athenaeum* ; F.S.A., 1910 ; went to Egypt in 1912 to assist Naville at Abydos ; a good Greek scholar ; pub. a translation of the *Philosophumena* of Hippolytus (2 vols., 1921), and a valuable introduction to Horner's translation of *Pistis Sophia*, 1924, which was published after his death, unfortunately without revision ; his principal work was *Forerunners and Rivals of Christianity*, 2 vols., 1915 ; Legge was a very able man, and was Foreign Sec. S.B.A. ; during the war he was employed in the Censor's office ; died by his own hand, 21 Nov. 1922.

JRAS. 1923, 151 ; *Newberry Corresp.*

LEGH, Thomas (*d.* 1857)

Traveller and scholar ; of Lyme Park, Co. Chester ; J.P., LL.D. ; M.P., 1819–31 ; F.R.S., 1817 ; F.S.A. ; visited Egypt and Nubia, 1812, and again 1814, and also Palestine ; pub. *Narrative of a Journey in Egypt and the Country beyond the Cataracts*, 1816 ; obtained Coptic papyri, now in B.M. (Crum, *Cat.* Nos. 447–454) ; died 8 May 1857.

Budge, *Eg. Sudan*, i, 26 ; *Henniker*, 97 ; *Hilmy*, i, 364 ; *Finati*, ii, 79, 225, 231, 234 ; *Irby*, 5, 100, 101, 103, 109, 148, 150.

LEGRAIN, Georges (1865–1917)

French Egyptologist ; born Paris, 4 Oct. 1865 ; studied art and architecture in Paris under Gerôme and Choisy, and Egyptian archaeology and philology under Pierret and Revillout; his first published work was on a demotic subject (*Rev. Arch.* 5, 1888, 89); he was for many years employed by the Service des Antiquités in Egypt and from 1895 was engaged in clearing and restoring the Temple of Karnak, and made the famous find of a hoard of statues in 1903; pub. many inscriptions and papers in *ASA* and other journals, and wrote a popular work on the Christian and Muslim dwellers in modern Thebes; died of pneumonia at Luxor, Aug. 1917.

ASA. 19, 105 (Bibl. 118); *Bull. Inst. Eg.* Ser. 5, 11, 425; *JEA*. 4, 276.

LEMM, Oskar Eduardovich von (1856–1918)

Russian Egyptologist; born St. Petersburg 5 Sept. 1856; educ. Alexandrewski Lyzeum; in 1877 went to Germany to study and took the D.Ph. degree at Leipsic, 1882; keeper of the Asiatic Museum of the Russian Imperial Academy of Sciences, 1883–1918; Member of Imp. Acad., 1906; from 1887 to 1891 lectured in the Oriental Faculty of St. Petersburg on Egyptian, Coptic and Semitic languages; his principal published works were Coptic; died 3 June 1918.

B. Turaev, in *Christianski Vostok*, 6, pt. 3 (1917–20), Leningrad, 1922, 325–333 (Bibl.).

LEMOYNE, Arnaud Hilarie Auguste (1800–1891)

French diplomatist; born Paris, 20 Floréal, Ann. VIII (= 10 May 1800); French Consul-General in Egypt 1849–52, when he left to become Minister Plenipotentiary at Lima, Peru; retired, 1862; was very helpful to Mariette on his first arrival in Egypt; died at Orleans, 27 Jan. 1891.

French F.O. Records; *Carré*. ii, 28; *Bibl. Ég.* 18, pp. xxvii, xlix.

LELORRAIN, Jean Baptiste (*fl.* 1820–1823)

French engineer; was sent to Egypt in 1820–1 by Saulnier to remove and convey to Paris the Circular Zodiac of Dendereh; in order to disarm suspicions of his intentions, he first proceeded up the Nile as far as Assuan, and bought antiquities at Thebes, some of which were studied by Champollion; on his return journey, he detached with great skill the heavy blocks inscribed with the Zodiac and successfully embarked them, but his operations were discovered by Luther Bradish (q.v.) who carried the news to Cairo, where Lelorrain met with great opposition by Salt and Drovetti, but succeeded in the end in carrying his booty to France.

S. L. Saulnier, *Notice sur le voyage de M. Lelorrain en Égypte*, Paris, 1822; *Champollion*, i, 6, 38, 57; ii, 155.

LENOIR, Marie Alexandre (1762–1839)

French archaeologist; born Paris, 26 Dec. 1762; studied art and archaeology on which he pub. many works, including the following relating to Egypt: *Antiquités Ég. apportées à Paris by M. Passalacqua*, 1821; *Essai sur le Zodiaque de Dendereh*, 1822; also wrote on decipherment, on which he held erroneous views, *Nouvelle explication des Hiéroglyphes*, 4 vols., 1809–10, and *Nouveaux Essais sur les Hiéroglyphes*, 1826; died 1839.

BIFAO, 5, 85; *Hilmy*, i, 368.

LENORMANT, Charles (1802–1859)

French archaeologist and numismatist ; born 1802 ; accompanied Champollion to Egypt, 1828 ; Librarian to the Arsenal, 1830 ; editor of the *Correspondant*; Professor of Eg. Archaeology, Coll. de France, 1848 ; his journal of the voyage in Egypt was posthumously published in 1861 ; amongst his many publications there are several dealing with Egyptology, of great value in their time ; it was at his suggestion that Mariette was first sent to Egypt ; died of fever at Athens while travelling with his son in Greece, 24 Nov. 1859.

Champollion, ii, passim ; *Carré*, passim (see index) ; *Hilmy*, i, 368.

LENORMANT, François (1837–1883)

French orientalist ; son of Charles L. ; born Paris, 17 Jan. 1837 ; began to learn Greek at the age of 6, and at 14 pub. a paper on Greek Inscriptions from Memphis in *Rev. Arch.* ; accompanied his father on a voyage to Greece, 1859, on which the latter died, and revisited Greece several times afterwards ; served in the Army, 1870 and was wounded at the seige of Paris ; Professor of Archaeology at the Bibl. Nat., 1874 ; founded *Gazette Archéologique*, 1875 ; as early as 1867 he had studied cuneiform, and this, with Egyptian and other oriental languages, occupied him all his life ; his knowledge was encyclopaedic, and his published works very numerous, the most celebrated is *Les Premières Civilizations*, 2 vols., Paris, 1874 (vol. i, Egypt ; vol. ii, Assyria, Chaldea and Phoenicia) ; was injured in an accident whilst exploring Calabria, he returned to France and died in Paris after a long illness, 9 Dec. 1883.

Gaz. Arch. 8, 361 ; *Academy*, 1883, No. 599, 280 ; *Athenaeum*, No. 2929, 783 ; *Hilmy*, i, 369.

LEPSIUS, Karl Richard (1810–1884)

German Egyptologist ; born Naumburg-am-Saale, 23 Dec. 1810 ; educ. Leipsic, Göttingen and Berlin Univs. ; Ph.D., 1833 ; went to Paris 1833 to collect materials on ancient weapons for the Duc de Luynes ; under the influence of Bunsen and Humboldt studied Egyptology, spending four years visiting the Eg. collections in England, Holland and Italy ; in 1842–5 he led the Prussian Expedition to Egypt and Nubia, when a large store of epigraphic material was collected and pub. in 1859 in the 12 vast volumes of *Denkmäler* ; the work consists entirely of plates, the letterpress did not appear until after his death, when it was compiled from his papers by Naville and others, and pub. in 5 vols. 1897–1913 ; in 1865 on the death of Passalacqua he was appointed Keeper of the Eg. collections of Berlin and in 1873, Keeper of the Royal Library ; visited Egypt again in 1866 when he discovered the celebrated Decree of Canopus ; he was more interested in archaeology, chronology and history than in philology and most of his many writings are concerned with these subjects, he did, however, study the Nubian dialects, and pub. his *Nubische Grammatik* in 1880 ; for many years he edited *ZÄS.* ; died in Berlin, 10 July 1884.

Richard Lepsius : ein Lebensbild, by Georg Ebers, Leipsic, 1885, translated by Underhill, N.Y. 1887 ; *ZÄS.* 22, 45 ; *Rev. Hist. des Relig.* 10, 238 ; Brugsch, *Mein Leben*, 32, 46, 74, 91, 262, 270, 272, 375 ; *Hilmy*, i, 375 ; ii, 431.

LESQUIER, Jean (1879–1921)

French Egyptologist; born at Lisieux, 1879; studied chiefly Graeco-Roman Egypt and papyrology, on which he published many works; excavated in Egypt for the Inst. Français d'Arch. Orient., 1908; pub. an adaptation of Erman's Egyptian Grammar for the *Bibl. d'Études* of the Institute, 1914; died at Neuilly-sur-Seine, 28 June 1921, buried at Lisieux.

JEA. 7, 218.

LESUEUR, Jean Baptiste Cicéron (1794–1883)

French architect; born Claire-Fontaine, Rambouillet, 1794; was interested in Egyptian art and chronology, and pub. *Chronologie des Rois d'Égypte,* Paris, 1848–50 and a work on the origins of art with special reference to Egyptian architecture; died Paris, 1883.

Chron. des Arts, 1883, 333; *Larousse* 19 *cent.*; *Hilmy,* i, 380.

LETRONNE, Antoine Jean (1787–1848)

French archaeologist and classical scholar; son of an engineer; born Paris, 25 Jan. 1787; Professor at Collège de France, 1831; Keeper of National Archives, 1840; pub. many archaeological works, those relating to Egypt being: *Recherches . . . l'histoire de l'Égypte pendant la domination des Grecs et Romains,* 1823; *L'hist. du Christianisme en Égypte,* 1832; *Sur l'origine grecque des Zodiaques prétendus égyptiens,* 1837; his most important work was *Recueil du Inscriptions grecques et latines de l'Égypte,* 2 vols., 1842–8; he took a prominent interest in the decipherment of hieroglyphics by Champollion and Young; died, Paris, 14 Dec. 1848.

Rev. Arch. 1848, 637; *Mem. Acad. des Inscr.* 18, 396; *Hilmy,* i, 380; *Hartleben,* see index.

LETHIEULLIER, William (*d.* 1755)

Of Huguenot extraction, a member of a very intellectual family that included Dr. Charles L., LL.D., F.S.A., of All Souls Coll. Cantab. (1718–59), Smart, L., F.R.S., F.S.A. (1701–60) a donor to the B.M., Pitt, L., also a donor to the B.M., and John L., Remembrancer to the City of London; William L. travelled in Egypt in 1721 and brought back from Sakkara a fine mummy which was engraved and pub. by Alexander Gordon (q.v.) in 1737, and other antiquities, which he presented to the B.M. (6695–6).

Nichols, *Lit. Anecd.* v, 372; Edwards, *Lives of the Founders,* 347.

LEUCHTENBERG, (*Duke*) **Maximilien Eugène Joseph Napoléon Beauharnais** (1827–1852)

Born Munich, 2 Oct. 1827; a member of the ancient French family de Beauharnais, one of whom, Eugène, was a stepson of Napoleon, on whose downfall the family settled at Munich and assumed the title of Duke (Hertzog) von Leuchtenberg; Maximilien had some important Egyptian antiquities, which passed to the Hermitage Museum; died St. Petersburg, 20 Oct. 1852.

L'HÔTE, Nestor (1804–1842)

Draughtsman and archaeologist; uncle of Mariette; born 1804; accompanied Champollion to Egypt as draughtsman, and returned to Egypt twice to complete his drawings, the second occasion being 1838–9; he had frail health, on which the climate of Egypt and the hardships of travel and camping put a great strain; pub. *Notice sur les Obélisques,* 1836; *Lettres écrites en 1838 et 1839* (with notes by Letronne), 1840; his manuscripts and drawings are in the Bibl. Nat. (*Nouv. acq. franç.*, 20394); died in Paris, 1842.

Hartleben, ii, 112 et passim; *Champollion,* ii, passim; *Carré,* passim (see index).

LIEBLEIN, Jens Daniel Carolus (1827–1911)

Swedish Egyptologist; born 1827; until his 20th year he was a workman in a sawmill, and later a clerk; at age 28 he became a student at the Univ. of Christiania, and in 1876, professor; published many articles, but his most useful contribution to Egyptology was his *Dictionnaire des noms propres,* 1871; died, Christiania, 1911.

Rec. Trav. 34, 114; *Sphinx,* 15, 161 (Bibl.); *Hilmy,* i, 385.

LIEDER, (*Rev.*) **Rudolph Theophilus** (1797–1865)

German missionary; born Erfurt, Prussia, 1797; worked in Cairo for many years under the Church Missionary Society, 1825–62; ordained priest in the Church of England, 1842; revised the New Testament in Coptic and Arabic for the S.P.C.K.; translated into Arabic the Homilies of St. Chrysostom and other works; Member of the Egyptian Society of Cairo, 1836; collected antiquities, and was hostile to Mariette; in 1861 Lord Amherst purchased his collection of 186 items for £200, the inventory of which is now in the Eg. Dept., B.M.; in the preface to the Amherst Sale Catalogue (1921) he is wrongly called "the Rev. W. Leider"; died of cholera in Cairo, 6 July 1865.

Inf. by Church Miss. Soc.; *Bibl. Ég.* 18, p. xxxvii; *Lepsius,* 36, 47, 74; Sophia Poole, *Englishwoman in Egypt,* ii, 183; iii, 33, 40, 41; *Lindsay,* 22, 33, 34, 37.

LIGHT, Henry (*c.* 1780–*c.* 1820)

Army officer; Capt. R. Artillery; while serving with his regiment in Malta, obtained leave to explore Egypt, Nubia and Palestine, 1814; went up the Nile as far as Derr; pub. *Travels in Egypt, Nubia and the Holy Land,* 1818; he obtained a painted coffin at Thebes which he presented to Col. Misset (q.v.) from whom it probably passed to Salt; part of Light's notes were used by the Rev. Robert Walpole in his works on eastern travel, 1817–20; died before 1825.

Hilmy, i, 386; *Army Lists*; *Legh,* 79; *Westcar Diary,* 111.

LIGHT, William (1784–1838)

Army officer; Colonel, 4th Dragoons; employed by Mohammad Ali to organize the Egyptian Navy, 1823–36; Surveyor-General, S. Australia, 1836–8; founded the City of Adelaide, where he died in 1838.

DNB. 33, 228; *Bonomi Diary,* 1831, Nov. 23.

LINANT DE BELLEFONDS, (*Bey*) **Louis Maurice Adolphe** (1799–1883)

French explorer and engineer; born Lorient, 1799; served in the French Navy till 1817 when he joined the Comte de Forbin's expedition to the East; came to Egypt as a draughtsman, 1818, and took part in many geographical expeditions in Egypt, Arabia, Nubia and the Sudan, 1821–6; explored the White Nile, 1827, and the goldmines between the Nile and the Red Sea, 1831; executed many drawings of monuments and inscriptions for W. J. Bankes; appointed Minister of Public Works, 1859, and many important irrigation and other undertakings were carried out under his direction; he kept a fine establishment in Cairo, and he and his family always wore Turkish dress; his first wife died of cholera in 1831; rendered much help to Champollion in 1828; many of his drawings and a diary are among the Bankes papers in the Griffith Institute, and many more in those of Burton in the B.M.: died, 1883.

Larousse 19th cent. 10, 531; *Carré*, ii, 24 etc. (Portr.); *Champollion*, ii, 78 and often; *Lepsius*, 14, 92; *Proc. R.G.S.* 6, 381; *Journ. R.G.S.* 2, 171; *Hilmy*, ii, 387; Brugsch, *Mein Leben*, 159; *Finati*, 301, 320, 345, 354, 394, 427; *Clot-Bey*, i, 41; ii, 479.

LINCKE, Arthur Alexander (1853–1898)

German orientalist; born Dresden, 13 Nov. 1853; a pupil of Ebers and Delitzsch; pub. the hieratic papyri of Bologna and other works on Egyptian epistolography; he afterwards forsook Egyptology for Assyriology; died 2 June 1898.

OLZ. 1898, 224; *Hilmy*, i, 387.

LINDSAY, (*Lord*) **Alexander William Crawford (afterwards 25th Earl of Crawford and 8th Earl of Balcarres)** (1812–1880)

Traveller and writer on Art; e. s. James, 24th Earl of Crawford and 7th of Balcarres; born 16 Oct. 1812; educ. Eton and T.C.C.; M.A., 1833; travelled much and collected books for the celebrated Lindsay Library; in 1836–7, he travelled in Egypt and Palestine and pub. *Letters from Egypt, Edom and the Holy Land*, 1838, 4th ed., 1847, which contains interesting particulars of Caviglia; his best known works are *Progression by Antagonism*, 1846 and *History of Christian Art*, 1847; succeeded to the earldoms, 1869; died in Florence, 13 Dec. 1880.

DNB. 33, 285; *Hilmy*, i, 149 (wrongly entered under *Crawford* instead of *Lindsay*).

LLOYD, George (1815–1843)

Botanist and traveller; son of Sir William Lloyd of Brynestyn, Wales; born 17 Oct. 1815; member of the Cairo Literary Society; excavated at Thebes with Prisse d'Avennes, 1839–43; died through the accidental discharge of his gun at Gurneh, 31 Oct. 1843; his papers and botanical collections were given by his parents to the Botanic Garden of Montpellier.

Carré, i, 307; Prisse, *Oriental Album* (1851) (portr.).

LOAT, William Leonard Stevenson (*d.* 1932)

Naturalist and archaeologist ; visited Egypt in 1899 as assistant to Dr. G. A. Boulenger, F.R.S., in the ichthyological survey of the Nile ; excavated at Gurob for Petrie, 1903 and at Abydos for E.E.F., 1908–9 and 1912–3 when he found and published the Ibis Cemetery ; in retirement he settled at Mevagissy, Cornwall and took up horticulture ; in 1927 visited the Andes ; F.Z.S. 1895–1902 ; died 10 Apl. 1932.

JEA. 18, 190 ; *Petrie*, 190.

LOFTIE, (*Rev.*) **William John** (1839–1911)

Clergyman and archaeologist ; born 25 July 1839 ; educ. T.C.D. ; B.A. ; F.S.A. ; Chaplain of the Chapel Royal, Savoy, 1871–95 ; pub. many works on the history and antiquities of London ; spent several years in Egypt and was closely associated with Sayce, Budge and Petrie ; pub. *A Ride in Egypt*, 1879 ; *Essay on Scarabs*, 1884 and contributed to the *Arch. Journ.* on Meydûm and the Pyramids ; died 16 June 1911.

WWW. i, 436 ; *Budge N & T*. i, 76, 82, 151 ; ii, 290 ; *Petrie*, 30.

LONGPÉRIER, Henri de (*fl.* 1860–1870)

French archaeologist ; son of Henri Adrien de Longpérier ; a pupil of de Rougé and of Maspero at the Collège de France ; did not follow Egyptology as a profession, but wrote on various archaeological subjects in scientific journals.

Maspero, *L'Égyptologie*, (1915), 7.

LONGPÉRIER, Henri Adrien Prévost de (1816–1882)

French archaeologist and numismatist ; Assistant, Cabinet de Medailles, and from 1847 Director of Musée du Louvre, where he made great improvements in the arrangement of the Eg. collections ; made numerous contributions to archaeological journals which were collected, with a biographical notice by G. Schlumberger, in 7 vols., Paris, 1883.

Oeuvres, ut supra ; *Bibl. Ég.* 21, pp. xvii, xviii ; *Hilmy*, i, 169.

LORD, John Keast (1818–1872)

Naturalist and Veterinary Surgeon, in which capacity he served in the Crimean War ; a man of many activities ; the first manager of the Brighton Aquarium ; naturalist to the Boundary Commission of British Columbia, 1858 ; carried out archaeological and scientific researches in Egypt on which he wrote in the popular press, and his results were utilized by Chabas and Maspero.

DNB. 34, 136 ; Maspero, *Hist. Anc.* i, 356, *n*. 1.

LORET, Victor (1859–1946)

French Egyptologist, naturalist and musician ; born Paris, 1859 ; studied Egyptology under Maspero ; an original member of the Mission archéologique ; Director, 1886 ; Reader in Egyptology at Lyons, 1886–1929 ; Director General, Service des Antiquités, 1897–9, but he was unfitted for the post and antagonized both Europeans and natives; wrote on many aspects of Egyptology, especially botany; founded a school of Egyptology in Lyons; died Lyons, 3 Feb. 1946.

ASA. 47, 7–13 (Portr.); *Chron*. 21, 202; *Sayce*, 306; *Budge N & T*. ii, 365, 392; *Petrie*, 168, 173.

LORTET, Louis Charles (1836–1909)

French naturalist; born Oullins (Rhône), 1836; Doyen Honoraire Faculté de Med., Lyons; Professor of Nat. Hist., Lyons, 1867; Director, Musée d'Hist. Nat. de Lyon, 1869–1909; studied the mummified animals of Egypt and the zoological and archaeological data provided by them in collaboration with his assistant Claude Gaillard (q.v.); pub. memoirs thereon in *ASA*, the Lyons *Annales du Musée* and the Cairo *Cat. Gen.*; died 1909.

Private information.

LOWE, (*Sir*) **Hudson** (1769–1844)

Army officer and traveller; born Galway, 28 July 1769; entered Army, 1787; Capt., 1795; served in Toulon, Corsica, Elba, Portugal and Egypt, 1805–12; Major-Gen. 1814; K.C.B., 1817; Governor of St. Helena during the confinement of Napoleon, 1815–21; governor of Antigua, 1823; on staff in Ceylon 1825–30; Lieut.-Gen. 1830; visited Egypt in 1826 and explored Thebes with Hay and Bonomi; died 10 Jan. 1844; his library was sold 1 May 1844.

DNB. 34, 189; Madden, *Travels*, i, 339; ii, 37; *Hay Diary*, 1826, May.

LOWRY-CORRY, Somerset, 2nd Earl of Belmore (1774–1841)

Born 11 July 1774; succeeded 1802; Governor and Custos Rotulorum, co. Tyrone; sometime Governor of Jamaica; in 1816–8 visited Egypt, Syria and Palestine and excavated in Western Thebes; ascended the Nile as far as Second Cataract; he brought back a number of antiquities, including a stone sarcophagus found by Belzoni (now B.M. 39, presented 1820); a considerable number of stelae (both of stone and wood), and five papyri (B.M. 9906, 10000, 10030, 10043-4); he had lithographic plates of these objects prepared intending to issue them for private circulation; after his death, the B.M. bought the whole collection, including the lithographic blocks: the latter were used in two official publications *Papyri from the Collection of the Earl of Belmore* and *Tablets*, ditto (1843); Lord Belmore also brought home on his yacht a considerable collection of antiquities for Henry Salt; his party, besides his own family and several relatives, included a chaplain (Rev. R. Holt), a physician, (Robert Richardson), and many servants; died 18 April 1841.

R. Richardson, *Travels along the Mediterranean . . . with the Earl of Belmore*, 2 vols. 1822; *Salt*, i, 487; ii, 40–47; *Athanasi*, 15; *Belzoni*, i, 386, 435; Belmore (4th Earl), *Hist. of Two Ulster Manors*, 1881, 275–284; Cailliaud, *Oasis*, 51; *Irby*, 52, 72, 100, 101.

LUCAS, Alfred (1867–1945)

Chemist; born Manchester, 17 Aug. 1867; educ. R. Coll. of Science; went to Egypt in 1897; in charge of the laboratories of the Survey

Dept. and Assay Office ; chemist to the Service des Antiquités, 1923–37 ; O.B.E. ; F.I.C. ; Membre Inst. Ég. ; his *Ancient Eg. Materials and Industries* and his many contributions on chemical problems in archaeology and mummification have been of high value ; examined and reported on the chemistry of the Tomb of Tutankhamen ; died 1945.

ASA. 47, 1–6 (portr.) ; *Ant. Journ.* 26, 231 ; *Chron.* 21, 205.

LUCAS, Paul (1664–1737)

French traveller ; son of a goldsmith at Rouen ; travelled in the Levant, 1696 and 1699, in Greece and Asia Minor, 1710 and Palestine and Egypt, 1714 ; he was not a scholar, but he took an interest in coins, manuscripts and antiquities, and although unable to read their inscriptions, he collected some good specimens ; he pub. accounts of all his voyages which were very popular and translated into several languages ; Lucas having no literary skill, his works were drawn up by Baudelot de Dairval, Étienne Fourmont and the abbé Antoine Banier.

Carré, i, 44–7, 75 ; *Hilmy*, i, 393.

LUSHINGTON, Edmund Law (1811–1893)

Classical scholar ; born 1811 ; educ. Charterhouse and T.C.C. ; Professor of Greek at Glasgow, 1838–75 ; Hon. LL.D., Glasgow, 1875 ; Lord Rector, Glasgow Univ., 1884 ; married Cecilia, sister of Lord Tennyson, 1842 ; took up Egyptology late in life ; pub. papers in *TSBA* and contributed to *Records of the Past* (1st ser. vols. ii and xii) ; died, Park House, Maidstone, 13 July 1893.

DNB. Suppl. iii, 114 ; *Hilmy*, i, 396.

LUYNES, (*Duc de*) **Honoré Théodore Paul Joseph** (1802–1867)

Archaeologist and collector ; born 1802 ; his collection, at Château Dampierre, consisted mainly of Greek and Roman antiquities, but he bought a collection of Eg. antiquities in 1863, some of which were forgeries ; he travelled in Egypt and Palestine in 1863–4, and met de Rougé in Egypt ; he employed Mariette to excavate the Sphinx to ascertain whether it was the tomb of Harmais as stated by Pliny ; he was a generous patron of archaeology ; his name is associated with the Papyrus Luynes, part of which he gave to the Louvre (3661) and part to the Bibl. Nat. (139–140) ; died 1867.

Bibl. Ég. 18, p. lviii, 125, 131 ; 21, lxxv ; Tristram, *Land of Israel*, 506, 514 ; *Rec. Trav.* i, 89.

LYONS, (*Sir*) **Henry George** (1864–1944)

Colonel R.E., geologist, meteorologist and archaeologist ; born 11 Oct. 1864 ; educ. Wellington and Woolwich ; entered R.E. 1884 ; posted to Egypt, 1890 ; served for some years in Nubia from 1891 ; cleared the temples of Buhen, 1892 ; visited the Dakhleh Oasis ; surveyed the temples of Philae, 1895–6 ; organized and directed the Geological and Cadastral Surveys of Egypt, 1897–1909 ; organized and directed the Archaeological Survey of Nubia, 1907 ; retired from Egypt, 1909 ; Asst. Director, Science Museum, London, 1911 ;

Director, 1919–33 ; F.R.S., 1906 ; For. Sec. R.S., 1928–9 ; Treas. R.S., 1929–39 ; Knighted, 1926 ; Treas. E.E.S., 1925–30 ; V.-P., 1931–40 ; while in Egypt, Lyons discovered many antiquities of importance ; of his great services to science and to the R.S. a full account has been given by Sir Henry Dale ; died at Gt. Missenden, Bucks, 10 Aug. 1944.

JEA. 31, 98 (Portr.) ; *OFRS*. 4, 795–809 (Portr. and Bibl.).

LYTHGOE, Albert Morton (1868–1934)

American Egyptologist ; educ. Harvard, 1892, A.M., 1897 ; a pupil of Wiedemann at Bonn ; assisted Reisner in the Hearst Expedition at Naga ed-Dêr, 1899–1904 ; entered the service of the Metrop. Museum of Art, N.Y., 1906 ; Curator of Egyptian Art, 1906–29 ; Curator Emeritus, 1929–33 ; conducted excavations for the M.M.A. at Lisht, Thebes, and other sites.

JEA. 20, 107 ; *Bull. M.M.A.* 29, 42.

MACCALLUM, Andrew (1821–1902)

Landscape painter ; born, Nottingham, 1821 ; began life in a factory ; studied art in Nottingham, Manchester and R.A. schools ; settled in London, 1852 and exhibited many works ; travelled in Europe and visited Egypt several times between 1870 and 1875 with Lord Alfred Paget ; in 1874 he procured the hieratic tablet and Canopic jars of Princess Eskhons (Nesikhonsu) from the cache of Royal Mummies ; these are associated with his name : the former is now in the B.M. (16672) and the latter he disposed of to Dillwyn Parrish, and were sold at Sotheby's, 5 July 1928 ; in 1874 he discovered a painted chamber on the S. side of the Temple of Abu Simbel ; died in London, 22 Jan. 1902.

DNB. Suppl. ii ; Edwards, *Thousand Miles*, ed. 2, 325 ff., 493 ; Budge, *Greenfield Papyrus*, p. xv ; Maspero, *Momies Royales*, 594 ; *Rec. Trav.* 4, 81.

McCLURE, (*Mrs.*) **Mary Louise Dora** (*d.* 1918)

Née Herbert, wife of Canon Edmund McClure, Secretary, S.P.C.K. ; joined the E.E.F. in 1884 and was for many years on the Committee ; translated Maspero's *Hist. Anc.* in 3 vols., entitled *The Dawn of Civilization*, *The Struggle of the Nations*, *The Passing of the Empires* ; died, 1918.

JEA. 5, 140 ; *Newberry Corresp.* ; *PEFQS*. 1920–1, 45.

MACE, Arthur Cruttenden (1874–1928)

Egyptologist ; born 1874 ; educ. St. Edward's School and Keble Coll. Oxon. ; joined Petrie at Dendereh, 1897–8, Hu, 1898–9 and Abydos 1899–1901 ; in 1901 joined Reisner with whom he continued to work on the California Univ. excavations at Gizeh and Naga ed-Dêr ; in 1906 worked for Metrop. Museum, N.Y. at Lisht until 1908 ; Asst. Conservator, M.M.A. ; returned to England 1912 ; served in the Artists Rifles in First World War ; returned to N.Y., 1919 and in 1920–2 excavated at Lisht, but left the site to assist Howard Carter in the Tomb of Tutankhamen ; after serving thus for two winters, his health failed and the next four years were spent in England and the Riviera ; contributed to the reports of the excavations in which he took part, and collaborated with Carter in vol. i of the *Tomb of Tutankhamen* ; died 6 April 1928.

JEA. 15, 105.

MACGREGOR, (*Rev.*) **William** (1848–1937)

Collector of antiquities ; born 1848 ; Exeter Coll. Oxon. ; M.A., 1874 ; Vicar of Tamworth, 1878–87 ; on Committee of E.E.F. 1888–1930 ; in his house, Bolehill Manor, Tamworth, he formed one of the most remarkable collections of Eg. antiquities ever made by a private individual ; the ceramic portion was described by Henry Wallis (q.v.), *Eg. Ceramic Art,* 1898 ; subscribed funds for many excavations in Egypt and Nubia ; the collection was sold at Sotheby's, June 1922, in a 7 days' sale (1800 lots, Cat. with 53 plates) ; it was full of choice pieces, one of which, the obsidian head of a king, fetched £10,000, out of a total of £34,000 ; died 26 Feb. 1937.

JEA. 4, 71 ; *Chron*. 13, 132 ; *Sayce*, 294, 307.

MACIVER, David Randall (1873–1945)

Egyptologist and antiquary ; born 1873 ; Queen's Coll. Oxon. ; Laycock Student of Egyptology, 1900 ; F.S.A. ; Director of the Eckley B. Coxe expedition to Egypt and the Sudan, 1907–11 ; Librarian, American Geographical Soc. ; settled in Italy and wrote on Italian archaeology ; died in New York, 30 Apl. 1945.

Ant. Journ. 26, 231.

MADDEN, Frank Cole (1873–1929)

Surgeon ; born Melbourne, 1873 ; Melbourne Univ., M.B. and Ch.B., 1893 ; St. Mary's Hospital, London ; M.R.C.S. and L.R.C.P., 1896 ; F.R.C.S., 1898 ; held many surgical appointments in Egypt ; Professor of Surgery, Cairo School of Med. ; Consulting Surgeon Kasr el-Ainy Hospital, Cairo ; his book, *The Surgery of Egypt,* Cairo 1919, with its lucid text and abundant illustrations, although dealing with modern Egypt, is of the utmost value in studying the Egyptian Medical Papyri ; died Cairo, 20 Apl. 1929.

BMJ. 1929, i, 833.

MADDEN, Richard Robert (1798–1886)

Traveller and administrator ; born 1798 ; studied medicine in Paris and London ; M.R.C.S., 1829 ; F.R.C.S., 1855 ; he never practised as a surgeon ; travelled extensively and was a personal friend of Lady Blessington (whose biography he published), Byron and D'Orsay ; travelled in Egypt 1827–8 and again in 1840 ; attended Henry Salt in his last illness ; held administrative appointments in the West Indies and in Ireland and was Colonial Secretary of Western Australia, 1847–50 ; pub. his *Travels*, 2 vols., 1829 in which there is much of interest to Egyptologists ; died in Ireland, 1886.

DNB. 35, 295 ; *BMJ*. 1929, ii, 628 ; *Salt*, ii, 282, 286 ; *Mem. Inst. Eg.* 13, 27 ; *Hilmy*, ii, 3.

MAGARIOS, Shenudeh (*fl. c.* 1863)

A Catholic Copt of Luxor who was Consular Agent for Austria about 1863 ; he offered his services to de Rougé as a copyist during his voyage in Egypt, but the offer was declined as de Rougé had seen a stela in a collection in Cairo which was ascertained to have been fabricated by Magarios.

Inf. by P. E. Newberry.

MAHAFFY, (*Sir*) John Pentland (1839–1919)

Classical scholar ; born Switzerland, 26 Feb. 1839 ; T.C.D., scholar, graduate and Provost ; G.B.E. ; C.V.O. ; M.D. ; D.D. ; D.C.L. ; LL.D. ; Fellow of Queen's Coll. Oxon. ; hon. member of many foreign academies ; pub. many works on Greek history and literature ; edited the Petrie Papyri (*Cunningham Memoirs*, 8, 9, 11, R.I.A.), 1891–1905 ; wrote vol. iv of Petrie's *History of Egypt*, on the Ptolemaic period ; Pres. R.I.A., 1911–16 ; died 30 April 1919.

WWW. ii, 693 ; *Sayce,* passim (see index) ; *Aegyptus,* i, 217 ; *Rev. Ég.* N.S. i, 259.

MAHLER, Eduard (1857–1945)

Hungarian mathematician and chronologer ; born 28 Sept. 1857 ; Doctor of Math. and Nat. Sci., 1880 ; pupil of Theodor Oppolzer in Vienna, 1882 ; Member of the Royal Commission on Measures, etc. ; began the study of oriental languages, returned to Hungary and worked at the Math. Inst. ; on staff of Archaeological Dept. of Nat. Museum of Hungary and Professor of History and Chronology of the ancient oriental nations at Pazmuny Univ. ; Member Hungarian Acad. of Sciences, 1909 ; a Festschrift was presented on his 80th birthday, 1937, which contains an account of his career and a bibl. of his works (275 items of which 37 are separate works) ; he wrote much on the Eg. calendar and chronology ; died 1945.

Dissertationes in Honorem Eduardi Mahler, Budapest, 1937 (Portr.).

MAILLET, Benoît de—*See* DE MAILLET

MALAN, (*Rev.*) Solomon Caesar (1812–1894)

Of Swiss origin, baptized César Jean Solomon Malan ; orientalist and biblical scholar ; born Geneva, 23 April 1812 ; came to England as tutor in the family of the Marquess of Tweeddale, 1830 ; St. Edmund's Hall, Oxon. 1833–7 ; ordained in the Church of England, 1838 ; lecturer at Bishop's Coll., Calcutta, 1838–40 ; left India and travelled in Egypt and Palestine, 1841–2 ; entered Balliol Coll. Oxon., M.A. 1843 ; after holding various curacies, Vicar of Broadwindsor, Dorset, 1845–85 ; travelled in the East, 1849–50 ; retired to Bournemouth where he died 25 Nov. 1894 ; Malan studied many oriental languages : Hebrew, Arabic, Syriac, Chinese and various Indian dialects, and was much interested in Egyptology, on which he corresponded with Birch and Chabas.

DNB. Suppl. i, 3, 133 ; *Chabas,* 52, 146 ; *Hilmy,* ii, 9.

MALASPINA, (*Marchese*) **Tommaso** (1749–1834)

Italian architect and author; born Villafranca di Lunigiana, near Spezia, 1749; had a collection of antiquities, some of the Egyptian items of which came from Nizzoli and which was inspected by Champollion in 1825; died at Modena, 1834.

Garollo, *Diz. biog. universale*; *Champollion*, i, 116, 181, 183.

MALCOLM, (*Sir*) **John** (1769–1833)

Indian administrator and diplomatist; born 2 May 1769; entered the service of the H.E.I. Co. as a boy, 1783 and rose to very important military and administrative positions in India and Persia; returned to England, 1821 and occupied himself in literary work, but returned to India in 1827 as Governor of Bombay; in 1830 he retired, and on his way home he spent some time in Egypt and brought a collection of antiquities to England, which included a mummy presented to the R. Asiatic Soc., and several papyri, now in the B.M. (9971–2, 10081, 10384, 10466); died 30 May 1833.

DNB. 35, 404; Pettigrew, *Hist. Eg. Mummies*, Introd., i.

MALET, (*Sir*) **Edward Baldwin** (1837–1908)

Diplomatist; born 10 Oct. 1837; 4th Bart.; G.C.B.; G.C.M.G.; P.C.; educ. Eton and C.C.C. Oxon.; held many important posts in the diplomatic service; Consul-General in Egypt, 1879–82; died 29 June 1908.

WWW. i, 469; *Hilmy*, ii, 9; *Khedives and Pashas*, 75–7 and often.

MALLET, (*Baron*) **Alphonse** (*fl.* 1852–1870)

French amateur Egyptologist; attended the classes of de Rougé at the Coll. de France; he discovered the Papyrus Judiciaire de Turin in the reserves of the museum and made a tracing of it which he offered to de Rougé in exchange for a copy of the Dorbiney Papyrus; the exchange did not eventuate and he handed his tracings to Devéria who edited the text; he also copied the long inscription of Bakenkhons at Munich which was also pub. by Devéria; Mallet's name is attached to the hieratic papyrus which he bought at the Anastasi sale of 1857 and afterwards presented to the Louvre, it was pub. by Maspero in 1870; he also owned a Book of the Dead, which was used by Naville (*Todtb*. Ph.); whilst always ready to place material at the disposal of his colleagues, he apparently published nothing himself; he was elected Membre Associé de l'Inst. Ég., 18 Oct. 1861.

Devéria, *Mem. et Fragm*. i, 263, 276, 302; *Hincks*, 99; *Bibl. Ég*. 21, p. lv.

MANGLES, James (1786–1867)

Naval officer; born 1786; entered the Navy, 1800; saw much service until 1815; travelled with Hon. Charles Leonard Irby in Egypt, Nubia, Syria and Palestine, 1817–8; F.R.S., 1825; F.R.G.S.; died 1867.

DNB. 36, 33; O'Byrne, *Naval Biogr*. 718; for other references see IRBY, C. L.

MARCEL, Jean Jacques (1776–1854)

French orientalist ; writer on Arabic language and history ; author of a dictionary and many other works ; he and Silvestre de Sacy did much to promote the study of Arabic in France ; Member of Napoleon's Commission in Egypt, of which he wrote a history ; Marcel's name is associated with a papyrus in the Bibliothèque Nationale, Paris.

Carré, i, 123, 147, 156, 162 ; ii, 36 ; *Hilmy*, ii, 14.

MARCELLUS, (*Comte de*) **Marie Louis André Charles** (1795–1865)

Diplomat and historian ; born Marseilles, 1795 ; was the means of acquiring the Venus de Milo for the Louvre ; visited Egypt as secretary to Comte de Forbin, 1828 ; pub. *Souvenirs de l'Orient*, 1839, and other works ; died in Paris, 1865.

Carré, i, 194.

MARIETTE (*Pasha*), **Auguste Ferdinand François** (1821–1881)

French Egyptologist ; born Boulogne, 11 Feb. 1821 ; nephew of Nestor l'Hôte ; educ. Coll. de Boulogne ; visited England 1839–40 ; Professor at Coll. de Boulogne, 1841 ; became interested in Egyptology from a study of Nestor l'Hôte's papers and in 1849 obtained a minor post in the Louvre ; in 1850 was sent to Egypt, nominally to collect Coptic MSS., but he engaged in excavations and discovered the Serapeum at Memphis ; he succeeded in raising funds and excavated for 4 years, most of his finds being sent to the Louvre ; in 1858 appointed by the Khedive Conservator of Eg. monuments (the virtual beginning of the Service des Antiquités), and settled in Egypt ; he started simultaneous excavations in numerous sites from Nubia to the Delta, and made many important finds which became the nucleus of the Bulak Museum ; the story of Mariette's activities in Egypt is long and interesting and is well summarized by Maspero, who succeeded him and published many of his unfinished works ; most of Mariette's papers were destroyed when his house at Bulak was flooded in 1878 ; he died at Bulak, 19 Jan. 1881 ; his remains were interred in a sarcophagus which stands in the forecourt of the Cairo Museum, surmounted by a bronze statue by Xavier Barthe unveiled 17 Mar. 1904.

Maspero, *Bibl. Ég.* 18 ; *Guide . . . au Musée du Caire*, (1915), pp. vii–xxv ; *Rev. Ég.* 2, 317–320 ; *Gaz. des Beaux-Arts*, Ser. 2, 24, 239–265 ; *Rev. Deux Mondes*, 1881, 768–792 ; *Comptes Rend. des Inscr.* Ser. 4, 11, 481–584 ; Maspero, *Rapports sur la Marche du Serv. des Antiquités*, 147–159 ; Brugsch, *Mein Leben*, 125, 137, 168 and often ; *Hilmy*, ii, 16.

MARMONT, Auguste Frederic Louis Viesse de, Duc de Raguse (1774–1852)

French Marshal ; born Chatillon-sur-Seine, 20 July 1774 ; became Napoleon's aide-de-camp ; fought with N's army in Italy and Egypt and in subsequent campaigns ; created Duc de Raguse, 1808 ; fell into disgrace by concluding a secret convention in 1813, but was reinstated under the restoration of the Bourbons ; pub. *Voyages en*

Hongrie . . . Égypte et en Sicile, 5 vols., 1837 (2nd ed. 1839) ; died at Venice, 22 Mar. 1852.

Hilmy, i, 170.

MASARRA, Youssef (*fl.* 1828–1840)

Dragoman to the French Consulate in Cairo ; a dealer in antiquities ; he exploited many tombs in the Gizeh necropolis ; his collection was examined by Lepsius in 1840.

Champollion, ii, 73 ; Vyse, *Pyramids,* i, 187, 201, 256, 266 ; Pückler-Muskau, *Travels,* i, 243 ; *Bonomi Diary,* 1830, July 12, 30 ; *L.D., Text,* i, 14, 16.

MASPERO, (*Sir*) **Gaston Camille Charles** (1846–1916)

French Egyptologist, of Italian origin ; born 23 June 1846 ; educ. Lycée Louis-le-Grand and École Normale, Paris ; Prof. of Egyptology, École des Hautes Études, 1869 ; Prof. of Egyptology, Collège de France, 1874 ; went to Egypt as Director of the Mission Archéologique, 1880 ; succeeded Mariette as Director of the Service des Antiquités, 1881–6 ; returned to France, 1886–99 ; again Director in Egypt, 1899–1914 ; Secretaire Perpetuel, Acad. des Inscr. (of which he was a member from 1883), 1914–16 ; Hon. Fellow, Queen's Coll. and Hon. D.C.L., Oxon., 1887 ; K.C.M.G., 1909 ; his activity, industry and learning were enormous ; in addition to countless scientific memoirs, he pub. a large number of popular books and reviews, of which a bibliography was pub. by Henri Cordier in 1922 ; Maspero in France and Adolf Erman in Germany are rivals for the premier place in Egyptology in their generation, but Maspero was the greater man of letters and had a greater instinctive understanding of the oriental mind ; Maspero died suddenly whilst addressing a meeting of the Académie, 30 June 1916.

JEA. 3, 227 ; 33, 66 (Portr.) ; H. Cordier, *Bibliographie de Gaston Maspero,* 1922, 127–135, enumerates a long list of Obituary Notices of Maspero ; most of these contain portraits.

MASPERO, Jean (1885–1915)

Papyrologist ; second s. Sir Gaston Maspero ; born Paris, 20 Dec. 1885 ; at an early age he showed great interest in archaeology and numismatics ; he was attached to the Inst. Français d'Archéologie Orientale, and was for a time assistant to Chassinat ; he specialized in Greek papyri, especially those of the Byzantine period ; he was engaged by the Catalogue Commission of the Service des Antiquités to catalogue the rich store of Byzantine papyri in the Cairo Museum ; he completed two volumes, but died before the publication of the third, which was seen through the press by his father, who prefixed a portrait and biographical memoir and a bibliography ; he joined the French Forces early in the war, and was killed in action during the French attack on Vauquois in the Argonne, 18 Feb. 1915.

[Maspero's eldest son, Henri, an eminent sinologist, lost his life in the second world war ; born 1884 ; he and his wife were deported by the Germans in July 1944 : she was imprisoned at Ravensbruck, and he in the concentration-camp of Buchenwald, where he succumbed to brutal treatment aggravated by dysentery, **15 Mar. 1945.** *JEA*. 33, 78.]

G. Maspero in *Papyrus grecs d'époque byzantine* (Cairo Mus. Cat.), iii, 1916, pp. i–xxxvi (Portr. and Bibl.) ; *JEA*. 2, 119.

MAUNIER, V. G. (*fl.* 1840–1865)

French resident in Egypt ; according to Maspero he was French Consular Agent in Luxor, and as such he resided for nearly 20 years in the Maison de France there, but there is no mention of his name in the consular records at Quai d'Orsay, and Brugsch (who first met him in 1853) states that he was a money-lender and dealer in antiquities, well-known to all the residents and very hospitable to European travellers ; he was very helpful to Mariette and superintended his Theban excavations in his absence ; it was Maunier who first heard of the discovery of the jewellery of Queen Aahotpe, and he took immediate steps to protect it and inform Mariette of the find ; from 1863 he was agent to Halîm Pasha, a large landowner, and lived in a fine house at Matâna, on the estate : from this service he retired a rich man and returned to France ; he is frequently mentioned in the letters of Lady Duff-Gordon, who resided for some years in the Maison de France after he had vacated it ; his name is attached to the important " Stèle Maunier " (Louvre C.256), which was for many years in his house at Luxor, he also presented the statue A.159.

Maspero, *Bibl. Ég.* 18, p. cii ; *Momies Royales*, 702, *n*. 6 ; Devéria, *Mem. et Frgm.* i, pp. xvi, 336, 357, 358 ; *Rec. Trav.* 12, 214 ; Brugsch, *Mein Leben*, 190–2 ; Duff-Gordon, *Letters from Eg.*, 3rd ed., 138, 145, 154, 160, 163, 184, 235, 265, 271, 279, 371.

MAXWELL, (*Sir*) **John Grenfell** (1859–1929)

Military officer ; born 12 July 1859 ; educ. Cheltenham ; entered the Army, 1879 ; Lieut., Royal Highlanders, 1881 ; Capt. 1887 ; served in the Egyptian War and was present at Tell el-Kebir, 1882 ; in Nile Expedition, 1884-5 as Staff-Captain ; Aide-de-Camp of Major-Gen. Grenfell in Egyptian Frontier Field Force, 1884–5 ; D.S.O. ; Dongola, 1896 ; commanded 2nd Eg. Brigade at Omdurman ; commanded 14th Brigade, S. Africa 1900–1 ; Military Governor of Pretoria ; K.C.B. ; C.M.G. ; commanded Force in Egypt, 1908–12 ; First World War, 1914–8 ; K.C.M.G. ; Commander-in-Chief, Ireland, 1916 ; G.C.B. ; Commander-in-Chief, Northern Comd. 1916–9 ; Lord Milner's Mission to Egypt, 1920 ; retired 1922 ; President, E.E.S. 1925–9 ; he had a choice collection of antiquities which was sold in 1929 ; died at Cape Town, 21 Feb. 1929.

WWW. iii, 920 ; *JEA*. 15, 103.

MAYER, Joseph (1803–1886)

A goldsmith of Liverpool ; born Newcastle-under-Lyne, 23 Feb. 1803 ; a lifelong collector of coins and antiquities ; his fine coll. of Greek coins sold to French Govt., 1844 ; his great collection of Roman, Saxon, Egyptian and other antiquities exhibited in the house in Liverpool until 1867 when he presented it entire to the City of Liverpool ; it was valued at £80,000 ; most of it was destroyed by enemy action, in 1940 ; the Eg. collection, amongst many first-rate objects, contains the two famous judicial papyri that bear his name ; he purchased specimens at many sales and from the collections of Lord Valentia, Rev. H. Stobart, Joseph Sams, Bram Hertz and others ; founder of the Historical Soc. of Lancashire and Cheshire, President, 1866-9 ; F.S.A. ; died at Bibington, Cheshire, 19 Jan. 1886.

DNB. 37, 149 ; C. T. Gatty, *The Mayer Collection*, 1877 ; Liverpool Mus. *Handbook to the Eg. Coll.*, 1st ed. (by Newberry), 1919, 2nd ed. (by Peet), 1932.

MENASCÉ, (*Baron*) **James** (*fl*. 1880–1891)

A member of a family who were considerable landowners in Alexandria, and whose name is attached to a street and a gallery in the town ; resided in Egypt for many years and made a considerable collection of antiquities, which were sold at the Hôtel Drouot, 23–4 Feb. 1891 (511 lots) ; an exhibition of the collection was made at the Palais des Arts Libéraux in 1889 ; the catalogue was drawn up by Georges Legrain ; Menascé settled in Paris in 1891 ; some of his antiquities were acquired by the Louvre.

Wilbour, 471 ; *Rev. de l'Art*, 43, 172.

MENGEDOHT, Henry William (1870–1939)

Believed to be of Hungarian origin, born in London, 1870 ; a man of good education who took up the study of Egyptology and Assyriology in which he had considerable proficiency, but he spoiled his prospects and reduced himself to poverty by life-long habits of intemperance, his principal associate being W. St. Chad Boscawen, whose career was similarly blighted ; for years he studied in the Dept. of Eg. and Assyr. Ant., B.M., but was eventually excluded from the Students' Room owing to his behaviour ; all his life he earned a precarious living by translating Eg. and Assyr. inscriptions for dealers, etc., and by conducting visitors round the B.M., where he was for many years a familiar figure, commonly known as " Egyptian Jack "; he published two short papers in the *Babylonian and Oriental Record*, 5, 13, 151 ; died 1939.

Inf. by George Salby and Dr. Margaret Murray.

METTERNICH-WINNEBERG, (*Prince*) **Clemens Wenzel Lothar** (1773–1859)

The famous Austrian statesman and diplomatist who played a prominent part in European affairs ; born, Coblenz, 15 May 1773 ; in Egyptology his name is associated with the great magical stela found in Alexandria in 1828, and given to him by Mohammad Ali, and first published by Golenischeff in 1877 ; this is now in the Metropolitan Museum, New York ; other Egyptian antiquities which belonged to him are in the Museum of Königswarth, Bohemia ; died 11 June 1859.

EB. ; *ZÄS*. 53, 146.

MEUX, (*Lady*) **Valerie Susie** (*d*. 1911)

Wife of Sir Henry Bruce Meux (1858–1900) ; he had inherited a collection of Egyptian antiquities in which Lady M. took great interest and commissioned Budge to catalogue it in 1893 ; she added considerably to it and in 1895, Budge bought a number of objects in Egypt ; a second edition of the catalogue was pub. in 1896 ; Budge also procured for Lady M. a collection of Ethiopic MSS. which were sumptuously printed for private circulation ; after her death the whole collection was sold in 1911, many of the objects being bought by William Randolph Hearst, whose collection was sold at Sotheby's, 11–12 July 1939 ; Lady Meux died in 1911.

Budge N & T. i, 29 ; ii, 339.

MEYER, Eduard (1855–1930)

German historian and chronologer ; born 25 Jan. 1855 ; his most important works were his *Geschichte des Alterthums,* 1884–1902 ; and *Ægyptische Chronologie,* 1904 (*Nächträge,* 1907–8), this was translated into French by A. Moret and pub. by the Musée Guimet, 1912 ; he made numerous contributions to journals on ancient oriental history and chronology, especially of Egypt ; died 31 Aug. 1930.

ZÄS. 66, 73 (Portr.) ; *Erman,* 112, 169.

MEYRICK, Augustus William Henry (1826–1902)

Army officer ; born 27 Oct. 1826 ; Scots Fusiliers, ensign 1846 ; Lieut., 1850 ; Capt., 1855 ; Colonel, 1868 ; Major-Gen., 1877 ; retired Lieut.-Gen., 1881 ; fought in the Crimean War, 1854-6 ; in 1878 he presented to the B.M. a large collection of oriental arms, Greek, Roman and Egyptian antiquities ; the papyrus 9969 bears his name ; died at 9 Wilbraham Place, London, 26 Mar. 1902.

R.U.S.I. Records.

MEZGER, John Maximillian (1869–1935)

Of West Kirby, Cheshire, formerly of Liverpool and Alexandria ; born 11 Oct. 1869 ; cotton broker and merchant with offices at Liverpool, Alexandria and Khartûm ; he was at one time (1910–2) the largest exporter of Egyptian cotton from Alexandria ; collected antiquities ; his collection sold at Sotheby's, 8 June 1925, lots 1–44 ; he died at West Kirby, 1935.

Inf. by R. Mezger (*son*).

MIDDLEMASS, (*Bey*) **Arthur Charles** (1850–1906)

Naval officer ; born 1850 ; entered R.N. as Cadet, 1866 ; served in Ashanti War, 1873–4 and Egyptian War, 1882 ; Inspector of the Coast Guard at Alexandria, 1884–9 ; retired with rank of Commander, 1889 ; in 1886 he discovered at Abukir a colossal statue of the Middle Kingdom usurped by Ramesses II ; it is now in the Cairo Museum (*Guide,* 1915, No. 1) ; the B.M. purchased from him a number of Coptic (Or. 5638–44) and Arabic (Or. 5645–54) manuscripts ; in retirement he lived at Dorking, and died at Drayton Gardens, S. Kensington, 28 Mar. 1906.

Private information ; *Wilbour,* 336, 342.

MIGLIARINI, Angelo Michele (1779–1865)

Antiquary and Etruscologist ; born Rome, 1779 ; in the service of the Grand Duke of Tuscany and afterwards Conservator of the Florence Museum ; he was acquainted with Champollion and well disposed to him ; pub. *Museo di Sculture . . . Ottavio Gigli,* 1858 ; *Indication succincte des Monuments Ég. de Florence,* 1859 and a very full account of the unrolling of a mummy, with Notes by Samuel Birch (*Archaeologia,* 36, 161–174), 1855 ; died, Florence, 1865.

N. Nieri, *Mem. Acad. Lincei,* Ser. 6, 3, 401–543 (1931) ; *Hilmy,* ii, 34 ; *Champollion,* i, 91, 235, 236, 238.

MILLIN DE GRANDMAISON, Aubin Louis (1759–1818)

French archaeologist ; his publications are concerned chiefly with Roman, French and other Western monuments, but he was interested in Egypt, and pub. *Ægyptiaques,* 12 plates of Eg. antiquities (1816) and *Pierres gravées égyptiennes* ; a friend and supporter of Champollion.

Hilmy, ii, 35.

MILLINGEN, Julius Michael (1800–1878)

Surgeon and archaeologist, of Dutch origin ; born London, 19 July 1800 ; studied at Rome and Edinburgh ; M.R.C.S. Ed., 1821 ; attended Byron in his last illness ; settled in Constantinople, 1827 ; Court Physician to five successive Sultans ; discovered the ruins of Aezani and excavated the Temple of Jupiter Urius on the Bosphorus ; his name is associated with the Papyrus Millingen, the master-text of the Instruction of Ammenemes, the original is lost, but a good tracing of it made in Italy, it is believed by Amadeo Peyron, was first pub. by Maspero (*Rec. Trav.* ii) ; died in Constantinople, 30 Nov. 1878.

DNB. 37, 439.

MILNE, Joseph Grafton (1867–1951)

Archaeologist, numismatist and historian ; born 23 Dec. 1867 ; educ. Manchester Grammar School and Corpus Christi Coll. Oxon. ; M.A. ; D.Litt. ; Senior Examiner and Asst. Sec., Board of Education, 1893 ; retired, 1926 ; Deputy Keeper of Coins, Ashmolean Museum, 1931–51 ; served for many years on Committee of E.E.S., Treas. 1912–19 ; Librarian, C.C.C., Oxford, 1933–46 ; published many books and papers on the history and inscriptions of Graeco-Roman Egypt and on Greek and Roman numismatics, contributing many articles to *JEA* on Ptolemaic coins ; died, 7 Aug. 1951.

The Times, 14 Aug. 1951.

MIMAUT, Jean François (1774–1837)

French diplomatist, son of a physician ; born Méru (Oise), 1774 ; educ. Coll. of Beauvais and Paris ; entered diplomatic service ; Sec. to Legation in Italy, 1804 ; Consul-General at Cagliari, 1814 ; at Carthagena, 1817 ; at Venice, 1826 ; Consul-General in Egypt, 1829 ; it was through his influence with Mohammad Ali that the obelisk now in the Place de la Concorde was obtained ; made a large collection of Eg. antiquities, which was sold in Paris after his death (588 lots), many important pieces, including the Table of Kings, were obtained by the B.M.; Mimaut was friendly to Champollion; his name is attached to a Greek Magical Papyrus in the Louvre (2391); died in Paris, 31 Jan. 1837.

Biogr. Notice prefixed to Sale Cat. by L. J. J. Dubois, Paris, 1837 (Portr.); *Carré* (see index); *Champollion*, ii, 248, 407, 412, 420.

MINUTOLI, (*Baron*) **Heinrich Carl Menu** (1772–1846)

German military officer, of Neapolitan origin; born Geneva, 12 May 1772; entered Prussian army in which he won distinction and came under the personal notice of the king; in 1820 sent by the Prussian Govt. on a scientific mission to Egypt, 1820–1, and visited the Siwa Oasis; an account of the journey pub. in 1824–7; his wife (née Comtesse de Schulembourg) pub. *Mes Souvenirs en Égypte*, Paris, 1826, English ed., 1827; he collected large quantities of antiquities, some of which were sold in Paris and seen by Champollion, others were acquired for the Berlin Museum; the remainder were retained in the collection of Dr. Alexander von Minutoli, which was sold in Cologne in 1875.

Hilmy, ii, 36.

MISSETT, Ernest (*d.* 1820)

Army officer; 97th Regt. of Foot; Capt. 1799; Major, 1803; Lieut.-Col. 1810; British Consul-General in Egypt, 1803–15; resigned owing to ill-health, and was succeeded by Henry Salt; died in Florence, 22 Sept. 1820.

GM. 1821, i, 185; *Legh*, 10 and often; *Athanasi*, 3, 4; *Salt*, i, 133, 403, 451, 455, 465; *Henniker*, 201; *Valentia*, iii, 456 and often; *Light*, 23, 27, 111, 115, 123.

MOHAMMAD MOHASSIB (*Bey*) (1843–1928)

Dealer in antiquities at Luxor; began life as a donkey-boy and served Lady Duff-Gordon who taught him English; became an itinerant dealer in anticas, and about 1880 opened a shop in Luxor; many important monuments in museums in Europe and America were procured through him; he was much persecuted and was arrested by Grébaut when he was director of the Serv. des Antiquités, but was released as he bore the highest character all his life; died 6 April 1928.

JEA. 14, 184; *Wilbour*, 48 and often (see index); *Budge N & T*. i, 138–9, 143, 145, 150.

MÖLLER, Georg (1876–1921)

German Egyptologist; born Caracas, 5 Nov. 1876; on staff of Berlin Museum; excavated in Egypt, particularly at Abusir el-Melek; pub. an important monograph on hieratic palaeography and an edition of the Rhind Bilingual Papyri as well as many contributions to journals, etc.; at the time of his death he was preparing works on hieroglyphic palaeography and on the hieratic graffiti in the quarry of Hat-nub; died at Uppsala, 2 Oct. 1921.

JEA. 7, 231; 8, 283; *ZÄS*. 57, 142 (Portr.).

MOND, (*Sir*) **Robert Ludwig** (1867–1938)

Chemist and archaeologist ; e. s. Dr. Ludwig Mond, F.R.S. ; born Farnworth, Lancs., 9 Sept. 1867 ; educ. Cheltenham, Peterhouse, Cambridge, and the Univs. of Zurich, Edinburgh and Glasgow ; of his services and contributions to chemistry and other branches of science, accounts will be found elsewhere ; for many years his chief recreation was Egyptian archaeology ; visited Egypt frequently from 1901 and in 1902 began work on clearing and recording Theban tombs, and discovered several new ones ; he had the assistance of Newberry, Howard Carter, Mackay, Emery, Yeivin and others ; he defrayed the cost of repairing, restoring and safeguarding many tombs and other monuments in Egypt, and was a generous supporter of many archaeological expeditions in Egypt and elsewhere : those of the E.E.S., of Prof. Garstang in Meroë and Asia Minor, of the Liverpool Inst. of Archaeology, of Miss Garrod at Atklit and Lydda and of Dr. H. Winckler in the Eastern and Libyan deserts ; in 1925 he ceased working at Thebes and transferred his activities to Armant, and in 1929 handed over the concession to the E.E.F. of which he was elected President that year ; he was also Treasurer of the Palestine Exploration Fund and of the British School of Archaeology in Palestine ; he defrayed the cost of many archaeological publications, and presented many antiquities to museums ; he was a great benefactor of the Royal Institution, of the British Inst. in Paris, and of many other scientific and cultural bodies ; LL.D., F.R.S.E. ; F.R.S., Knighted 1932 ; a large collection of his notes, photographs and other material relating to the Theban Tombs is now in the Griffith Inst., Oxford ; died in Paris, 22 Oct. 1938.

WWW. iii, 954 ; *JEA*. 24, 208 (Portr.) ; *AAA*. 25, 69 ; *Chron*. 14, 40 ; *Nature*, 12 Nov. 1938 ; *OFRS*. No. 7, Jan. 1939 (Portr.) ; *DNB* 1931–40, 622.

MONRO, (*Rev.*) **Vere** (1802–1841)

Son of Thomas Monro of Thaxted, Essex, born 1802 ; University Coll. Oxon., B.A., 1823 ; travelled in Egypt and Nubia with J. A. St. John, 1832–3, whose book is dedicated to him ; his name is carved on the rock of Abu Sir, 2nd Cataract ; parted from St. John at Cairo, 31 Mar. 1834 and proceeded alone to Palestine and Syria ; pub. *A Summer Ramble in Syria*, London, 1835 ; died at Malta, 20 Oct. 1841.

Al. Oxon. ; St. John, *Eg. and Moh. Ali*, 1834, i, 79 ; ii, 344 et passim.

MOORE, William (1768–1848)

Army officer ; born 1768 ; 2nd W. India Regt. transferred to 14th Foot then in India, 1802 ; Capt., 1806 ; Major, 1816 ; returned to England with dispatches and went on half-pay, 1819 ; on his way from India, stayed in Cairo, visited the Pyramids with Belzoni and conveyed the latter's report thereon to Lord Aberdeen, Pres. S.A. ; died, a Lieut.-Col., 7 April 1848.

Army Lists ; *GM*. 1848, i, 560 ; *Belzoni*, i, 391 ; *Journ. Soc. for Bibliogr. of Nat. Hist.* 2, 57, 59.

MORET, Alexandre (1868–1938)

French Egyptologist ; born Aix-les-Bains, 1868 ; studied Egyptology under Maspero ; Maître des Conférences, Faculty of Letters, Lyons, 1897–9 ; Director of École des Hautes Études, 1899–38 ; Professor, Coll. de France, 1923 ; Membre de l'Acad., 1927 ; Keeper of the Musée Guimet, 1918–38 ; Frazer Lecturer, Oxford, 1926 ; author of many popular books on Egyptian history and religion ; translated Meyer's *Chronologie* and Mahler's *Calendrier* into French ; died 2 Feb. 1938.

BIFAO, 20, 155 ; *Chron.* 13, 322 ; *Journ. Savants*, 1938, 38 ; *Chron.* 13, 322.

MORRISON, Walter (1836–1921)

Banker and philanthropist ; born 21 May 1836 ; educ. Eton and Balliol Coll. Oxon. ; J.P. ; M.P. for various constituencies, 1874–1900 ; a great benefactor to hospitals, to Oxford Univ., and the Bodleian Library ; a generous supporter of excavations in Egypt and financed many costly publications, died 18 Dec. 1921.

DNB. Suppl. ; *WWW.* ii, 751.

MORTON, Alice Anderson (*fl.* 1884–1902)

Student at University Coll., London, 1884–1902 ; translated Maspero's *Au Temps de Ramsès et d'Assourbanipal* under the title *Life in Ancient Egypt and Assyria*, 1890 ; collaborated with Mary Brodrick in *A Concise Dictionary of Eg. Archaeology*, 1902.

JEA. 33, 87.

MOSCONAS, Demetrius (1839–1895)

Greek Egyptologist and interpreter ; born Island of Leros, 1839 ; went to Egypt as a young man and studied hieroglyphic writing under H. Brugsch, having a gift for languages, of which he knew ten ; Chief Interpreter to Thomas Cook & Son ; went to U.S.A. in 1892 with Egyptian exhibits for Chicago Fair ; he knew General Gordon ; his eldest son George, a Lieutenant, served under Hicks Pasha and died fighting the Dervishes ; another son, Theodorus Demetrius, is now Librarian to the Greek Patriarchate at Alexandria ; died 1895.

Inf. by Dr. T. D. Mosconas (son).

MUNIER, Henri (1884–1945)

French bibliographer and Coptic scholar ; born 14 July 1884 ; Librarian of the Cairo Museum, 1908–1925 ; succeeded Cattaui-Bey as secretary of the Soc. Royale de Géographie de l'Égypte, 1925–45 ; published many papers chiefly on Coptic texts and early Christianity in Egypt ; died 20 Aug. 1945.

ASA. 48, 258 (Portr. and Bibl.) ; *Bull. Soc. Roy. Géogr.* 21, 313.

MURCH, (*Rev.*) **Chauncey** (1856–1907)

American missionary in Luxor ; born Alexander, Pa., 1 Jan. 1856 ; educ. Muskingum Coll. ; A.B., 1876 ; A.M., 1879 ; after attending various theological seminaries, was sent in Oct. 1883 to Egypt by the United Presbyterian Board of Foreign Missions ; while in Egypt, he made a collection of antiquities, of which the large series of scarabs was acquired by the B.M. in 1906 ; all the other items went to the Metrop. Museum of Art, New York, of which a description was pub. by A. C. Mace in 1911 ; the Art Institution of Chicago bought a collection of scarabs from Murch in 1894 ; he was very helpful to European travellers and collectors in Egypt, and he negotiated the payment by the B.M. of many Coptic and Greek MSS. obtained in Egypt by Budge ; died 1907.

WWWA. i, 881 ; *Budge N & T*. i, 87, 135, 411 ; ii, 148, 154, 33, 341, 347.

MURE, William (1799–1860)

Classical scholar ; educ. Edinburgh and Bonn ; travelled in Italy and Greece, 1838 and pub. a large work on Greek language and literature, 1850–7 ; an opponent of Champollion whom he criticised in a work on the Egyptian Dynasties which claimed to demonstrate "the falacy of the system laid down by Champollion," 1829 ; he also wrote a treatise on the Egyptian Calendar and Zodiac, 1832.

DNB. 39, 330 ; *Hilmy*, ii, 53.

MURRAY, (*Sir*) **Charles Augustus** (1806–1895)

Diplomatist ; 2nd s. 5th Earl of Dunmore ; born 22 Nov. 1806 ; educ. Eton and Oriel Coll. Oxon ; Fellow of All Souls Coll. 1827 ; M.A., 1837 ; called to the Bar, Lincoln's Inn, 1827 ; Sec. Brit. Legation, Naples, 1844 ; Consul-General in Egypt, 1846–63 ; afterwards in the diplomatic service in other countries ; C.B., 1848 ; K.C.B., 1866 ; P.C., 1875 ; died 3 June 1895 ; Murray's name is attached to a fine funerary papyrus in the B.M., purchased in 1861 (10010).

DNB. Suppl. ii, 313 ; Brugsch, *Mein Leben*, 152.

MUSTAFA AGHA AYAT (*d*. 1887)

Consular Agent in Luxor for Britain, Belgium and Russia ; he had travelled in Europe and spoke fluent English, French and Italian ; a merchant of much wealth and influence, who under cover of diplomatic immunity, conducted a considerable illicit trade in antiquities and many important papyri and other objects are known to have passed through his hands : he also played a hidden part in the exploitation of the cache of Royal Mummies for which he was deprived of his Belgian agency ; he lived in a house built between the columns of the Temple of Luxor which was demolished after his death ; he was exceedingly helpful and courteous to British travellers in Egypt, and spared no expense in entertaining them and providing for them everything they required, and in this connection A. H. Rhind and Lady Duff-Gordon were especially indebted to him ; he died at an advanced age in 1887, having held his consular appointments over 50 years.

Edwards, *Thousand Miles*, 2nd ed., 144, 455 ; Maspero, *Momies Royales*, 513 ; Lady Duff-Gordon, *Letters*, 3rd ed., passim, esp. 190 ; *Wilbour*, 73 et passim (see index).

MUTLOW, Thomas (*fl.* 1840–50)

Member of the firm of Thomas, Henry and James Mutlow of York St., Covent Garden, copperplate and seal engravers, etc.; Lee's Egyptian papyri were mounted by him.

Hartwell Register, ii, No. 1837; iv, No. 4070.

MYERS, William Joseph (1858–1899)

Army officer; of Porter's Park, Herts.; born 4 Aug. 1858; educ. Eton; Major in King's Royal Rifles; served in Zulu War and Nile Expedition; killed in action in the Boer War, 30 Oct. 1899; formed a choice collection of Egyptian antiquities which he bequeathed to Eton College.

JEA. 5, 145; *Eton Coll. Chron.* No. 2394, 29 Oct. 1936, 243.

NAHMAN, Maurice (*d.* 1948)

Dealer in antiquities in Cairo; formerly chief cashier at the bank of Crédit Lyonnais at Cairo, from which he resigned and became one of the principal dealers in Cairo; died March 1948.

Chron. 24, 300; *Inf. by P. E. Newberry.*

NASH, Davyd William (*d.* 1876)

Barrister-at-law, naturalist and scholar; A.L.S., 1832; F.L.S., 1849; a member of the Syro-Egyptian Society; wrote on the Geology of Egypt, on Eg. chronology and on the Pharaoh of the Exodus; his library was sold at Sotheby's 20 Jan. 1888; died at Cheltenham, 16 July 1876.

Hilmy, ii, 58; *Private information.*

NASH, Walter Llewellyn (*d.* 1920)

Medical practitioner in Hong Kong; on retirement took much interest in ancient Egypt and visited Egypt several times; he often bought antiquities at sales and made up small collections which he sold; many of his own objects he pub. in *PSBA*; in 1898 he succeeded W. H. Rylands as Sec. of S.B.A. and remained in office until the society was virtually extinguished by being merged in the R. Asiatic Soc.; a small Coptic papyrus, now at Cambridge, bears his name; some of his antiquities were bought by the B.M. after his death; F.S.A. 1895–1918; died at Northwood, Middlesex, 8 April 1920.

Inf. by P. E. Newberry.

NAUS, (*Bey*) **Henri** (1875–1938)

Belgian official and administrator in Egypt; born Hasselt, 27 Mar. 1875; held many important administrative posts in Egypt; President of the Fondation Égyptologique Reine Élisabeth, Brussels; died at Brussels, 22 Sept. 1938.

Chron. 14, 5 (Portr.).

NAVILLE, Henri Édouard (1844–1926)

Swiss Egyptologist; born Geneva, 1844; educ. Geneva, King's Coll. London, Bonn, Paris and Berlin; a pupil and literary executor of Lepsius; D.C.L.; LL.D.; excavated in Egypt for the E.E.F. from

1883 to 1913; his chief publications, besides excavation memoirs are *Todtenbuch*, 1886; *Litanie du Soleil*, 1875; *Mythe d'Horus*, 1870; he refused to move with the times and obstinately maintained all his life obsolete views and theories, and was very impatient of criticism; he married in 1883, Marguerite, d. Count Alexandre de Pourtales, who executed the plates for most of his publications: she died 14 Dec. 1930; he died at Geneva, 17 Oct. 1926.

WWW. ii, 770; *JEA*. 13, 1 (Portr.); *Hilmy*, ii, 58.

NEEDHAM, John Turberville (1713–1781)

Roman Catholic priest and scientist; F.R.S. 1746; F.S.A.; published learned works on a great variety of subjects, and attempted to prove the identity of Egyptian hieroglyphic and Chinese writing.

DNB. 40, 157; *BIFAO*. 5, 82; *Griffith Studies*, 467; *Hilmy*, ii, 61.

NEWBERRY, John Ernest (1862–1950)

Architect; elder brother of Percy E. Newberry; visited Egypt in 1881 and again 1890–3 as draughtsman and assistant to his brother at Beni Hasan, and to Naville at Deir el-Bahri; F.R.I.B.A.; died, Ilford, Essex, 28 Dec. 1950.

Newberry Corresp.

NEWBERRY, Percy Edward (1869–1949)

Botanist and Egyptologist; born 23 Apl. 1869; educ. King's Coll. School and King's Coll., London, M.A.; O.B.E.; studied botany and archaeology; assisted R. S. Poole with secretarial work of the E.E.F. 1884–6; appointed to take charge of the Archaeological Survey expedition at Beni Hasan and El Bersheh, 1890–4; carried out a survey of the Theban Necropolis and superintended excavations for Lord Amherst, the Marquis of Northampton, Margaret Benson, Theodore Davis and Mrs. Tytus, 1895–1905; Brunner Professor of Egyptology, Liverpool, 1906–19; Pres. Section H. British Assn., 1923; Prof. of Ancient Hist. and Archaeology, Cairo Univ., 1929–32; wrote or contributed to many excavation memoirs; pub. *Life of Rekhmara*, 1900; *Amherst Papyri*, 1900; *Scarabs*, 1905 and many contributions to journals; and several vols. to the Cairo Museum Catalogue; died 7 Aug. 1949; his scientific correspondence is now in the Griffith Institute, Oxford.

JEA. 36, 101 (Portr.).

NEWTON, Francis Giesler (1878–1924)

Architect and excavator; born Ipswich, 4 Apl. 1878; educ. Repton, R.A. Schools and as pupil of Sir Aston Webb; practised as an architect; excavated at Rome, 1905; for Palestine Exploration Fund at Beth Shemish and Petra, where he made drawings; with Sir Arthur Evans at Knossos; with joint B.M. and Pennsylvania Expedition to Ur; with E.E.S. at Amarna, 1920–1 and 1923–4 as director; during the last expedition he was taken ill and died in hospital at Assiut, 25 Dec. 1924; his coloured drawings of the mural paintings at Amarna were published as a memorial volume, with a memoir and portrait, in 1929.

JEA. 11, 70 (Portr.).

NICHOLSON, (*Sir*) **Charles** (1808–1903)

Physician and archaeologist ; born Bedale, Yorks, 23 Nov. 1808 ; studied medicine ; M.D., Edinb., 1833 ; emigrated to Australia, 1834, and practised as physician ; played a great part in the development of education and the founding of Sydney Univ., of which he was Provost in 1851 and Chancellor, 1854–62 ; returned to England, 1860 ; Knighted, 1852 ; created baronet, 1859 ; Hon. D.C.L. Oxon., 1857 ; Hon. LL.D. Cantab. and Edinb. ; visited Egypt 1854–5 and brought home a collection of antiquities described in a catalogue by Bonomi, 1858, reprinted with additional matter as *Aegyptiaca,* 1891 ; the collection was presented to Sydney Univ. ; died Totteridge, Herts, 8 Nov. 1903.

WWW. 1, 525 ; *DNB*. Suppl. ; *Hilmy,* ii, 65.

NIEBUHR, Karsten (1733–1815)

German geographer and traveller ; born Lüdingworth, Holstein, 17 Mar. 1733 ; the son of a farmer, he had little education, but instructed himself, particularly in mathematics and surveying, and learned Arabic ; joined the expedition sent by Frederick V of Denmark for scientific exploration in Egypt, Arabia and Syria, which sailed in Jan. 1761 ; by May 1763, Niebuhr was the only surviving member of the party, the others (including the botanist Forskal), having died of disease ; on his return he lived in Copenhagen, but eventually went back to Germany ; he was a careful observer, and his valuable *Reisenbeschreibung nach Arabien und andern umliegenden Ländern* was pub. in 2 vols. in Copenhagen, 1774–8, the third vol. appeared posthumously in 1737 ; it contains valuable information on Egypt, including a survey of the Pyramids ; died 26 Apl. 1815.

Life, by his son Barthold, N., Keil, 1817 ; English ed., 1838 ; *Hilmy,* ii, 66.

NIZZOLI, Giuseppe di (*fl.* 1818–1828)

Chancellor of the Austrian Consulate in Egypt, 1818–28 ; he made considerable collections of Eg. antiquities : the first part was purchased in 1820 for the Vienna collection, the second in 1824 by the Grand Duke of Tuscany, now in Florence, and the third by Pelagi, now in Bologna ; he met Champollion in Italy in 1824 ; a catalogue by Champollion of the Nizzoli collection was published by Pelegrini in 1903 (*Bessarione,* Ser. 2, 5, 187).

JEA. 24, 12 ; *Champollion,* i, 24, 39, 61, 181, 393.

NORDEN, Frederik Ludwig (1708–1742)

Captain in the Danish Navy ; born Gluckstadt in Holstein, 22 Oct. 1708 ; entered the Navy, 1722 ; a man of exceptional ability ; sent by Christian VI to Egypt in 1738 to obtain a full and accurate account of that country, and stayed about a year ; afterwards attached to the British Navy and resided in London ; F.R.S., 1740 ; a member of the [First] Egyptian Society ; his *Travels,* first pub. in 1751, were reissued several times and translated into English and German ; died in Paris in 1742.

Nichols, *Lit. Anecd.* ii, 297 ; *JEA*. 23, 259 ; *Hilmy,* ii, 73.

NORTHAMPTON, Marquis of—*See* COMPTON

NUGENT, Baron—*See* GRENVILLE

OPPENHEIMER, Henry (*d.* 1932)

Banker and art-collector ; born in Washington, educ. Frankfurt and became a partner in the London house of Speyer Bros. ; collector of antiquities and works of art ; in 1912 purchased a large number of Heseltine's drawings by the old masters ; purchased Eg. antiquities at the Rustaffjaell and other sales ; his collections sold at Christie's, 22–23 July 1936 ; some of the Eg. antiquities were bought by E. L. Paget and re-sold at the Paget sale, Sotheby's, 18 Oct. 1949 ; Oppenheimer was elected F.S.A. in 1914 and died in London, 23 Mar. 1932.

Sale Cat. Preface ; S.A. Records.

OPPERT, Jules (1825–1905)

French Assyriologist ; of Jewish origin, born Hamburg, 9 July 1825 ; studied at Heidelberg, Bonn and Berlin ; settled in Paris, 1848 ; one of the most prominent Assyriologists of his time and made many valuable contributions to the science as well as much field-work ; his association with Egyptology is the important memoir presented to the Acad. des Inscr., *Memoire sur les Rapports de l'Égypte et de l'Assyrie*, 1869 ; died in Paris, 21 Aug. 1905.

Budge R & P. 206 (Portr.).

ORCURTI, Pier Camillo (1822–1871)

Italian Egyptologist ; on the staff of Turin Museum ; published a catalogue of the Eg. collection in 1852.

Brugsch, *Mein Leben*, 104 ; *Hilmy*, ii, 81.

OSBURN, William (*fl.* 1828–1854)

Archaeologist ; F.R.S.L. ; Member of the Arch. Inst. ; his earliest Egyptological work, the description of the " Leeds Mummy," 1828, is very good for its time ; his later works are mainly devoted to the relations of Egypt and the Bible, on which he pub. three books, 1846–54 and the *Monumental History of Egypt*, 2 vols., 1854.

Hilmy, ii, 82.

OSMAN, (*Effendi*) (*d.* 1835)

The name adopted by a Scottish soldier, Donald Donald of Inverness, who went to Egypt as a drummer-boy in the forces under Gen. Alexander Mackenzie Fraser in 1807 ; he was taken prisoner and suffered great hardships, and was given the choice of death or becoming a Muslim ; he chose the latter and to the end of his life assumed the religion and customs of Islam and wore Turkish dress ; Legh met him at Minieh in 1814, and offered to pay the ransom for his release and to convey him to England, but his master married him to one of the women of his harîm and as he showed no inclination for release, he remained in Egypt ; he was afterwards in the service of Burckhardt until the death of the latter in 1817 ; he then settled in Cairo where he prospered and owned a number of houses ; he was very helpful to British travellers in Egypt, Robert Hay being especially indebted to him on his first arrival in Cairo ; Kinglake was entertained by him during his visit to Cairo ; died of plague in Cairo, 1835.

Legh, 129 ; *Madox*, i, 107, 115, 255 ; ii, 49 ; *Westcar Diary*, 258, 270 ; *Hay Diary*, 1824, Nov. 24 *et seq.* ; *Bonomi Diary*, 1833, May 27 ; Kinglake, *Eothen*, Ch. 18 ; *Sherer*, 160, 176 ; Madden, *Travels*, i, 345.

OUARDÉ, Antoun—*See* WARDI

PACHO, Jean Raymond (1794–1829)

French traveller ; born Nice, 3 Jan. 1794 ; educ. Collège de Tournon ; visited Italy and came to Paris in 1816 ; his first interests were drawing and botany ; in 1818 he went to Egypt with the intention of exploring that country, but being unable to obtain the necessary funds, he returned to Paris and lived by portrait-painting and journalism until the end of 1820, when he returned again to Egypt, funds having been provided by a French merchant in the service of the Pasha ; he explored Lower Egypt, making drawings of the monuments and collecting plants ; the death of his patron in 1823 interrupted his explorations, but another supporter having appeared, he continued them for another year ; returning to Cairo, he planned the exploration of Cyrenaica, which he accomplished between Nov. 1824 and July 1825 ; on the recommendation of Letronne he received a grant for further exploration, but his mind gave way, and he took his own life at Paris, 26 Jan. 1829 ; he pub. an account of his travels, Paris, 1827–9 with a large folio vol. of plates.

NBG. 39, 12 ; *Champollion*, i, 271, 295 ; ii, 74.

PAGET, Rosalind Frances Emily (*d.* 1925)

Daughter of the Rev. Francis Edward Paget, Rector of Elford, Staffs. ; student at Univ. Coll. London, 1893–8 ; went to Egypt 1895–6 with Miss Pirie (later Mrs. J. E. Quibell) for the Egyptian Research Account and copied the scenes in the tomb of Ptah-hotpe at Sakkara, pub. in the memoir *The Ramesseum* (1896) ; she visited the Temple of Dêr el-Bahri and made many coloured facsimiles which were used by Griffith in his *Hieroglyphs* (1898) ; died unmarried 29 Jan. 1925.

Burke's Landed Gentry ; *Petrie*, 158.

PALAGI, Pelagio (1775–1860)

Italian painter, sculptor and architect ; born Bologna, 24 May 1775 ; worked mainly in Rome ; collected works of art and antiquities, which he bequeathed to his native town of Bologna ; the Egyptian antiquities came from the collection of Nizzoli, and were therefore brought from Egypt between 1818 and 1828 ; died at Turin, 16 Mar. 1860.

Enc. It. 25, 943 ; Ducati, *Guida del Museo di Bologna*, 1923, 6.

PALANQUE, Charles (1865–1910)

French Egyptologist ; studied under Guieysse and Moret ; member of the Inst. Fr. d'Arch. Orientale, Cairo ; excavated with Chassinat at Assiût, 1903 and at El-Dêr, 1902 and Bawit, 1903 ; contributed to the *Bull.* and *Mem.* of the Institute ; died 9 Dec. 1910.

BIFAO, 7, 177.

PALIN, (*Comte de*) **Nils Gustaf** (1762–1842)

Swedish orientalist and diplomatist ; born Stockholm, 1762 ; Swedish Minister in Constantinople ; formed a rich collection of Eg. antiquities, part of which was lost in a fire at Para in 1818 ; received Dr. John Lee in Constantinople and travelled with him to Thebes, 1810 ; a futile precursor of Champollion, he claimed to have deciphered hieroglyphics and pub. several memoirs thereon, 1802–12 ; after retiring from official life he settled in a mansion at Bologna, where he was murdered, 16 Mar. 1842 and many of his antiquities were stolen ; his remaining collections were acquired by the Louvre in 1859.

Lee MSS. ; *Rev. de l'Art*, 43, 168 ; *BIFAO*, 5, 84 ; *Hilmy*, i, 175.

PALMER, William (1811–1879)

Roman Catholic theologian and archaeologist ; brother of 1st Earl of Selborne ; Magdalen Coll. Oxon ; M.A., 1833 ; visited Egypt 1853–4 and pub. *Egyptian Chronicles with a Harmony of Sacred and Eg. Chronology*, 2 vols., 1861 ; died and buried in Rome.

DNB. 43, 167 ; *Hilmy*, ii, 89.

PARAVEY, Charles Hippolyte de (*fl.* 1821–1868)

An officer in the Corps de Ponts et Chaussées ; wrote many works on Eg. hieroglyphs and the Zodiac of Dendereh and sought to find therein references to the Noachian Deluge and other biblical narratives ; he claimed to have established a common hieroglyphic origin of all forms of writing in his *Essai sur l'origine unique et hiéroglyphique des chiffres et des lettres de tous les peuples*, etc., Paris, 1826 ; he was de Rougé's first instructor in Egyptology.

Hartleben, ii, 137 ; *Chabas*, 47 ; *Hilmy*, i, 175.

PARISET, Étienne (1770–1847)

French physician ; Sec. perpetuel de l'Acad. de Med., Paris ; visited Egypt in 1828 intending to accompany Champollion on his journey to Upper Egypt, but remained in Cairo to study the plague ; pub. in 6 vols., Paris 1831, *La Contemporaine en Égypte*, a bitterly critical and sarcastic work ; he studied the technique of mummification and pub. *Lettre sur les Embaumements*, Paris, 1827.

Champollion, ii, 214 and often ; *Carré*, i, 216.

PARKE, Henry (1792–1835)

Architect ; visited Egypt and ascended the Nile to Wady Halfa with J. J. Scoles, and the Levant, 1824 ; on the journey to Upper Egypt Parke and Scoles travelled in company with Frederick Catherwood and Henry Westcar ; pub. a map of Nubia, 1829 ; his large collection of architectural drawings from antique subjects is in the library of the R.I.B.A. ; died 5 May 1835.

DNB. 43, 225 ; *Westcar Diary*, passim ; *Hay Diary* 1827, Aug. 23.

PARKER, John Henry (1806–1884)

Writer on architecture ; succeeded his uncle Joseph in the well-known printing and publishing house at Oxford ; F.S.A., 1849 ; C.B., 1871 ; pub. *The Twelve Egyptian Obelisks in Rome*, Oxf., 1879, with translations of the texts by Samuel Birch.

DNB. 43, 250 ; *Hilmy*, ii, 93.

PARRISH, Dillwyn (*d.* 1899)

Of Bickley, Kent, collector of antiquities and objets-d'art ; on the Committee of E.E.F. 1893–8 ; his collections were sold at Sotheby's 5 July 1928 ; the Egyptian objects (lots 55–63) included the four Canopic Jars of Princess Eskhons (Nesikhonsu) from the royal cache of Dêr el-Bahri, which he obtained in 1874 from Andrew MacCallum.

Rec. Trav. 4, 79 ; Maspero, *Momies Royales*, 712.

PARTHEY, Gustav Friedrich Constantin (1798–1872)

German classical and Coptic scholar ; born Berlin, 27 Oct. 1798 ; educ. Berlin and Heidelberg ; in 1820–4 visited England, Italy and Egypt ; pub. a number of Greek and Coptic texts, and several books, the best known of which is *Vocabularium Coptico-latinum et Latino-Copticum*, 1844, which for many years remained the best Coptic dictionary until it was superseded by more modern works ; his travel-book, *Wanderungen durch Sicilien und die Levant*, 1833–40, the second part of which is concerned with Egypt ; Member of Berlin Acad., 1857 ; died 2 April 1872.

Hilmy, ii, 94.

PASSALACQUA, Giuseppe (1797–1865)

Italian excavator and collector of antiquities ; born Trieste, 1797 ; went to Egypt as a horse-dealer, but as this business did not prosper, he took to excavating and collecting antiquities ; he made a large and important collection at Thebes and other sites and brought it to Paris for sale ; it was exhibited at 52 Passage Vivienne in 1826 ; he offered the collection to the French Govt. for fcs. 400,000, but it was rejected and afterwards bought for fcs. 100,000 by Friedrich Wilhelm IV for the Berlin Museum ; Passalacqua was in consequence installed as Conservator of the Eg. Collections, a position he held until the end of his life, when Lepsius, who from 1855 had been Assistant Conservator, succeeded him. The collection was described in the *Catalogue Raisonné* pub. in Paris in 1826 ; died Berlin, 1865.

Champollion, i, 297 ; *Westcar Diary*, 274 ; *Madox*, i, 278 and often ; *Hilmy*, ii, 95 ; Ebers, *Richard Lepsius* (trans. Underhill), 183 ; Brugsch, *Mein Leben*, 25–49, 189.

PATERSON, Emily (1860–1947)

Friend and associate of Amelia Edwards, and her private secretary, 1888–92 ; succeeded her as Secretary, E.E.F., 1892 ; retired, 1919 ; attended Griffith's classes at Univ. Coll. London, and gave lectures for the E.E.F., to the library of which she was also a donor ; died at Redruth, Cornwall, 3 Sept. 1947.

E.E.S. Ann. Rep. 1947, 7 ; *Newberry Corresp.*

PEET, Thomas Eric (1882–1934)

Born Liverpool, 1882 ; educ. Merchant Taylors' School, Crosby and Queen's Coll. Oxon., Jodrell Scholar ; Craven Fellow, 1906 ; Pelham Student, Brit. School in Rome ; excavated in Italy, 1909 ; Laycock Student in Egyptology, Oxon., 1923 ; Lecturer in Egyptology, Manchester Univ., 1913–28 ; Brunner Professor of Egyptology, Liverpool, 1920–33 ; Prof. of Egyptology, Oxford, 1933–4 ; excavated in Egypt ; for many years editor of *JEA*. ; Schweich Lecturer, 1929 ; a scholar of the highest calibre, he made many important contributions to Egyptology, and particularly in the study and publication of the series of papyri dealing with the tomb-robberies at Thebes under the later Ramessides ; died 22 Feb. 1934.

WWW. iii, 1061 ; *JEA*. 20, 66 (Portr.) ; *DNB*. 1931–40, 685.

PELLEGRINI, Astorre (1844–1908)

Italian Egyptologist of Florence ; born Leghorn, 5 June 1844 ; educ. Pisa Univ. ; pub. many short papers, chiefly in the *Bessarione* from 1906 onwards ; pub. a papyrus with a new text of the Book of Breathings, and some short Coptic texts ; died 22 Feb. 1908.

Sphinx, 12, 152 (Bibl.).

PENDLEBURY, John Devitt Stringfellow (1904–1941)

Excavator in Egypt and Crete ; born London 12 Oct. 1904 ; educ. Winchester, 1918–23, and Pembroke Coll., Cantab., 1923 ; travelled in the Balkans and Greece ; excavated in Crete and in Macedonia, 1928 ; joined E.E.F. expedition at Armant, 1928 and Amarna, 1928–9 ; directed Amarna expedition 1930–1 ; Curator of Knossos, 1930 ; pub. *Ægyptiaca*, a catalogue of Eg. objects found in the Aegean area ; excavated at Amarna until 1936, spending the summer months in Crete ; pub. *Tell el-Amarna*, 1935 ; worked thereafter exclusively in Crete ; pub. *Archaeology of Crete*, 1939 ; in 1939, joined the forces in Crete, Capt. 18th Infantry Brigade ; in May 1941 was severely wounded in action ; while dangerously ill, he was made to come from his bed and was questioned by the Germans as to the position of the British forces : he refused information and they shot him, on or about 24 May 1941.

JEA. 28, 61 (Portr.) ; 34, 2 ; *Chron*. 18, 272.

PERCIVAL, Francis William (1844–1929)

Born 1844 ; Queen's Coll. Oxon. ; M.A. ; F.S.A. ; a lifelong friend of Sayce with whom he travelled frequently to Egypt and elsewhere ; joined E.E.F. in 1886 and served on the Committee from 1894 ; Hon. Librarian, 1919 ; died in London, 1929.

Sayce, passim.

PERCY, Algernon, 1st Baron Prudhoe and 4th Duke of Northumberland (1792–1865)

Second son of Hugh Percy, 2nd Duke, by his second marriage ; born Syon House, 15 Dec. 1792 ; entered Navy, 1805 ; retired Captain, 1815 ; Rear Admiral, 1850 ; Vice-Ad., 1857 ; Admiral, 1862 ; created Baron Prudhoe, 1816 ; travelled in the East for some years with

Major Orlando Felix (q.v.) and met Champollion in Nubia in 1828 ; made an extensive collection of Eg. antiquities (over 2,000 objects) of which a catalogue by Samuel Birch was published in 1880 ; accompanied Sir John Herschel's expedition to the Cape, 1834 ; D.C.L., Oxon., 1841 ; F.R.S. ; F.S.A. ; F.G.S. ; F.R.A.S. ; financed E. W. Lane's Arabic Lexicon and sent him to Egypt to collect materials ; his wife, née Lady Eleanor Grosvenor, continued to support Lane after the Duke's death ; succeeded as 4th Duke, 1847 ; restored Alnwick Castle and greatly improved the estate ; First Lord of the Admiralty, 1852–3 ; a Trustee of the B.M. ; died at Alnwick, 12 Feb. 1865, buried in the Percy Chapel, Westminster Abbey 27 Feb. The Alnwick collection of antiquities was presented to the Univ. of Durham in 1950.

DNB. 44, 390 ; *Ann. Register*, 1865, 19–21.

PERNETTY, Antoine Joseph (1716–1801)

French Benedictine ; pub. a work on Egyptian and Greek fables and an attempt to decipher hieroglyphs, 2 vols., Paris, 1758, reissued in 1786.

BIFAO. 5, 82 ; *Hilmy*, ii, 104.

PÉRICHON, (*Bey*) **Jean André** (1860–1929)

French industrialist ; born Bessines near Limoges, 1860 ; educ. École des Arts et Métiers d'Angers ; worked for five years for the firm of Cail, Paris, by whom he was sent to Egypt, where for 22 years he directed the Khedive's sugar factory at Rodah ; while in Egypt he formed a collection of antiquities in which he was often assisted by Maspero and Lefébure ; his collection was bequeathed to the town of Limoges and since 1931 has been exhibited in the Musée de l'Évêché ; died 1929.

Limoges Museum, *Guide-Catalogue*, 9 ; *Chron*. 14, 150.

PEROFFSKY, Wassili Alexejewich (1784–1857)

Russian general ; born Charcov, 1784 ; for his retreat in the Khivan Expedition he was much censured, but was vindicated by the Duke of Wellington whose opinion the Czar had asked for ; Governor of Orenberg ; died in the Crimea, 1857 ; his name is known in Egyptology by the "Pierre Peroffsky," a large stone inscribed with § 64 of the Book of the Dead ; it was given to P. by Czar Nicolas and presented by his family to the Hermitage Museum in 1861.

Golenischeff, *Herm. Eg. Coll.* p. 169, No. 1101 ; Maspero, *Études de Myth.* i, 368, *n.* 1 ; *Larousse* 19*th Cent.* 12, 647 ; A. Geikie, *Life of Sir Roderick Murchison*, i, 344.

PERRING, John Shae (1813–1869)

Civil engineer ; born Boston, Lincs, 24 Jan. 1813 ; educ. Dorrington Grammar School and articled to a surveyor ; came to London in 1833 ; went to Egypt in Mar. 1836 under directions of Galloway Bros. of London, as assistant to Galloway Bey, manager of public works for Mohammad Ali and was engaged on various works in Egypt ; in Jan.–Aug. 1837 he assisted Col. Howard-Vyse in his survey and exploration of the Pyramids of Gizeh ; pub. *On the Engineering of the Anc. Eg.*, 1835 ; *The Pyramids of Gizeh,* a large oblong folio, 1839 ; part i deals with the Great Pyramid, part ii with the other Pyramids of Gizeh, and part iii with the Pyramids S. of Abu Roash, those of Middle Egypt and Campbell's Tomb ; Perring's work is acknowledged by Howard-Vyse in his own publication ; returned to England in 1840, and was thereafter employed in railway and other engineering works ; died Manchester, 16 Jan. 1869.

DNB. 45, 15 ; *Hilmy,* ii, 104 ; Vyse, *Pyramids,* passim (Portr. vol. iii, frontispiece).

PERROT, Georges (1832–1914)

French classical scholar and writer on ancient art ; born Villeneuve-St.-Georges, 12 Nov. 1832 ; joined the École d'Athènes and visited Greece, 1855–8 ; employed in educational work at Angoulême, Orleans and Versailles, 1858–60 ; went on a mission to Asia Minor, 1860–2 ; lecturer in ancient history, Éc. des Hautes Études, 1874 ; his principal work is his *Hist. de l'Art dans l'Antiquité,* in collaboration with Charles Chipiez, the first volume of which, dealing with Egypt, appeared in 1881 ; Sec. Perpetuel de l'Acad. des Inscr., 1904–14 ; died, 30 June 1914.

Maspero, *Notice sur . . . M. Georges Perrot* (*Mem. Acad.* 1915) (Portr.) ; *Hilmy,* ii, 104.

PERRY, Charles (1698–1780)

Traveller and medical writer ; pub. medical works and *View of the Levant,* 1743, which contains much interesting information on Egypt ; the mummy described and figured in that work passed into the hands of Richard Cosway, R.A., at the sale of whose effects, it was acquired by Pettigrew, who examined and published it ; the coffin was acquired by Dr. John Lee, and then by Lord Amherst, in whose sale in 1921 it was lot 348.

DNB. 45, 29 ; *JEA.* 20, 170 ; Pettigrew, *Hist. Eg. Mummies,* p. xvii ; *Hartwell Cat.* Nos. 589, 590 ; *Hilmy,* ii, 108.

PERSIGNY, (*Duc de*) **Jean Victor Gilbert Fialin** (1808–1872)

French statesman ; born 11 Jan. 1808 ; educ. at Limoges and became an officer in the Hussars, 1828 ; dismissed for the share taken by the regiment in the revolution of 1830 ; became a Bonapartist and suffered imprisonment, during which he wrote *De la destination et de l'utilité des Pyramides d'Égypte,* Paris, 1845, in which he sought to prove that the pyramids were built as screens against the desert sand to prevent the Nile from silting ; became Minister of the Interior, 1852–4 and 1860–3 ; exiled in 1870, and died at Nice, 11 Jan. 1872.

Delaroa, *Le Duc de Persigny,* 1865 ; *Carré,* ii, 120.

PETHERICK, John (1813–1882)

Usually known as " Consul Petherick "; traveller in Egypt and in East and Central Africa ; entered the service of Mohammad Ali in 1845 ; in 1848 he left the Egyptian service and established himself in Kordofan and thereafter explored Central and East Africa ; pub. *Egypt, the Sudan and Central Africa*, 1853–8 ; died in London, 15 July 1882.

DNB. 21, 305 ; *Proc. R. Geogr. S.* 4, 700 ; *Hilmy*, ii, 109.

PETRIE, (*Sir*) **William Matthew Flinders** (1853–1942)

Egyptologist ; s. William Petrie, a civil engineer, and Anne d. Capt. Matthew Flinders, the explorer of Australia; born Charlton, 3 June 1853 ; as a boy collected coins and was introduced by R. S. Poole to Amelia Edwards who founded the E.E.F. ; surveyed the Pyramids, 1880 and pub. *Pyramids and Temples of Gizeh*, 1883 ; excavated at Tanis and other sites for E.E.F. 1884–6 ; left E.E.F. and excavated independently with funds provided by friends 1887–95 ; first Edwards Professor of Egyptology, Univ. Coll., London, 1894–1933 ; rejoined E.E.F. 1896 and worked again for that body, but having founded the Egyptian Research Account in 1894, he finally left the E.E.F. as soon as it was well established, and in 1906 renamed it British School of Archaeology in Egypt ; he later abandoned Egypt and transferred his activities to Palestine ; in addition to the annual volumes describing his excavations, Petrie pub. a large number of books, both scientific and popular, and amassed a great collection of antiquities housed at Univ. Coll. London, though his most important finds are in the Cairo Museum and other museums in England and America ; F.R.S. ; F.B.A. ; Hon. D.C.L., LL.D., Litt.D., Ph.D., and hon. member of many foreign societies and academies ; died at Jerusalem, 28 July 1942.

Autobiogr. *Seventy Years in Archaeology*, 1931 ; *JEA*. 29, 67 (Portr.) ; *Man*, 43, 20 (No. 9) ; *ASA*. 41, 1–14 (Portr.).

PETTIGREW, Thomas Joseph (1791–1865)

Surgeon and antiquary ; born London, 28 Oct. 1791 ; practised as a surgeon in Savile Row ; surgeon to the Duke of Kent and vaccinated Queen Victoria ; Librarian to the Duke of Sussex ; F.R.C.S. ; F.R.S., F.S.A. ; Hon. Member, Inst. Eg. ; took an active part in most of the literary and archaeological movements of his time ; one of the founders of the Brit. Arch. Assn. ; was first interested in Egyptology by meeting Belzoni in 1818 ; studied the language etc. with assiduity ; was particularly interested in mummification ; pub. *Hist. of Eg. Mummies*, 1834 ; *Encyclopaedia Ægyptica*, 1842 and many shorter papers besides many works on other subjects ; unrolled and gave demonstrations on a large number of mummies ; had a collection of Eg. antiquities, which were sold 23 Aug. 1905, lots 205–212, but the principal items were disposed of in his lifetime ; died 23 Nov. 1865.

Autiobiography up to 1840, in *Medical Portrait Gallery*, iv : W. R. Dawson *Memoir of T. J. Pettigrew*, N.Y., 1931 (Portrs. and Bibl.) ; *JEA*. 20, 170 (Portr.) ; *Dawson MSS*. 18, f. 120–132 ; 30, f. 1–269 ; 27, f. 39 42 ; 39A, f. 97 ; 40, f. 174, 199 ; 63, f. 96–143 ; *Hilmy*, ii, 113.

PEYRON, Amedeo Angelo Maria (1785–1870)

Italian Coptic and Greek scholar ; born Turin, 2 Oct. 1785, the youngest of 11 brothers ; in 1800 attended classes in Greek and oriental literature given at Turin Univ. by the Abbot of Caluso, who remained a good friend to him ; ordained priest about 1810 ; from 1803 taught oriental languages ; assistant in Turin Univ. library, 1814 ; Professor 1815, and also taught Greek ; employed by Count Balbo to collect ancient MSS. ; Member of Turin Acad., 1816 ; of Inst. de France, 1854 on the recommendation of Cardinal Mai with whom he had been acquainted since 1820 ; began to collect materials at an early age for his Coptic dictionary which from 1825–35 was his chief preoccupation ; he arranged the words under radicals instead of the usual alphabet, a feature criticised by Letronne and Silvestre de Sacy, though they praised the final result ; in 1835 his *Lexicon Linguae Copticae* was pub. at the expense of the King ; after its completion, Peyron did little more work in Coptic, but turned his attention to Greek ; died 1870.

Atti R. Acad. Scienze Torino, 5, 1–32 ; *Hilmy*, ii, 113.

PICCININI, —— (*fl.* 1820–1830)

A native of Lucca, who excavated in Egypt and also bought antiquities for Giovanni Anastasi ; he had a house at Thebes at the S. end of Dira Abu'n-Naga, close to the tomb now numbered 161 ; nothing is known of his previous or later history, but he is frequently mentioned by travellers in Egypt, and was at Thebes some years earlier than Winlock (*JEA*. 10, 231, *n* 1) suggests.

Hartleben, ii, 292, 320 ; *Champollion*, ii, 149, 245 ; *Westcar Diary*, 72 ; *Hay Diary*.

PIEHL, Karl (1853–1904)

Swedish Egyptologist ; born 30 Mar. 1853 ; established in Sweden a School of Egyptology, a professorship and a journal—the *Sphinx* ; he was a careful copyist of texts and a painstaking editor, but he was very hostile to the methods of the new school which originated in Germany ; he had a persistent habit of acrimonious criticism of his colleagues, often carried to a deplorable extent ; he held the Chair of Egyptology at Uppsala from 1881 until his death, 5 Aug. 1904.

Sphinx, 8, 117 (Portr.) ; 9, 104 ; *Rec. Trav.* 27, 134 ; *Hilmy*, ii, 116.

PIEPER, Max (1882–1941)

German Egyptologist ; born 9 April 1882 ; educ. Berlin Univ. ; D.Phil., Berlin ; pub. with Max Burchardt *Handbuch der aeg. Königsnamen*, 1912 and contributions to *ZÄS*. ; died 31 May 1941.

Chron. 18, 273 ; *Kürschner*.

PIER, Garrett Chatfield (1875–1943)

American traveller and museum official ; born London 30 Oct. 1875 ; studied in Columbia Univ., N.Y., 1896–8 ; studied in European and Egyptian museums for four years, and Egyptology and Assyriology at Chicago Univ., 1906 ; Asst. Curator of Decorative Arts, M.M.A., 1907–10 ; travelled to Japan, China and Far East buying for the M.M.A., 1911–4 ; served in First World War, 1918–9 ; attached to U.S. State Dept. and the Peace Commission, 1919–21 ; formed a considerable collection of Eg. antiquities of which he published an account, *Eg. Ant. in the Pier Collection*, Chicago, 1906 ; pub. works on oriental ceramics and antique guns, and wrote works of fiction ; died 30 Dec. 1943.

Inf. by Dr. Dows Dunham.

PIERRET, Paul (1837–1916)

French Egyptologist ; a pupil of de Rougé ; conservator in succession to Devéria of the Egyptian collections of the Louvre ; did much to popularize Egyptology in France ; he pub. a translation of the Book of the Dead, a hieroglyphic vocabulary and books on Eg. mythology : died at Versailles, Feb. 1916.

Anc. Eg. 1916, 187 ; *Hilmy*, ii, 117.

PIÉTREMENT, Charles Alexandre (1826–1906)

French naturalist and ethnologist ; studied particularly the history of the domestication of animals, and especially of the horse ; in addition to many separate memoirs on these subjects he wrote : *Les Chevaux dans les temps préhistoriques et historiques*, Paris, 1808, On the horse in Egypt, *Rev. d'Ethnographie*, 3, 369–388, and *Les origines du cheval domestique, d'après la palaeontologie, la zoologie, l'histoire et la philologie*, Paris, 1870.

Hilmy, ii, 117–8.

PIETSCHMANN, Richard (1851–1923)

German Egyptologist ; born Stettin, 24 Sept. 1851 ; studied at Berlin and Leipsic ; librarian successively at Breslau, Griefswald, Marberg and Göttingen ; Professor of Egyptology and Oriental History, Göttingen ; Professor of Bibliography and Director of the Univ. Library, Göttingen, 1903–23 ; died 17 Oct. 1923.

Kürschners Deutscher Literaturkalendar ; *Chronik der . . . Univ. Göttingen*, 1921–3 ; *Hilmy*, ii, 119.

PILLAVOINE, Alexandre (1756–1838)

French merchant ; born 22 Jan. 1756 ; emigrated at the Revolution and took refuge in Aleppo, where he carried on his business until the time of the Expedition to Egypt ; he was made prisoner by the Turks, robbed and tortured, 1799 ; was set at liberty the same year for a large ransom, which brought ruin to him ; French Consul at St. Jean d'Acre, 1802 ; Acting Consul-General in Egypt, 1819–21 ; afterwards Consul at Baltimore, 1821, Philadelphia, 1825, and Larnaca, 1829 ; retired, 1831 ; in 1820 he received Lelorrain and procured for him the facilities for removing the Zodiac of Dendera ; died 4 Oct. 1838.

French F.O. Records ; *Lelorrain*, 15.

PIRIE, Annie Abernethie—*See* QUIBELL

PLEYTE, Willem (1836–1903)

Dutch Egyptologist ; born Hillegom, 26 June 1836 ; educ. Zalt-Bommel and Utrecht ; conservator of the Eg. collections at Leiden, 1868 ; Director of the Museum, 1891 ; D. ès L., Leiden, 1891 ; pub. many hieratic papyri in Leiden, Paris and Turin, the last in collaboration with Francesco Rossi ; pub. *Chapitres Suppl. au Livre des Morts,* 1881–2 ; died 11 Mar. 1903.

Sphinx, 7, 175 (Portr.) ; *Hilmy,* ii, 122.

POCOCKE, (*Rev.*) **Richard** (1704–1765)

Traveller and divine ; born 1704 ; C.C.C. Oxon. ; B.A., 1725 ; D.C.L. 1733 ; visited Egypt 1737–8 ascending the Nile as far as Philae ; visited Palestine, Asia Minor and Greece, 1738–40 ; explored Switzerland, 1741 ; Bishop of Ossory, 1756–65, of Meath, 1765 ; pub. his eastern travels, 1743–5 ; MS. journal of this travels, B.M. Add. MSS. 22995, 22997–8 ; member of the first Egyptian Society ; died 1765 and buried in Christ Church, Oxford.

DNB. 46, 12 ; *JEA.* 23, 260 ; *Hilmy,* ii, 124.

POINSINET DE SIVRY, Louis (1733–1804)

French littérateur and classical scholar ; born Versailles, 1733 ; wrote several tragedies ; translated Sappho, Anacreon and Bion (1758) ; Pliny (1781) ; Aristophanes (1784) ; *Nouvelles recherches sur la science de Medaikes, Inscriptions et Hiéroglyphes Antiques,* Paris, 1778 : in this work he claimed to be able to read the " hieroglyphs " on the Turin bust, previously studied by Needham, Stukeley and others, and which is a manifest forgery ; died in Paris, 1804.

Mem. IFAO. 66, 367 (*Mélanges Maspero*) ; *Hilmy,* ii, 125.

POITEVIN, Éphraim (*fl.* 1853–5)

French archaeologist ; contributed memoirs on the Table of Abydos, the inscription of Aahmes and the town of Avaris to *Rev. Arch.,* 1853–5 ; on his proposal a monument to Champollion was erected at the Coll. de France.

Hartleben, ii, 606 ; *Hilmy,* ii, 125.

POITOU, Eugène Louis (1815–*c.* 1880)

French poet and publicist ; born Antwerp, 9 Feb. 1815 ; travelled in Egypt in 1857 where he met Clot-Bey and travelled with him as far as the Cataracts ; pub. *Un Hiver en Égypte,* 1859, which was translated into English and reached a fourth edition ; he was the first Frenchman to describe the Serapeum ; died about 1880.

Carré, ii, 243 ; *Vapereau,* 1436 ; *Larousse 19th cent.,* 12, 1279 ; *Hilmy,* ii, 125.

PONIATOWSKI, (*Prince*) **Stanislaus** (1757–1833)

Polish statesman and general ; retired in 1793 and settled in Vienna and afterwards in Rome where he formed his famous collection of engraved gems in his house in the Via Flaminia ; the collection was sent to London for disposal and was sold at Christie's in a 17 days' sale commencing 13 Feb. 1839 ; the collection included many fine scarabs and gnostic gems from Egypt ; died at Florence, 13 Feb. 1833.

C. W. King, *Handb. of Engraved Gems,* 2nd ed., 193–7.

PONTCHARTRAIN, (*Comte de*) **Jérôme Phélypeaux** (1674–1747)

French statesman ; born Paris, 1674 ; succeeded his father as Secretary of State, 1693 ; resigned office in 1715 in favour of his son ;

died in Paris, 1747. He was the owner of Eg. antiquities, probably sent by Benoît de Maillet, French Consul-General ; among these was a mummy, which is described and depicted in an elaborate MS. by Florimond, now in the library of King's Coll. Cambridge ; the mummy was given to the Convent of the Petits Pères, Paris, which was destroyed during the Revolution and the mummy, which was believed to be that of Cleopatra, was buried in the convent garden.

Carré, i, 57 ; *Florimond MS.* ; *Dawson MS.* 15, f. 238–242 ; *Inf. by Mme. Noblecourt.*

POOLE, Reginald Stuart (1832–1895)

Numismatist and archaeologist; younger son of Rev. Edward Richard and Sophia Poole ; born 1832 ; went to Egypt as a boy and remained there several years studying the monuments with his uncle Edward William Lane ; entered the service of the B.M., 1852 ; Keeper of Coins and Medals, 1870 ; retired 1893 ; pub. a number of books and papers on Egypt and vindicated Champollion against the attacks of Sir G. Cornewall Lewis (*Archaeologia*, 39, 471) ; took an active part with Amelia Edwards in founding the E.E.F., 1882 ; Professor of Archaeology, Univ. Coll. London, 1889 ; Hon. Sec. E.E.F. ; introduced Newberry to Egyptology ; died 8 Feb. 1895.

DNB. 46, 101 ; *JEA.* 33, 72 ; *Hilmy*, ii, 128 ; *Newberry Corresp.*

POOLE, Sophia (1804–1891)

Sister of Ed. William Lane ; married 1829, Rev. Edward Richard Poole ; mother of Reginald Stuart Poole ; resided in Egypt with her brother, 1842–9 ; pub. *The Englishwoman in Egypt*, vols. i, ii, 1844, second series [vol. iii], 1846 ; she spent her last years in her son's official residence at the B.M.

DNB. 46, 104 ; *Romer*, ii, 3 ; *Hilmy*, ii, 130.

PORTER, Bertha (1852–1941)

Egyptological bibliographer ; born London, 9 Apl. 1852 ; had literary tastes and was acquainted with Dickens, Carlyle and the Brownings ; she was also interested in psychical research ; studied Egyptology under Griffith and under Sethe at Göttingen ; she spent many years in amassing the material for the *Topographical Bibliography of Ancient Hieroglyphic Texts, Reliefs and Paintings*, the first volume of which, dealing with the Theban Necropolis, appeared in 1927, with the collaboration of Miss Rosalind Moss, who has produced the many subsequent volumes ; died at Oxford, 17 Jan. 1941.

The Times, 22 Jan. 1941.

POSNO, Gustave (*fl.* 1873–1883)

Collector of antiquities ; a catalogue, *Collection de M. Posno*, Cairo, 1873, was issued ; the objects described are mostly Graeco-Roman ; the collection was sold in 1883 (cat. with plates) ; some bronzes were bought for the Louvre ; other objects are now in the Palais des Beaux Arts, Paris, Berlin (8438–9), and Copenhagen (A.99).

Rev. de l'Art, 43, 171 ; *Inf. by Miss R. Moss.*

POTOCKI, (*Comte*) **Jean** (1761–1815)

Polish scholar ; travelled in Egypt in 1784 and pub. an account of his journey in 1788 ; studied Manetho and Eg. chronology and pub. several memoirs thereon, 1803–8.

NBG. 40, 900 ; *Larousse, 19th cent.* 12, 1521 ; *Hilmy,* ii, 133.

POURTALÈS, (*Comte de*) **Albert Alexander** (1812–1861)

French diplomatist, of a Protestant family settled at Neuchâtel ; born Neuchâtel, 1812 ; Prussian Envoy at Constantinople and later in Paris, from 1854 ; formed a gallery of antiquities and works of art in Paris, which was sold in 1865, when some important Egyptian objects were bought by Lord Amherst ; died in Paris, 1861.

Larousse ; *Inf. by P. E. Newberry.*

PRICE, Frederick George Hilton (1842–1909)

Banker and antiquary ; born 20 Aug. 1842 ; entered Child's Bank in 1860 and eventually became senior partner ; F.S.A., and Director, S.A., 1894–1909 ; V.-P., Soc. Bibl. Arch. ; President, E.E.F., 1906–9 ; published several antiquarian works ; had a large collection of antiquities, those relating to London formed the basis of the London Museum ; his Eg. antiquities were very numerous and choice, many of them he described in *PSBA*, and the whole collection was catalogued in sumptuous privately-printed volumes (2 vols., 1897–1908) ; the collection was sold at Sotheby's, 12–21 July 1911 and realized £12,000 ; his numismatic library sold at Sotheby's, 20 April 1911 ; died at Cannes, 14 Mar. 1909.

WWW. i, 575 ; *AAA.* 2, 94.

PRICHARD, James Cowles (1786–1848)

Physician and anthropologist ; born Ross-on-Wye, 11 Feb. 1786 ; M.D., Edinb., 1808 ; matriculated at T.C.C. 1808 and afterwards at St. John's and Trinity Colls., Oxon., but did not graduate at either University ; Physician to St. Peter's Hospital, Bristol, 1811, and to Bristol Infirmary, 1814 ; a Commissioner of Lunacy, 1845 ; apart from his medical writings and his valuable contributions to anthropology of which his *Physical History of Mankind* and *Natural History of Man* are the most important, he seriously studied Eg. history, chronology and religion ; pub. *Analysis of Egyptian Mythology* (1st ed. 1819, transl. into German, 1837) ; died in London, 22 Dec. 1848.

DNB. 46, 344 ; Haddon, *Hist. Anthropology,* 104 (Portr.) ; *Man,* 1949, § 163 (Portr.) ; *Hilmy,* ii, 135.

PRINGLE, John Watson (1791–1861)

Army officer, Royal Engineers ; born 1791 ; Lieut., 1811 ; fought and wounded at Waterloo ; on half-pay as Captain, 1817 ; visited Egypt en route for Ceylon, 1824 ; pub. *Route de l'Inde par l'Égypte et la Mer Rouge* (*Bull. Soc. Géogr. Paris,* 1826, 651) ; died at Bath, 12 Oct. 1861.

Westcar Diary, 191–6, 200, 207, 218, 221 ; C. Dalton, *Waterloo Roll Call,* 2nd ed., 229 ; *Bull. Soc. Géogr. Paris,* 1826, 651–60 ; *Madox,* ii, 28, 33.

PRISSE D'AVENNES, Achille Constant Théodore Êmile (1807–1879)

French Egyptologist, of Welsh origin (Price of Aven); born Avesnes-sur-Helpe, 1807; educ. Châlons-sur-Marne, 1822–5, where he obtained the diploma of Engineer-Architect; took part in the Greek War of Independence, 1826; went to Egypt and obtained an appointment as engineer under Mohammad Ali till 1836; in 1842 founded with Dr. Henry Abbott the Association Littéraire in Cairo; discovered the Table of Kings at Karnak in 1845 and with great difficulty removed it to France; revisited Egypt in 1858; his name is particularly associated with the famous papyrus in the Bibliothèque Nationale (Cartons 183–194) and with the Table of Kings; produced a splendid series of publications, including, besides the facsimile of his papyrus, *Monuments Ég.* (1847); *Hist. de l'Art Ég.* (1858–77); *L'Art Arabe* (1867–79); his MSS. and drawings are in the Bibl. Nat. (Nouv. Acq. Fr. 20416–49); other papers were in possession of his son (*d.* 1919) from whom they were acquired by the Arch. Soc. of Avesnes, some of these papers and the portrait of Prisse, were stolen by the Germans from Avesnes in 1918 and have not been recovered.

Carré, i, 297–319 (Portr. and Bibl.); *Hilmy*, ii, 138.

PRUDHOE, Lord—*See* PERCY

PRUNER, (*Bey*) **Franz** (1808–1883)

Bavarian physician and anthropologist; born Pfreimdt, 8 Mar. 1808; educ. Munich; later studied at Paris 1860–70 under Grossi; went to Egypt to assist Clot-Bey in the medical service; in addition to his medical writings, Pruner wrote on the Egyptian race and its origin, on Neanderthal Man and on the general problems of race; he took hair to be the test of racial purity, " a single hair presenting the average form characteristic of the race might serve to define it " (*Mem. Soc. Athr. Paris,* 2); President, Soc. Anthr. Paris 1865; Hon. Fellow R.A.I., 1863; died at Pisa, 29 Sept. 1883.

Bull. Inst. Eg. 2nd ser. 1883, 81; *JAI.* 12, 561; Clot-Bey, *Aperçu*, ii, 417; Brugsch, *Mein Leben*, 159; *Lepsius*, 47, 98; *Hilmy*, ii, 144.

PUECKLER-MUSKAU, (*Prince*) **Hermann Ludwig Heinrich** (1785–1871)

German traveller and author; born Muskau, Lusatia, 30 Oct. 1785; after military service, settled on his estates; travelled extensively in England, America, Asia Minor and Egypt (1837); his account of his journey in Egypt was translated into English by H. E. Lloyd under the title *Travels and Adventures in Egypt,* 2 vols. 1845; visited Vyse during his operations at the Pyramids; died at Branitz, 4 Feb. 1871.

EB. 22, 632; *Vyse*, i, 170, 172; *Hilmy*, ii, 145.

PUGIOLI, G. (*fl.* 1874–1888)

Of Alexandria; collector of antiquities; his collection was seen by Wilbour in 1884; a collection of vases from Pugioli was acquired by the Cairo Museum in 1888; pub. *Esposizione del Governo di S.A. Ismaïl 1er,* Alexandria, 1874.

Wilbour, 313, 386; *Bull. Inst. Eg.* 9, (1888), pp. iv–xii; *Hilmy*, ii, 145.

QUATREMÈRE, Étienne Marc (1782–1857)

French scholar and antiquary ; born Paris, 1782 ; appointed to the Manuscripts Dept. of the Bibliothèque Nationale, 1807 ; Professor of Greek literature at Rouen, 1809 ; Membre de l'Acad. des Inscr., 1815 ; while his work was mainly classical, he studied Egyptian history and pub. *Recherches . . . sur la langue et la littérature de l'Égypte,* Paris, 1808 and *Mémoires géographiques et historiques sur l'Égypte,* Paris, 1811, based on Coptic and Arabic manuscripts ; died in Paris, 1857.

Larousse, 19 *cent.* s.v. ; *Hilmy,* ii, 147 ; *Hartleben* (see index).

QUIBELL, Annie Abernethie (1862–1927)

Née Pirie ; d. Rev. Prof. William Robertson, P. of Aberdeen ; born 12 Dec. 1862 ; married in 1900 James Edward Quibell ; did much excavating in Egypt as assistant to Petrie and contributed to several of his volumes ; assisted her husband in his archaeological work in Egypt ; her drawings of hieroglyphs from El Kab were used by Griffith in his monograph *Hieroglyphs* (1898) ; pub. *Egyptian History and Art,* 1923 ; *A Wayfarer in Egypt,* 2nd ed. 1926 ; arranged the Grant-Bey Collection at Aberdeen ; died 1927.

Petrie, *Seventy Years,* 158 ; *Inf. Aberdeen Univ.*

QUIBELL, James Edward (1867–1935)

Born 1867 ; educ. Christ Church, Oxon. ; excavated with Petrie at Coptos, Nakada, Ballas and other sites and contributed to several volumes of the E.R.A. ; discovered the Middle Kingdom papyri under the Ramesseum, the Palette of Narmer and other important antiquities ; on staff of Serv. des Antiquités as Inspector, 1898 ; on the Catalogue Commission, 1899 ; excavated at Sakkara for many years ; discovered the Tomb of Yuaa and Thuiu, 1905 ; Conservator, Cairo Mus., 1913–23 ; Secretary-General, 1913–25 ; retired, 1925 ; pub. many important volumes for the Serv. des Antiquités ; in all his work he had the able assistance of his wife, Annie A. Quibell (q.v.) ; died 1935.

JEA. 21, 115 ; *Chron.* 11, 100 ; *Sayce,* 298, 322 ; *Petrie,* 144, 148.

QUINTINO, Giulio de San—*See* CORDERO DI SAN QUINTINO

RADDI, Giuseppe (1770–1829)

Italian botanist ; visited Brazil about 1820 and pub. papers on Brazilian Cryptogams, 1822–3 ; Professor of Natural History at Florence ; accompanied Rosellini in Champollion's expedition to Egypt, 1828.

Atti Acad. Georgofili, Firenze, 8, (1830), 304–9 ; *Champollion,* ii, p. vii, 9, 16, 47, 398.

RAFFAELLI, Giuseppe (1750–1826)

Italian jurist and collector of antiquities ; at the sale of the collection in 1824, Champollion secured some items for the private collection of the Duc de Blacas.

Rec. Champ., 5 ; *Champollion,* i, 8.

RAGUSE, (*Duc de*)—*See* MARMONT

RAIFÉ, Alphonse (1802–1860)

French collector of antiquities ; he bought at the principal sales, particularly that of Anastasi in Paris, 1857 ; two important papyri in the Louvre bear his name (4889–90) ; his collections were sold in Paris in March, 1867 and fetched high prices, the Catalogue was drawn up by F. Lenormant (Eg. ant., lots 1–446).

Sale Cat. pp. v–xv (Portr.) ; *Rev. de l'Art,* 43, 168 ; *Bibl. Ég.* 17, pp. xliii–iv.

RAINER, (*Archduke*) (1827–1913)

Prince of the House of Habsburg ; 4th son of Rainer (1784–1864), Viceroy of Lombardy-Venetia and grandson of the Emperor Leopold II (1747–1792) ; born 11 Jan. 1827 ; made a large collection of papyri, hieratic, demotic, Coptic, Greek and Arabic ; the collection originated with a large find of papyri at Arsinoë in 1877–8 which were purchased from the dealer Theodor Graf in 1884 ; many subsequent additions were made, notably two large finds from El-Eshmûnen and Akhmîm ; the collection was acquired by the Imperial Library of Vienna, and in 1892 an account of it was published : *Papyrus Erzherzog Rainer : Führer durch die Ausstellung* ; the Archduke was Patron of the Arts and Crafts Museum, 1862–98, and Curator of the Acad. of Sciences, 1861–1913 ; died 27 Feb. 1913.

EB. ed. 12, 32, 241.

RAINIER, Peter (*d.* 1836)

Naval officer, nephew of the famous Admiral of the same name ; Capt. R.N., 1806 ; on active service throughout the Napoleonic wars ; C.B., 1815 ; Naval Aide-de-Camp to William IV, 1830 ; went up the Nile as far as Abu Simbel in 1828 and met Champollion in Nubia (Champ. mis-spells his name as Reynier) ; his name is carved on the rock of Abu Sir ; died Southampton, 13 April 1836.

O'Byrne, *Naval Biog.* 949 ; *Champollion,* ii, 190, 191.

RAWLINSON, (*Rev.*) **George** (1812–1902)

Scholar and divine ; born Chadlington, Oxon., 23 Nov. 1812 ; Trin. Coll. Oxon. ; B.A., 1838 ; M.A., 1841 ; Fellow of Exeter Coll. ; Camden Professor of Ancient History, 1861–89 ; Canon of Canterbury, 1872 ; pub. *Hist. of Egypt,* 1881, edited Herodotus and wrote many books on Egypt, Assyria and the ancient history of the Near East ; assisted his brother, Sir Henry C. Rawlinson, the pioneer of Assyriology ; died 6 Oct. 1902.

WWW. i, 588 ; *JEA.* 33, 71 ; *Hilmy,* ii, 152.

RAWNSLEY, (*Rev.*) **Hardwicke Drummond** (1851–1920)

Author and clergyman ; born 28 Sept. 1851 ; educ. Uppingham and Balliol Coll. Oxon. ; M.A. ; ordained 1875 ; held benefices in the Lake District ; Canon of Carlisle ; took a leading part in the foundation of the National Trust, and interested in many social, cultural and educational movements ; visited Egypt, Syria and Palestine, 1875 and Egypt again in 1890; in 1892 pub. *Notes for the Nile*, a book which has enjoyed great popularity; in 1896 pub. *Life of Bishop Harvey Goodwin*, brother of Charles Wycliffe G., containing valuable information about the latter; a voluminous writer on many subjects; died 28 May 1920.

WWW. ii, 872; *Life*, by E. F. Rawnsley, 1923 (Portr.).

RAYET, Olivier (*d.* 1887)

French scholar and archaeologist; Répétiteur pour les Antiquités grecques, École des Hautes Études, 1876; Directeur-adjoint, 1878; pub. *Monuments de l'Art Antique*, which appeared in parts and was completed in 2 folio vols. with 90 plates, Paris, 1884; Maspero contributed eleven important articles to this collection between 1879 and 1883; died 20 Feb. 1887.

Annuaire, Éc. des H.É., 1897, 53, 55; *Hilmy*, ii, 152.

REA, (*Rt. Hon.*) Russell (1846–1916)

Merchant of Liverpool and of Eskdale, Cumberland; born 11 Dec. 1846; P.C., 1909; visited Egypt 1907–8 and in subsequent years and purchased a considerable number of antiquities chiefly from Mohammad Mohassib, under the guidance of Howard Carter and Harold Jones; subscribed to excavations at Abydos and other sites; many of his antiquities were presented to the B.M. by his widow; died 5 Feb. 1916.

WWW. ii, 874; *JEA.* 14, 46; *Inf. by P. E. Newberry.*

REIL, Wilhelm (1820–1880)

German physician; born Schönwerda, Thüringen, 8 Apl. 1820; settled in Cairo about 1850 and practised amongst the European population; in 1860 erected a sanatorium for the treatment of chest complaints; physician to the Viceroy; interested in antiquities and carried out excavations, and was known to Mariette and other European excavators; he greatly damaged the pictures in the Tomb of Ti by taking wet squeezes which removed the colours; pub. *Aegypten als Winteraufenthalt für Kranke*, 1859; died in Cairo, 14 Jan. 1880.

Bibl. Ég. 18, pp. cx, clxxx; 21, p. lxxxvi; *Hilmy*, ii, 159.

REINISCH, Simon Leo (1832–1919)

Austrian philologist; born Syria, 26 Oct. 1832; Professor at Vienna Univ., 1865–80; Keeper of Miramar Egyptian Collection; made several expeditions to Egypt; for the last thirty years of his life he studied the languages of N.E. Africa, especially the Cushite group; made many contributions to Egyptological literature; died Lemkowitz, 1919.

E.E.F. Ann. Arch. Rep. 1902–3, 37; *Hilmy*, ii, 160.

REISNER, George Andrew (1867–1942)

American Egyptologist; born Indianapolis, 5 Nov. 1867; educ. Harvard Univ., Ph.D., 1893; Hearst Lecturer and Director of the Hearst expedition to Egypt, 1905–7; Director, Arch. Survey of

Nubia, 1907–9; excavated for Harvard Univ. for many years in Egypt, particularly at Gizeh; Professor of Egyptology, Harvard, 1914; Curator of Eg. Dept., Boston Museum of Fine Arts, from 1910; published many important works; died in Cairo, June 1942.

ASA. 41, 11–18 (Portr.); *Chron*. 18, 268.

RENOUARD, (*Rev.*) **George Cecil** (1780–1867)

Clergyman and orientalist; born Stamford, Lincs., 7 Sept. 1780; educ. St. Paul's School; Sidney Sussex Coll., Cantab; B.A. 1802; ordained 1804; Chaplain to Brit. Embassy, Constantinople, 1804–6, 1811–14; Professor of Arabic, Cambridge, 1815; Rector of Swanscombe, 1818–67; studied Hebrew, Arabic, Egyptian and Berber languages; Foreign Sec., R.G.S., 1836–46; a constant correspondent of Ed. Hincks and other orientalists; he had a large oriental library, which was sold at Sotheby's with that of Hincks, 12 Nov. 1867; died, unmarried, at Swanscombe, 15 Feb. 1867.

DNB. 48, 22; *Hincks*, passim (see index).

RENOUF, Ludovica Cecilia (1836–1921)

Wife of Sir Peter Le Page Renouf, née Brentano; d. Christian Brentano; born Marienburg, 3 Nov. 1836; married 25 July 1857 at Aschaffenberg; collected all her husband's Egyptological works and republished them in 4 vols., after his death; died in London, 8 Feb. 1921.

Inf. by Miss E. Renouf (*daughter*).

RENOUF, (*Sir*) **Peter Le Page** (1822–1897)

Orientalist and Egyptologist; born Guernsey, 23 Aug. 1822; educ. Elizabeth Coll., Guernsey and Pembroke Coll. Oxon., but left without taking a degree as he had become a Roman Catholic; Classical tutor, Oscott Coll.; Professor of Ancient Hist. and Oriental languages, Catholic Univ., Dublin, 1855–64; H.M. Inspector of Schools, 1864–85; succeeded Birch as Keeper of Oriental Antiquities, B.M., 1885–91; Pres. Soc. Bibl. Arch., 1885–97; visited Egypt, 1875; Hibbert Lecturer, 1879; made many contributions to Egyptology and translated the Book of the Dead, unfinished at his death and completed by Naville; his writings were collected and republished by his wife as *The Life-work of Sir P. Le Page Renouf*, 4 vols., 1902–7; died in London, 14 Oct. 1897.

WWW. i, 594; *PSBA*. 19, 271–9 (Bibl. and Portr.); *ZAS*. 35, 165; Biogr. [by his daughter], *Life-Work*, iv. pp. i–cxxxiii; Correspondence, *Dawson MS*. 18, f. 1–94.

REUVENS, Gaspard Jacobus Christian (1793–1837)

Dutch scholar and archaeologist; born The Hague, 22 Feb. 1793; director of the Leiden Museum of Antiquities; the Anastasi collection was acquired in 1828 under his directorship; studied Greek and demotic papyri on which in 1830 he pub. a valuable essay, *Lettre à M. Letronne sur les Papyrus bilingues et grecques*; he was succeeded by Conrad Leemans; died at Rotterdam, 28 July 1837.

NBG. 42, 63; *Hilmy*, ii, 162.

REVILLOUT, Charles Eugène (1843–1912)

French Egyptologist ; born 4 May 1843 ; studied oriental languages and Egyptology under Maspero, and in 1876 took up demotic ; copied most of the demotic material available in his day, and pub. a great number of texts and articles, but he was erratic and unsystematic and his work is full of inaccuracies ; in 1880 he founded the *Revue Égyptologique*, the greater part of which was written by himself ; he was for some years Conservateur-Adjoint in the Eg. Dept. of the Louvre ; died Paris 16 Jan. 1912.

Rev. Arch. Ser. 4, 21, 243 ; *Rev. Ég.* New Series, 1 (1919), 101 ; *Bull. Soc. d'Ethnogr. Paris*, N.S. 1, 81 ; *Stud. Pal. und Pap.* 13, 10.

RHIND, Alexander Henry (1833–1863)

Scottish lawyer and traveller ; born Wick, Caithness, 26 July 1833 ; educ. Pultneytown, Caithness, and Edinb. Univ., 1848–50 ; studied law and was intended for the Scottish bar, but abandoned law owing to ill-health and was obliged to winter in the south ; visited Egypt, 1855–6 and 1856–7 ; travelled in Spain, France and Italy, 1858–62 ; F.S.A. Scot., 1852 ; excavated at Thebes and acquired a fine collection of antiquities which he bequeathed to the Nat. Museum of Antiquities, Edinburgh (now removed to the Royal Scottish Museum) ; pub. *Thebes its Tombs and their Tenants*, 1862 ; revisited Egypt, 1862–3 where he had a serious illness and died on the way home at Majolica, 3 July 1863 ; his body was brought home and buried at Wick. By his will, Rhind bequeathed £5,000 for two scholarships at Edinburgh, £7,000 for an orphanage at Wick, £400 to the Soc. Ant. Scot. and his large library and collections, and a substantial sum to found a Lecturership in Archaeology in Edinburgh, which began in 1874 and still continues ; Rhind's name is associated with the Egyptian coll. at Edinburgh, with the lecturership, and with certain important papyri : the two bilingual hieratic-demotic papyri at Edinburgh (908–9), the Mathematical Papyrus (B.M. 10057–8) and leather roll (10250) and the long magical papyrus generally called Bremner-Rhind (10188) ; the papyri now in the B.M. for some reason unknown, were not sent to the Edinb. Museum with the rest of the collection, but were sold by David Bremner, Rhind's executor.

DNB. 48, 82 ; *Hilmy*, ii, 171 ; *Inf. obtained in Edinburgh.*

RHONÊ, Arthur (1836–1910)

French author and traveller ; a close friend of Mariette whom he frequently accompanied on his tours of inspection in Upper Egypt, as he did also Maspero ; he thus made many journeys between 1865 and 1882 ; in 1881 he was attached to the Mission archéologique, Cairo ; contributed many accounts of discoveries in Egypt to the *Gaz. des Beaux Arts*, *Le Temps*, *Mag. Pittoresque*, etc., and published work on travel in Egypt, *L'Égypte à petites journées*, which enjoyed great popularity, and of which there were several editions ; died 7 June 1910.

Rev. Arch. Ser. 4, 16, 152 ; *Wilbour*, 64, 92 et passim ; *Hilmy*, ii, 171.

RICARDI, Francesco (*fl.* 1821–1843)

A Genoese who claimed to have discovered the decipherment of hieroglyphs ; he pub. between 1821 and 1843 a number of pamphlets attacking Champollion's system and defending his own.

Hilmy, ii, 172 ; *Hartleben*, i, 545, 580 ; ii, 19, 420 ; *Champollion*, i, 41, 67, 72.

RICCI, Alessandro (*d.* 1832)

Italian physician and explorer, a native of Sienna ; accompanied Bankes in his travels in Egypt, 1815 ; employed by Bankes to draw the paintings of Beni Hasan ; associated with Belzoni and made drawings in the tomb of Sety I ; made several journeys in Egypt and Nubia 1819–21 ; visited the Oasis of Ammon and accompanied Linant to Sinai, 1820 ; a member of the Champollion-Rosellini expedition to Egypt, 1828–30 ; died as the result of a scorpion-sting at Thebes, 1832. Ricci's collections are partly in Florence and partly in Dresden ; his journal and many documents relating to him have been pub. by the Soc. Royale Géogr., edited by Angelo Sammarco, 2 vols., Cairo, 1930 where full references will be found.

Athanasi, 25, 27 ; *Belzoni*, i, 371, 388 ; ii, 24, 38, 105 ; *Hay Diary*, 1825, Dec. 1 ; *Finati*, ii, 301, 335, 344, 357, 394 ; *Champollion*, passim ; *Hartleben* (see index) ; other references in Sammarco *ut supra*.

RICCI, Seymour de (1881–1942)

Bibliographer and antiquary ; he resided chiefly in Paris, and published many bibliographical works on rare books and MSS. ; he had a fine library and his knowledge of book collectors and sales of books and MSS. was unrivalled ; he visited Egypt several times and obtained many important papyri, chiefly Greek, some of which he published ; Sandars Lecturer, Cambridge, 1929–30 ; pub. a bibliography of Egyptology (*Rev. Arch.* v–viii (1917–18), and of Champollion (*Rec. Champ.* 763–784) ; died in Paris, 26 Dec. 1942.

JEA. 31, 1 ; *The Library*, 1943–4, 187–194 ; *Chron*. 19, 96.

RICHARDS, Thomas Bingham (1781–1857)

Of Lamb's Conduit Place, London, and Langton, Tunbridge Wells, Kent ; son of Wm. Clavell Richards of Smedmore and Sophia, d. Richard Bingham, barrister-at-law ; London agent of Henry Salt ; he carried out the prolonged and difficult negotiations with the Trustees of the B.M. for the purchase of Salt's collections in 1821–4 ; died at Langton, April 30 1857.

Salt, i, 413 ; ii, 40 et passim ; *GM*. 1857, i, 740.

RICHARDSON, ROBERT (1779–1847)

Physician and traveller ; born Stirling, 1779 ; educ. Glasgow and Edinburgh Universities ; M.D., 1807 ; L.R.C.P., 1815 ; travelling physician to Viscount Mountjoy and to the Earl of Belmore with whom he travelled in Egypt as far as the Second Cataract and in Palestine, 1816–8 ; practised in London ; died Gordon St., Bloomsbury, 5 Nov. 1847, buried in Highgate Cemetery ; his library was sold at Sotheby's, 11 Apl. 1849 ; pub. narrative of Lord Belmore's travels, 2 vols., 1822.

Munk, *Roll Coll. of Phys.* iii, 134 ; *DNB.* 48, 242 ; *Hilmy,* ii, 172 ; Cailliaud, *Oasis,* 51 ; *Westcar Diary,* 250 ; *Lindsay,* 114 ; *Belzoni,* i, 386, 436 ; ii, 292.

RIFAUD, Jean Jacques (1786–*c.* 1845)

French excavator, a sculptor by profession ; a native of Marseilles, born 29 Nov. 1786 ; carried out excavations for Drovetti, whom he accompanied to the Second Cataract in 1816 ; spent over 40 years in Egypt and did an immense amount of digging ; his work, however, was hasty and unscientific as his only object was the acquisition of portable antiquities ; he pub. a number of large works, notably *Voyages en Égypte, en Nubie . . . depuis 1805 jusqu'en 1827,* Paris, 1830, 5 vols. 8vo and a large folio vol. of plates ; *Tableau d'Égypte* etc. 1830 ; *Rapport . . . sur les ouvrages et collections rapportés de l'Égypte et de la Nubie,* 1829 ; many of the antiquities found by Rifaud are in the Drovetti Coll. at Turin, but others are dispersed in many museums ; he sometimes carved his name on the statues he found, and the date, e.g. three at Turin and one at Munich ; he died about 1845.

Irby, 5 ; Hartleben, *Champollion,* ii, 192, 414, 426 ; Devéria, *Mem. et Fragm.* i, 276–9 ; *Carré,* i, 172, 197, 223, 240 ; *Richardson,* ii, 92 ("Ripaud") ; *Sherer,* 81, 84, 89, 91, 113 ; *Hilmy,* ii, 173.

RIPAULT, Louis Madelène (1775–1823)

French antiquary ; a member of Napoleon's Commission in Egypt ; afterwards librarian to the Imperial Palace ; took part in the Commission's expedition to Upper Egypt and pub. reports on the monuments.

Carré, i, 147, 148, 152 ; *Hartleben,* i, passim (see index) ; *Hilmy,* ii, 174.

RIQUET, Adolphe de—*See* CARAMAN

ROBERTS, David (1796–1864)

Artist ; born Stockbridge, Edinburgh, 24 Oct. 1796 ; apprenticed to a house-painter ; he began his art as a scene-painter ; came to London, 1822, and began to exhibit in R.A. and Brit. Inst., 1826 ; travelled in the East, 1838–9 ; A.R.A., 1838 ; R.A., 1841 ; his eastern drawings were lithographed and pub. in a series of volumes : *Egypt and Nubia,* 3 vols. 1846–9, *The Holy Land, Syria, Egypt and Nubia,* 1842–9, with text by the Rev. George Croly ; another ed. with 250 plates, 1855 ; his remaining works were sold at Christie's, 13 May 1865 (five days' sale, 1040 lots) and his library 20 May (305 lots) ; died in London, 25 Nov. 1864.

Life, by James Ballantine, 1866 ; *DNB.* 48, 376 ; *Hilmy,* ii, 176.

ROBIOU DE LA TRÉHONNAIS, Félix Marie Louis Jean (1818–1894)

Commonly called Félix Robiou ; French classical scholar and orientalist ; born Rennes, 10 Oct. 1818 ; Asst. Director of Ancient History, École des Hautes Études, 1871, resigned 1874 ; wrote much on Egyptian and Greek chronology, religion and history ; contributed the text to F. Lenormant's *Chefs-d'oeuvre de l'Art Antique*, Paris, 1867 ; died 30 Jan. 1894.

Vapereau, 1349 ; *Hilmy*, ii, 177 ; *Annuaire, Éc. Hautes Études*, 1897, 5, 54.

ROCHEMONTEIX, (*Marquis de*) **Maxence du Chalvet** (1849–1891)

French Egyptologist ; born Clermont-Ferrand, 5 Feb. 1849 ; educ. at the Lycées St. Louis, Louis-le-Grand and d'Alger ; learned Arabic and various African dialects including Berber and Nubian and studied Egyptology ; began life in a bank, but his linguistic tastes made him seek employment in Egypt ; sent to Egypt by the Ministre d'Instruction Publique in 1875 and joined Mariette ; visited many sites and settled at Edfu on his second journey, 1877 ; returned to Egypt in 1879 with a civil appointment (Sous-Administrateur de la Commission des Domaines de l'État) and retired in 1885 ; became a pupil of Maspero at the Coll. de France and began the publication of the Temple of Edfu which was continued by Chassinat after his death ; his works were collected by Maspero in the *Bibl. Ég.* in 1892 ; died in Paris, 30 Dec. 1891.

Bibl. Ég. 3, pp. xi–xxxix (Biogr. and Portr.) ; *Wilbour*, pl. facing p. 240 (Portr.).

ROCHETTE, Désiré Raoul (1789–1854)

French archaeologist ; Membre de l'Institut, author of *Hist. des Colonies Grecques*, 1813 and translator of Baroness Minutoli's *Souvenirs de l'Égypte*, 1826 ; an opponent of Champollion's claims and sided with Quatremère and Jomard against Silvestre de Sacy and the Duc de Blacas.

Rev. Arch. 3, 118, 194 ; *Champollion*, i, 45, 129, 324 ; ii, 250 ; *Hilmy*, ii, 151.

ROGERS, (*Bey*) **Edward Thomas** (1831–1884)

Consular official ; born 1831 ; entered Consular Service 1848 as British Consul in Jerusalem ; Vice-Consul at Caiffa, 1853–7 ; V.-C. at Beyrout, 1857 ; engaged in several special missions to the East, 1857–61 ; Consul at Damascus, 1861–7 ; Acting Consul-General in Syria, 1867–8 ; Consul at Cairo, 1868–74 ; in 1874 the Cairo consulate was abolished, and Rogers returned to England, acting for a short time as agent for the Eg. Govt., after which he returned to Egypt and was appointed Minister of Public Instruction ; he was interested in oriental art and a collector of antiquities and Mohammedan coins ; contributed to *Academy, Art Journal* and *Bull. Inst. Eg.* ; his name is associated with the " Tablette Rogers," a hieratic text of Dyn. XXI from the cache of Royal Mummies, pub. by Maspero, *Rec. Trav.* 2, 13–18, and afterwards acquired by the Louvre ; died in Cairo, 10 June 1884.

Academy, 14 and 28 June, 1884 ; *Athenaeum*, 14 June and 22 Sept. 1884 ; *Hilmy*, ii, 179.

ROLLIN, Claude Camille (1813–1883)

Dealer in coins, gems and antiquities in Paris ; took into partnership Félix Feuardent and in 1867 opened a branch in London, 27 Haymarket, later removed to 10 Bloomsbury Street, under the style Rollin & Feuardent ; on the death of Rollin, the firm continued under F. Feuardent and became Feuardent Frères in Rue Louvois, Paris, until the business ceased about 1945 ; the firm had a high reputation and supplied coins and antiquities to the leading museums ; in 1872 Rollin & Feuardent sold to the Louvre a gold collar of Osorkon II for fcs. 25,000 ; Rollin's name is attached to papyri in the B.M. (10257, 10371) and to several in the Bibl. Nat., Paris, viz. a portion of the Harîm Conspiracy texts (part of Pap. Lee, B.N. 195), a group of account papyri of the XIX Dyn., pub. by Pleyte and by Spiegelberg (B.N. 203–213) ; he died in Paris, 1883.

E. Babelon, *Traité des Monnaies gr. et rom.* pt. i, t. i, Paris, 1901 ; *Rev. de l'Art*, 43, 170.

ROMER, Isabella Frances (*d.* 1852)

Miscellaneous writer ; y. d. Major-Gen. Robert Frank Romer, Royal Artillery ; married Major William Medows Hamerton of the 67th Foot and soon after separated ; travelled in the East and pub. *A Pilgrimage to the Temples and Tombs of Egypt, Nubia and Palestine*, 2 vols., 1846, 2nd ed. 1847 ; died in London, 27 April 1852.

DNB. 49, 184 ; *Hilmy*, ii, 181.

ROMIEU, Auguste (*fl.* 1866–1902)

French scientist and mathematician ; Professor of Hydrography at the Collège de Agde (Hérault) ; a disciple of Chabas ; wrote on Eg. astronomy and calendar in *Rec. Trav.* and *ZÄS*, and pub. a memoir on the calendar, 1902.

Chabas, 58 ; *Hilmy*, ii, 181.

ROSELLINI, Niccolo Francesco Ippolito Baldessare (1800–1843)

Italian Egyptologist, a native of Pisa ; born 1800 ; studied under Mezzofanti at Bologna ; Professor of Oriental Languages, Pisa, 1824 ; explored Egypt as head of the Tuscan delegation in Champollion's mission to Egypt, 1828–9 ; on his return he published his materials in the great *Monumenti dell' Egitto et della Nubia*, 1832–40 ; his papers and journals are in the Library of Pisa University ; died 1843.

G. Gabrieli : *Ippolito Rosellini e il suo giornale*, etc. Rome, 1925 ; *Hartleben*, passim ; *Champollion*, ii, passim ; *Aegyptus*, 5, 65 ; *Hilmy*, ii, 182.

ROSIGNANI, —— (*fl.* 1818–1824)

Piedmontese adventurer in Egypt ; agent for Drovetti at Thebes where he worked with Antonio Lebolo (q.v.) and joined him in hostility to Belzoni, who always calls him " the renegade "; nothing is known of his history.

Belzoni, i, 385 ; ii, 129, 132, 235, 237 ; *Salt*, ii, 23.

ROS(S)ETTI, Carlo (1736–1820)

Venetian merchant who came to Egypt in the time of Ali Bey ; he gained the confidence of Murad-Bey whom he warned of Napoleon's impending invasion of Egypt ; Consul-General in Egypt for Austria and other powers ; Napoleon employed him in various missions during the French occupation ; the Rosetti (or Rossetti) who received Champollion in 1828 was his son, and was Consul for Tuscany ; the elder R. died, blind and paralysed, in his palace at Bulak in 1820.

G. Guimard, *Les Reformes en Égypte*, Cairo, 1936, 65 *n.* ; Hamilton, *Ægyptiaca*, 343 ; *Legh*, 131, 132 ; *Athanasi*, 15 ; *Champollion*, ii, 21, 22, 24, 36, 50, 62, 64 ; *Clot-Bey*, ii, 174.

ROSSI, Francesco (1827–1912)

Italian Egyptologist ; born Turin, 18 May 1827 ; Assistant in Turin Museum, 1865 ; Vice-director, 1867 ; Professor extraordinary of Egyptology, Turin, 1876–7 ; Professor in ordinary, 1906–9 ; collaborated with Willem Pleyte in *Les Papyrus de Turin*, 1869–76, for which he executed the facsimiles ; died Turin, 11 Jan. 1912.

Enc. It. 30, 142 ; *Hilmy*, ii, 194.

ROTH, Henry Ling (1855–1925)

A man of versatile interests ; made several valuable communications to *JAI.*, and studied ancient textiles ; pub. a handbook on ancient Eg. and Greek looms for the Bankfield Museum, Halifax, of which he was Curator, and with G. M. Crowfoot contributed an article on the same subject to *Anc. Eg.* (1921, 97–101).

JEA. 11, 333 ; *Man*, 1925, 97 (Portr. and Bibl.).

ROUELLE, Guillaume François (1703–1770)

French chemist ; began life as an apothecary ; appointed Demonstrator in Chemistry, Jardin du Roi, Paris, 1742 where Lavoisier was one of his pupils ; his most important work was that on the *salts* which form the basis of the modern chemical acceptation of that term ; in 1750 he communicated to the Acad. des Sciences a memoir on Egyptian embalming which contains some good observations and is very creditable for its period.

Mem. Inst. Eg. 13, 38 ; *Hilmy*, ii, 195.

ROUSSEL, —— (*fl.* 1814–1819)

French Consul-General in Egypt, 1814–9 ; he held office in the interval between the two periods of the consulship of Drovetti, and was much under his influence.

Belzoni, ii, 235, 236 ; *Cailliaud*, 65.

ROUSSET, (*Bey*) **——** (*fl.* 1845–1868)

French accountancy expert who was sent to Egypt about 1845 to audit the Egyptian Government accounts and finances ; while he was in Egypt, he formed a collection of antiquities which was sold in Paris, 15 July 1868 (1208 lots) ; some of these antiquities were acquired by the Louvre.

Inf. by R. Hill ; *Rev. de l'Art*, 43, 169.

RUFFER, (*Sir*) **Marc Armand** (1859–1917)

Pathologist ; son of Baron Alphonse de Ruffer ; born 1859 ; educ. Brasenose Coll. Oxon., Univ. Coll. London ; President, Sanitary and

Quarantine Council of Egypt ; M.A. ; M.D. ; C.M.G. ; Professor of Bacteriology, Cairo Medical School ; investigated traces of ancient disease in Eg. mummies and skeletons and pub. a number of papers thereon which were collected after his death as *Studies in the Palaeopathology of Egypt*, edited by Roy L. Moodie, Chicago, 1921 ; died 2 May 1917.

WWW. ii, 915.

RÜPPELL, Wilhelm Peter Eduard Simon (1794–1884)

German zoologist and traveller ; he travelled in Egypt, Nubia and Abyssinia and made great contributions to the knowledge of the fauna of those regions ; an account of his travels was pub. in 1829, and a large atlas of plates, 1826–31 ; in his honour the Ruppell-stiftung zur Forderung wissenschaftlicher Reisen was founded at Frankfurt-a-M. in 1871.

Irby, 38, 39, 41, 48 ; *Westcar Diary*, 174 ; *Hilmy*, ii, 200.

RUSTAFJAELL, Robert de (*d.* 1943)

Collector of Egyptian antiquities ; lived for some time in Egypt studying principally predynastic sites and pub. *Palaeolithic Vessels of Egypt*, London, 1907, *The Light of Egypt*, 1909 ; he lived for some years before his death in America and at one period changed his name to Col. Prince Roman Orbeliani ; his collections were dispersed in three sales : Sotheby's, 19 Dec. 1907 (three days), Sotheby's, 20 Jan. 1913 (five days, 1051 lots), and New York, 29 Nov. 1915 (3 days) ; the first sale produced £1,843 and the second, £2,748 ; died 10 Feb. 1943.

Inf. by R. Geogr. Soc.

RYLANDS, William Harry (1847–1922)

Archaeologist ; born Warrington, 20 Dec. 1847 ; M.R.A.S. ; F.S.A. ; Secretary of Soc. Bibl. Arch. in succession to W. R. Cooper, 1878–98 ; contributed a few papers on Egyptian subjects to the Society's *Proceedings*, and a memoir and bibliography of Renouf ; also interested in Heraldry and edited some of the Visitation volumes for the Harleian Society ; died 1922.

JEA. 9, 223 ; *JRAS.* 1922, 637 ; *PEFQS.* 1923, 1.

SABATIER, Raymond Gabriel Baptiste (1810–1879)

French diplomatist ; born Béziers (Hérault) 1810 ; Capitaine, Corps d'État Major ; travelled in the East including Egypt and Nubia, 1840–1 ; sent on a mission to the Morea, 1836 ; Consul-General for France in Egypt, 1852 ; minister plenipotentiary, 1862 ; resigned 1864 ; Comm. Légion d'Honneur, 1854 ; had permission from the Viceroy to excavate in Egypt and amassed a large coll. of antiquities for which a special gallery was constructed in his house, 35 Avenue Hoche, Paris ; his coll. sold at Hôtel Drouot, Paris, 31 Mar.–4 Apl. 1890 (615 lots) ; many items were acquired for the Museum at Copenhagen, but some went elsewhere (e.g. the stela B.M. 656) ; a papyrus, not in the sale, was recently acquired by the Louvre from his grandson ; died in Paris, 12 Jan. 1879.

Inf. by Comte de Jumilhac (grandson) ; *Carré*, i, 43 ; *Bibl. Ég.* 18, p. xlix.

ST. ASAPH, Viscount—*See* ASHBURNHAM

SAINT-FERRIOL, (*Comte de*) **Jacques Louis Xavier** (1814–1877)

Eldest son of Joseph Armand Gaspard Vincent de Paule; born Château de Clelles (Isère), 9 May 1814; educ. at Freiburg and Paris; inherited the Château d'Uriage from the Marquise de Gautheron, 1828; travelled in Germany and Russia, 1839–40; travelled in Egypt and Nubia, 1841–2 and made a choice collection of antiquities, of which the famous Stela of Kûban is the most important; this collection, long in the Château d'Uriage, is now mainly in the Museum of Grenoble, to which it was presented in 1916; the count left a MS. journal of his voyage to Egypt; died suddenly at Evian (Haute-Savoie), 26 Apl. 1877 and buried at St. Martin d'Uriage.

P. Tresson, *Bull. Acad. Delphinale*, Grenoble, 1928; *Carré*, i, 321; *Rev. Ég.* N.S. i, 1.

ST. JOHN, Bayle (1822–1859)

Son of next, born 1822; travelled in Egypt in 1846 and 1851; pub. *Adventures in the Lybian Desert and the Oasis of Jupiter Ammon*, 1849, new ed., 1853; also wrote works on modern Egypt.

DNB. 50, 128; *Hilmy*, ii, 204; Maspero, *Ét. de Myth.* vi, 265.

ST. JOHN, James Augustus (1801–1875)

Father of last; assisted James Silk Buckingham in the editorship of the *Oriental Herald*, 1824; travelled extensively in Egypt and Nubia, mostly on foot, 1832–3; pub. *Egypt and Mohammed Ali*, 2 vols., 1834; *Egypt and Nubia*, N.D.; wrote the letterpress of Prisse's *Oriental Album*, 1848.

DNB. 50, 145; *Hilmy*, ii, 204; *Vyse*, ii, 310.

SALLIER, François (*d.* 1831)

Revenue official of Aix-en-Provence, of which he was Mayor in 1802 and 1806; rendered many important public services to his native town; owned a collection of antiquities, now in the Museum of Aix, and five papyri, four of which, known as Sallier I–IV, are historic and were first studied by Champollion who twice visited Sallier, in July 1828 and Jan. 1830, in order to inspect them; the papyri were purchased by the B.M. in 1839 (B.M. 10181–2, 10184–5 and a demotic pap. 10226); Sallier died at Aix, 20 Feb. 1831.

JEA. 35, 160.

SALT, Henry (1780–1827)

British Consul-General in Egypt, and collector of antiquities; born Lichfield, 14 June 1780; trained as a portrait-painter and went to London in 1797 as a pupil of Joseph Farrington, R.A., and afterwards of John Hoppner, R.A.; in 1802 accompanied George Annesley, Visct. Valentia, as secretary and draughtsman, on a long tour in the East, visiting India, Ceylon and Abyssinia and Egypt, and returned 1806; made many drawings to illustrate Lord V.'s *Voyages and Travels*, 1809; sent by Govt. on a mission to Abyssinia, 1809–11 and pub. *Voyage to Abyssinia*, 1814; in 1815 appointed to succeed

Missett as Consul-General in Egypt and arrived there in 1816 ; did much excavating in Egypt to procure antiquities for the B.M. ; with Belzoni and Burckhardt removed colossal bust of Ramesses II from Thebes and presented it to B.M., 1817 ; employed Belzoni at Thebes and financed his explorations in Nubia, and those of Caviglia at the Pyramids ; in 1819, d'Athanasi excavated at Thebes under his direction ; in 1818, he sent a large collection of antiquities to the B.M., but the Trustees objected to the price demanded, and after protracted delay, they gave £2,000 (less than the cost of excavation and transport) for the collection, but rejected the finest piece—the sarcophagus of Sety I—which was bought by Sir John Soane ; Salt's second collection, formed 1819–24, was reported upon by Champollion and bought by the French Govt. ; his third collection was sold at Sotheby's in a nine days' sale in 1835 and realized £7,168 : many objects were bought by the B.M. ; he published an essay on Young's and Champollion's systems of decipherment, 1825 ; F.R.S. 1812, F.L.S. ; died Alexandria, 30 Oct. 1827.

Biogr. by J. J. Halls, 2 vols. 1834 (Portr.) ; *DNB*. 50, 212 ; *GM*. 1835, ii, 187 ; *Hilmy*, ii, 208 ; references to Salt, many of them important, abound in the Diaries and books of travel of his period.

SALVOLINI, François Pellegrin Gaspard (1809–1838)

Italian orientalist ; born Faenza, 9 Mar. 1809 ; studied oriental languages at Bologna ; went to Paris in 1830 as a pupil of Champollion ; visited Leiden to copy papyri, 1834 ; after Champollion's death certain important MSS. of his were found to be missing, and it was eventually proved that Salvolini had stolen them, and after his benefactor's death, published the discoveries they contained as his own ; a good summary of this discreditable episode will be found in the Introduction to Budge's *Eg. Hieroglyphic Dictionary* (1920), pp. xxii–xxv ; Salvolini died in Paris, 24 Feb. 1838.

Encyc. It. 30, 589 ; *Hartleben*, see index ; *Hilmy*, ii, 209

SAMS, Joseph (1784–1860)

Bookseller and dealer in antiquities ; born Somerton, Somerset, 1784 ; settled in Darlington where he opened a school, but soon closed it and opened a bookseller's shop ; travelled in Egypt and Palestine, 1832–3 and brought back a valuable collection of antiquities, many of which were purchased by the B.M. with a Parliamentary grant of £2,500 in 1834 : among these were many papyri and the Coffin of Amamu (B.M. 6654) ; his remaining collections were exhibited in London and a catalogue issued ; many important articles were bought by Joseph Mayer of Liverpool ; Sams also dealt largely in MSS., and many famous specimens passed through his hands, including many Coptic, bought by the B.M. ; his books, pictures, tapestries and other antiquities were sold at Puttick & Simpson's in two sales, 5 Nov. 1860 and 18 Feb. 1861 ; died at Darlington, 18 Mar. 1860.

DNB. 50, 236 ; *GM*. 1833, 312 ; Edwards, *Lives of the Founders*, 34 ; *Athanasi*, 127 ; *Hilmy*, ii, 209.

SAN QUINTINO—*See* CORDERO DI SAN QUINTINO

SANTONI, Pietro (*fl.* 1820–30)

Banker of Leghorn ; brother-in-law of Henry Salt ; he negotiated the sale of Salt's second collection to the French Govt., in 1825 ; met Champollion in Alexandria in 1828.

Salt, ii, 250, etc. ; *Champollion*, i, 239 and often ; ii, 22, 37.

SAULCY, Louis Frédéric Joseph Caignart de (1807–1880)

French archaeologist and numismatist ; born Lille, 1807 ; Keeper of the Artillery Museum, Paris, 1840 ; Senator, 1854 ; Membre de l'Acad. ; wrote many important numismatic works, also wrote on the Egyptian language, especially demotic ; travelled in Egypt in 1863 and 1869, the MS. journal of these voyages is in the library of the Inst. Fr. (2259–63) ; died Paris, 1880.

Larousse, XXth cent., 6, 206 ; Brugsch, *Mein Leben*, 54, 88, 91 ; *Hilmy*, i, 180.

SAULNIER, Sebastien Louis (1790–1835)

French archaeologist ; born Nancy, 29 Jan. 1790 ; held several prefectures, including that of Mayenne ; financed explorations in Egypt and imported antiquities ; sent Lelorrain to take down and bring to Paris the Circular Zodiac of Dendereh, now in Paris ; he hoped his Eg. collections would be acquired for the Louvre, but at the sale in Paris in 1839, most of them went to Berlin ; besides an account of the expedition of Lelorrain, he pub. works on roads and railways ; died at Orleans, 23 Oct. 1835.

Quérard, viii, 467 ; *Hartleben*, i, 395, 547 ; ii, 473 ; *Champollion*, i, 6, 11 ; ii, 155 ; *Hilmy*, ii, 213.

SAUVAJOL, Henri (*d.* 1860)

Commissariat official in Algeria ; he communicated to Devéria some Egyptian antiquities discovered in Algeria ; died 1860.

Devéria, *Mem. et Fragm.* i, 143.

SAYCE, (*Rev.*) Archibald Henry (1845–1933)

Assyriologist, but intimately connected with Egypt ; born Shirehampton, 25 Sept. 1845 ; educ. Grosvenor Coll., Bath and Queen's Coll. Oxon. ; Professor of Assyriology, Oxford, 1891–1919 ; D.Litt. ; LL.D. ; D.D. ; Hon. F.B.A. ; member of O.T. Revision Company, 1874–84 ; Hibbert Lecturer, 1887 ; Gifford Lecturer, 1900–2 ; Rhind Lecturer, 1906 ; Huxley Lecturer, 1931 ; travelled extensively and spent many winters in Egypt copying inscriptions, etc. ; pub. many works on the Assyrians, Egyptians, Hittites and other ancient nations, and his *Reminiscences*, 1923 ; died 4 Feb. 1933.

WWW. iii, 1201 ; Autobiogr., *Reminiscences*, 1923 (Portr.) ; *Budge R & P*, 185 (Portr.) ; *JEA*. 19, 65 ; *DNB* 1931–40, 786.

SCHACK-SCHACKENBORG, (*Graf*) Hans (1853–1905)

German Egyptologist ; born 12 Dec. 1853 ; the son of a large landowner, he took over the management of his paternal estates at the age of 21 ; educ. Dresden and Göttingen ; he devoted all his leisure to Egyptology in which he was self-taught ; he was not a mere amateur, but all his work was thorough and scholarly ; his first publications date from 1883, and he devoted special attention to the Pyramid Texts of which he co-ordinated and numbered the sections (*ZÄS*. 42, 87) ; he served on the Wörterbuch Commission from 1898, and collated many mathematical and astronomical texts, as well as the mythological texts in the Tombs of the Kings ; in later years, he was confined by a long illness, but continued his work to the end ; died 28 Jan. 1905.

ZÄS. 42, 87 ; E.E.F. *Arch. Report,* 1905–6, 51.

SCHARFF, Alexander (1892–1950)

German Egyptologist ; born Frankfort, 26 Feb. 1892 ; educ. Halle and Berlin ; Ph.D. ; Asst. Professor of Egyptology at Munich, 1923 ; Professor, 1932–50 ; author of a number of books and contributions to *ZÄS* and other journals ; died 11 Nov. 1950.

Kürschner, 1950, 1759.

SCHEIL, (*Père*) **Jean Vincent** (1858–1940)

French Assyriologist ; born Königsmacker, Lorraine, 10 June 1858 ; studied Egyptology in Paris under Maspero ; joined the Mission Archéologique at Cairo, 1883 ; employed chiefly in copying Theban Tombs, some of which he pub. in *Mem. Miss, Arch.* t. 5 ; he then concentrated on Assyriology, became eminent in that science, in which he spent the rest of his life ; died in Paris, 21 Sept. 1940.

Rev. d'Assyr. 37, 81 ; *Orientalia,* N.S. 11, 80 (Bibl.) ; *Archiv f. Orientforschung,* 13, 353 ; *Budge R & P,* 215 (Portr.).

SCHIAPARELLI, Ernesto (1856–1928)

Italian Egyptologist ; son of the historian Luigi S., and cousin of the astronomer, Giovanni S. ; born 1856 ; studied Egyptology in Paris under Maspero, 1875–80 ; was for many years director of the Turin Museum, and was in charge of the Italian expedition in Egypt, 1903–20 ; excavated at Kau el-Kebir, Heliopolis, Assûan and the Valley of the Queens at Thebes ; he was engaged in preparing the reports of these excavations, of which two vols. appeared up to 1927 ; a senator of the National Parliament and an ardent patriot ; of his earlier works, the best known is his *Libro dei Funerali,* 3 vols., 1881–90 ; died 14 Feb. 1928.

Ægyptus, 8, 337 ; *Hilmy,* ii, 218.

SCHMIDT, Carl (1868–1938)

German Coptic scholar ; born Hagenow, Mecklenburg, 26 Aug. 1868 ; studied at Leipsic and Berlin, 1887–1894 ; Privat-docent, Berlin, 1889 ; Professor-extraordinary, 1909 ; Hon. Professor, 1921 ; full Professor, 1928 ; retired 1935 ; he edited and published many important Coptic texts, and in 1930 discovered the famous Manichaean papyri ; visited Egypt several times to obtain Coptic MSS. ; some of his MSS. went to Louvain, and were edited by Lefort, but most of these were destroyed by enemy action ; the rest of his MSS.

were sold to Michigan Univ. after his death ; died in Egypt, 17 Apl. 1938.

Chron. 13, 335 ; *Bull. Soc. d'Arch. Copte*, 4, 195 ; *JEA*. 24, 135.

SCHMIDT, Valdemar (1836–1925)

Danish Egyptologist ; born Hammel, N. Jutland, 7 Jan. 1836 ; had a brilliant University career and was a great linguist, and knew, it is said, 28 languages ; in 1860–9 travelled in Greece, Western Asia and Egypt ; sec. to Arch. Congress at Copenhagen, 1869 ; Professor, Copenhagen Univ., 1869–1922 ; for many years Keeper of the Ny-Carlsberg Egyptian collection ; pub. many archaeological works, including a history of Assyria, 1872, and Egypt ; his last important work was an elaborate treatise on Eg. sarcophagi ; visited Egypt several times, and England almost annually ; died at Copenhagen, 26 June 1925.

JEA. 13, 80 (Portr. pl. ii) ; *L'Anthropologie*, 36, 168.

SCHOW, Niels Iversen (1754–1830)

Swedish scholar and archaeologist ; a pupil of C. G. Heyne ; Professor of Archaeology, Copenhagen Univ., 1805 ; Professor of Greek, 1813–27 ; a friend of Zoëga ; when on a visit to Rome he was given the first Greek papyrus from Egypt to edit, which he pub. as *Charta Papyracea Graecae scripta in Musei Borgiani Velitris*, etc., Rome, 1789.

Preisendanz, *Papyrusfunde und Papyrusforschung*, 1933, 72 ; *Chron.* 7, 324 ; *Hilmy*, ii, 222.

SCHWEINFURTH, Georg August (1836–1925)

German traveller and botanist ; of Russian origin, born Riga 29 Dec. 1836 ; educ. Univs. of Heidelberg, Munich and Berlin, 1856–62 ; specialized in botany and palaeontology ; explored shores of the Red Sea, Egypt, and the Sudan as far as Khartûm, 1863–6 ; explored interior of Africa 1869–71, when many important geographical and scientific discoveries were made, but his collections lost by fire ; explored the Libyan Desert with Rohlfs, 1873–4 ; settled in Cairo, 1875, and founded the Geographical Soc. there under the auspices of the Khedive ; between 1876 and 1888, explored the Arabian Desert and conducted botanical and geological researches in the Fayûm and the Nile Valley and pub. many valuable papers thereon ; removed to Berlin, 1889, died 19 Sept. 1925.

Bull. Soc. Geogr. Eg. 14, 65 (Portr.) ; 72 (Bibl.) ; 129 ; 135 ; 139 ; *Ægyptus*, 6, 251 ; *OLZ*. 29, 1 ; *JEA*. 12, 304 ; *Rev. Arch.* 23, 124 ; *Hilmy*, ii, 224.

SCOLES, Joseph John (1798–1863)

Architect ; born London, 27 June 1798 ; studied in Italy and Egypt with Bonomi ; practised his profession in London ; F.R.I.B.A., 1835 ; pub. architectural works ; he with Henry Parke accompanied Henry Westcar and Frederic Catherwood up the Nile as far as Wady Halfa, and afterwards with Parke visited the Levant ; died in London, 29 Dec. 1863.

DNB. 51, 3 ; *Westcar Diary*, 27 et passim ; *Hilmy*, ii, 225.

SENKOWSKI, Joseph (*fl.* 1819–1826)

Polish traveller ; visited Egypt and Nubia in 1819 ; pub. an account of his travels in *Petersburger Zeitung,* 1822 ; obtained in Egypt a funerary papyrus which was presented to the Museum of Cracow and pub. by the Petersburg Acad. in 1826.

Hartleben, ii, 111 ; *Hilmy,* ii, 228.

SETHE, Kurt Heinrich (1869–1934)

German Egyptologist ; born Berlin, 30 June 1869 ; educ. Berlin University ; Ph.D. ; Member of the British Acad. ; studied Egyptology under Erman ; Professor of Egyptology at Göttingen and afterwards at Berlin in succession to Erman ; a great scholar and a voluminous writer : of his many philological works, his *Verbum* (3 vols. 1899–1902) is the most important ; he collated and re-edited the Pyramid Texts, first pub. by Maspero, a work in several volumes the first of which appeared in 1908 ; he founded and edited the *Untersuchungen zur Geschichte und Altertumskunde Aegyptens* to which he made many important contributions from 1896 onwards ; in 1904–5 he visited Egypt and copied and collated a large number of historical texts which he pub., 1905–9, as *Urkunden der 18. Dynastie* ; Sethe's contributions to all periods of Egyptian history and philology from the earliest to Roman times are enormous, and appeared in *ZÄS* and other journals and as separate publications ; died in Berlin, 6 July 1934.

JEA. 20, 43 ; *ZÄS.* 70, 132 (Portr.) ; *Chron.* 10, 77.

SEYFFARTH, Gustav (1796–1885)

German archaeologist ; born Uebigau, 13 July 1796 ; entered Liepsic Univ. 1815 and in 1825 appointed to an archaeological chair ; resigned, 1854 and emigrated to America, where he held a professorship at Concordia Coll., St. Louis ; promulgated a fantastic system of Egyptian decipherment and attacked Champollion's system in a number of curious but worthless publications ; the arrangement of the fragments of the canon of Kings at Turin is mainly due to him ; his papers are now in the Brooklyn Museum ; died 1885.

ZDMG, 41, 193 ; Knortz, *Gustav Seyffarth : eine biogr. Skizze,* N.Y., 1886 ; *Hartleben,* passim ; Renouf, *Life-Work,* i, 1–80 (Bibl.) ; *Hilmy,* ii, 229 ; *Champollion,* i, 119 and often.

SEYMOUR, Henry Danby (*d.* 1878)

Author and politician, of 39 Upper Grosvenor Square, London ; M.P. for Poole ; previously Under-Sec. of State for India ; pub. *Russia and the Black Sea,* 1855 ; translated Brugsch's History under the title *Egypt under the Pharaohs,* 2 vols., 1879, but died just before completing it ; in 1869 presented to B.M. four painted plaster slabs from Theban tombs (919–922) which were pub. by Budge, *Wall Decorations of Egyptian Tombs,* B.M., 1914, 14–15 ; a foundation-member of Soc. Biblical Arch. ; died 1878.

SHARPE, Samuel (1799–1881)

Banker and antiquary ; born 8 Mar. 1799 ; entered the banking-house of Samuel & Henry Rogers, 1814 ; partner, 1821–61 ; much interested in ancient history and Egyptology ; pub. many popular works on Egypt, including *History* (1852 and later editions) ; his *Egyptian Inscriptions* (series 1 and 2) was one of the first large bodies of Eg. texts to be produced in England and was of great service to students ; pub. a Hebrew Grammar and a new translation of the Bible ; died 28 July 1881.

Life by P. W. Clayden, 1883 ; *DNB*. 51, 425 ; *Hilmy*, ii, 231.

SHELLEY, George Ernest (1840–1910)

Ornithologist ; y. s. Sir Timothy Shelley ; born 1840 ; Capt. Grenadier Guards ; made four expeditions to Egypt and in 1870 pub. his standard work, *The Birds of Egypt*, which has been of the utmost value to Egyptologists in determining the species represented on the monuments ; African birds being his special study, he visited Gold Coast, Natal, etc. ; his large collections are now in the B.M. (Nat. Hist.) ; died 29 Nov. 1910.

Ibis, 9th ser. 5, 369 ; *Hist. Coll. B.M. Nat. Hist.* ii, 484.

SHERER, Moyle (1789–1869)

Army officer and traveller ; Major in the 34th Foot (Cumberland) ; served in the Peninsula War and made a prisoner at Puerta de Mayer, 1813 ; afterwards went to India and returned by the overland route ; pub. *Sketches in India*, 1821 ; *Scenes and Impressions of Egypt and Italy*, 1824 (2nd ed. 1825), (selections from both these works republished in one vol., 1825), and other works ; died at Southampton, 18 Feb. 1869.

DNB. 52, 73 ; *Hilmy*, ii, 233.

SHORTER, Alan Wynn (1905–1938)

Born London, 8 June 1905 ; educ. St. Paul's School ; Queen's Coll. Oxon. ; joined the E.E.S. expedition to Armant and Amarna, 1928 ; Asst. in the Eg. Dept. B.M., 1929–38 ; pub. several popular books on Egyptian life and mythology and was engaged in a catalogue of the B.M. papyri of the Book of the Dead, one part of which was completed ; died 31 May 1938.

JEA. 24, 211.

SICARD, (*Père*) **Claude** (1677–1726)

French Jesuit ; professor at Lyons for a time, then went as a missionary to Syria ; in 1707 he transferred to Cairo where he remained for the rest of his life ; made extended journeys to Upper Egypt, 1708, 1712, 1720 and 1731 ; his principal object was to make converts amongst the Copts, but was ordered also by the Regent, Philippe of Orleans, to survey the ancient monuments and to make plans and drawings of them ; he was the first European traveller to reach Assuan and to describe Philae, Elephantine and Kom Ombo ; his papers were mostly lost, a matter for great regret as he shows himself, in such papers as have survived, to be an excellent observer ; he has left a complete list of all the monuments and sites he explored, both Christian and pagan ; died of plague in Cairo, 1726.

Carré, i, 67–70 ; Bibl. 75 ; *Hilmy*, ii, 233.

SICKLER, Friedrich Karl Ludwig (*fl.* 1820–1832)

German antiquary; wrote on the hieroglyphs in the astronomical texts at Dendereh and on mummy-cases in the Hammer collection, a work on Egyptian and Ethiopian hieroglyphic writing, etc.; these appeared between 1820 and 1832.

BIFAO, 5, 86; *Hilmy*, ii, 234.

SILVESTRE DE SACY, (*Baron*) **Antoine Isaac** (1758–1838)

French orientalist; born Paris, 21 Sept. 1758; began life as a civil servant, studying oriental languages in his spare time; Professor of Arabic at the École des Études Orientales, 1795, to which Persian was afterwards added; he gave great stimulus to Arabic studies by his *Grammaire Arabe*, 1810, and *Chrestomathie*, 1806; Sec. Perpetuel, Acad. des Inscr. (in succession to Dacier), from 1832; founded with Rémusat the Société Asiatique; pub. many works in various oriental languages, including the celebrated edition of Abd-Allatif, *Relation sur l'Égypte*; played a prominent part in the controversies arising out of Champollion's decipherment of hieroglyphics; died 21 Feb. 1838.

EB. ed. xi, 25, 119; *Hartleben* (see index); Renouf, *Life-Work*, i, 44, 88, 151, 167–9; *Hilmy*, ii, 235.

SIMONIDES, Constantine (1824–1867)

Forger of papyri and manuscripts; he himself gave the date of his birth as 11 Nov. 1824, but subsequently "emended" this to 5 Nov. 1820 so as to justify his claim that he wrote the *Codex Sinaiticus* in 1839; certain papyri belonging to Joseph Mayer being suspect, a committee of the R. Soc. Literature investigated the matter, and C. W. Goodwin detected the forgery; in 1856 the Berlin Acad. bought from S. on the advice of Lepsius a manuscript of the lost work of Uranius; this was afterwards found to be a forgery, and S. was arrested on the instigation of Lepsius who obtained repayment of the sum he had advanced; after a short detention in Berlin, S. was released and came to England; another forged MS., the *Persae* of Aeschylus, reached Leipsic by way of Egypt; this was exposed by Ritschl; S. himself declared that the *Codex Sinaiticus* was a forgery made by himself in 1839, an absurdity exposed by Henry Bradshaw; S. was nevertheless a clever man: he pub. in London in 1860 a dissertation, written in Greek, on hieroglyphic writing, a work on Horus of Nilopolis, 1863, and a translation of the *Periplus of Hanno*, 1864; he died in Alexandria, in 1867.

Charles Stewart, *Biogr. Memoir of Constantine Simonides*, London, 1859; J. A. Farrer, *Literary Forgeries*, 34–66; Ebers, *Richard Lepsius* (transl. Underhill), 194–5, 335; *Report of the Council of the R.S.L. on some of the Mayer Papyri and a Palimpsest MS. of Uranius*, 1863; F. Ritschl, *Rhein. Mus.* 27, 114–126; H. Bradshaw, *Guardian*, 26 Jan. 1863; two collections of press-cuttings on S.'s career in England, B.M. Press-marks 1700 b. 4 and 11899 g. 42; *The Mount Sinai MS. of the Bible* (B.M. pamphlet) 4th ed. 1935, 11–15; Corresp. on the forged papyri, *B.M. Add. MS.* 34098; Corresp. on other forgeries, with some actual specimens of them, *Add. MS.* 42502; the forged MS. of *Persae*, *Add. MS.* 41478; *Hilmy*, ii, 237.

SKRINE, (*Rev.*) Vincent Eccles (1850–1929)

Born 24 Aug. 1850 ; C.C.C. Oxon. ; B.A., 1875 ; M.A., 1877 ; ordained 1875 ; Vicar of Itchen Stoke, Hants and finally Rector of Claverton, Bath, where he died in 1929 ; presented a collection of papyri to the Bodleian in 1913 ; some of these came from the great find of mummies cleared by Grébaut in 1891, and as they were obtained by the donor's brother at the time of the Battle of Tell el-Kebir, it proves that the site was being exploited by the natives for some years before they disclosed the secret.

Clergy Lists ; *JEA*. 4, 122 ; 5, 24.

SLICHTEGROLL, Adolf Heinrich Friedrich von (1764–1822)

German antiquary ; pub. a work on Egyptian, Greek and Roman divinities, 1792–8 and a work on the Rosetta Stone with German translation and 7 plates, Munich, 1818.

BIFAO. 5, 85 ; *Hilmy*, ii, 219.

SLOANE, Charles (*fl.* 1820–1838)

Consular official in Cairo ; Secretary and later Chancellor of the British Consulate in Egypt, 1824–38 ; discovered with Caviglia in 1820 the colossus of Ramesses II at Mit Rahineh ; joined with Salt, Vyse, Briggs and others in financing Caviglia's excavations.

Hay Diary, 1824, Nov. 28 and Dec. 3 ; *Bonomi Diary*, 1831, Nov. 27 ; *Westcar Diary*, 243, 264, 275, 280 ; *Lindsay*, 39 ; *F.O. Records*.

SMELT, (*Rev.*) Charles (1784–1831)

Born York, 1784 ; Ch. Ch. Coll., Oxon. ; B.A., 1806 ; M.A., 1808 ; student, 1802–12 ; Rector of Gedling, Notts., 1824–31 ; accompanied Thomas Legh to Egypt and Nubia, 1812–13 ; died 6 Dec. 1831.

Alum. Ox. ; *Legh*, 73, 110, 117 ; *Belzoni*, i, 122, 129.

SMITH, (*Sir*) Charles Holled (1846–1925)

Army officer ; born 12 Sept. 1846 ; educ. Shrewsbury School, entered Army, 1865 ; Capt., 1877 ; retired, Major-General, 1900 ; served in Zulu and Boer Wars, 1879–81, Egyptian War, 1882 and Nile Expedition, 1884–5 ; in the Sudan, 1885–6, Suakim, 1888, Tollar, 1891 ; Governor of Red Sea Littoral and Commandant at Suakim, 1888–92 ; K.C.M.G., 1892 ; excavated at Assuan, 1887–8 ; in 1887 he presented to the B.M. some important stelae and other sculptured monuments (1015, 1019, 1021–2, 1055, 1188–9) ; died 18 Mar. 1925.

WWW. ii, 970 ; *Budge N & T*. i, 94, 100, 132.

SMITH, Edwin (1822–1906)

American adventurer in Egypt ; born Connecticut, 1822 ; settled in Egypt in 1858 and resided at Luxor till 1876, carrying on the business of a money-lender and dealer in antiquities ; he acquired two important medical papyri in Jan. 1862, one of which he sold to Ebers and the other he retained until his death, when his daughter presented it to the N.Y. Historical Society, and it was published in a sumptuous edition by Breasted in 1930 ; Smith had considerable knowledge of hieroglyphic and hieratic writing and Naville stated that he used that knowledge to assist the natives to make forged antiquities, and according to Adams, he was a forger himself; he died in 1906.

Devéria, *Mem. et Fragm.* i, 358 ; Breasted, *Edwin Smith Surgical Papyrus*, 20 ; *Goodwin*, 110 ff. ; A. L. Adams, *Notes of a Naturalist in the Nile Valley*, 56–8.

SMITH, (*Sir*) **Grafton Elliot** (1871–1937)

Anatomist and anthropologist ; born Grafton, N.S.W., 15 Aug. 1871 ; educ. Universities of Sydney and Cambridge ; Fellow (later Hon. Fellow) St. John's Coll. ; Prof. of Anatomy, Cairo School of Medicine, 1900–1909 ; at Manchester 1909–19 ; at Univ. Coll., London, 1919–36 ; M.A. ; Litt.D. ; D.Sc. ; M.D. ; L.R.C.P. ; F.R.S. ; one of the foremost authorities on the brain and the evolution of man ; while in Egypt he examined the human remains and mummies found at many sites, and particularly those found in the Arch. Survey of Nubia ; from an examination of the Royal Mummies in the Cairo Museum and many others, he explained and defined the technique of embalming in Egypt and corrected many long-standing errors ; he enunciated the hypothesis that Egypt was the place of origin from which most of the customs and beliefs of mankind spread to all parts of the world, which provoked much controversy, but is now widely accepted ; his contributions to the study of mummification are of great value, and include the volume *The Royal Mummies*, of the Cairo *Cat. Gen.* ; died 1 Jan. 1937.

WWW. iii, 1253 ; *Life*, by W. R. Dawson, 1938 (Portr. and Bibl.) ; *Nature*, 9 Jan. 1937, 57 ; *BMJ.* same date, 99 ; *Lancet*, same date, 113.

SMYTH, Charles Piazzi (1819–1900)

Astronomer ; s. Admiral William Henry Smyth, F.R.S. ; born Naples, 3 Jan. 1819 ; did distinguished work as an astronomer ; Astronomer Royal of Scotland, and Professor of Astronomy, Edinburgh Univ., 1845 ; visited and surveyed the Great Pyramid, 1865 ; pub. *Our Inheritance in the Gt. Pyr.*, 1864 ; *Life and Work at the Gt. Pyr.*, 3 vols., 1867 ; he made quite fantastic deductions from his measurements, etc. and propounded a theory that the builders of the pyramid could never have conceived or acted upon ; F.R.S., 1854, but resigned 1874 on the society refusing to accept a paper by him on his interpretation of the design of the Gt. Pyramid; retired 1888, and died near Ripon, Yorks, 21 Feb. 1900.

DNB. Suppl. 3, 350 ; *Hilmy*, ii, 239.

SOCIN, Albert (1844–1899)

German orientalist ; born Basle, Oct. 1844 ; studied oriental languages under J. H. Petermann ; Professor at Tubingen Univ. ; pub. a Grammar of Classical Arabic in the *Porta Linguarum Orientalium* series, it was translated into English by the Rev. Dr. T. Stenhouse ; contributed the chapter on the religion of Islam to Baedeker's *Egypt* ; died in Leipsic, 24 June 1899.

Larousse, 20th Cent. 6, 386.

SOLDI-COLBERT DE BEAULIEU, Émile (1846–1897+)

French sculptor ; born Paris, May 1846 ; studied Egyptology under Maspero and Guieysse at the École des Hautes Études, Paris, 1895–7 ; pub. works on Egyptian and oriental art and sculpture, 1874–83 ; not traced after 1897.

Annuaire École des H.E., 1897 ; *Hilmy*, ii, 244.

SONNINI DE MANONCOUR, Charles Nicolas Sigisbert (1751–1812)

French naturalist and traveller ; born Lunéville, Lorraine, 1751 ; trained as a lawyer at Nancy, but soon abandoned law and entered the navy as Officier-Ingénieur ; visited America and W. Africa, 1772–5 ; retired from the navy and devoted himself to natural history, which had always been his main interest, and studied under Buffon ; in 1777 he embarked for Alexandria, and spent three years exploring Egypt as far as Assûan ; returned to Paris, and produced a new edition of Buffon's great work in 127 vols., of which nearly 80 contained new matter contributed by himself, 1798–1808 ; his *Voyage dans la Haute et Basse-Égypte* did not appear until 1799, it deals largely with the nat. hist. and physical features of the country, but he visited and described many ancient sites ; the work was very successful and was translated into English, German and Russian ; died in Paris, 1812.

Carré, i, 107 (Portr.) ; *Hilmy*, ii, 245.

SOTTAS, Henri (1880–1927)

French Egyptologist ; born 1874 ; began life as an army officer, but retired through ill-health ; studied Egyptology under Moret and Guieysse at Éc. des Hautes Études, 1903–14, where he took his diploma with the thesis *La Preservation de la propriété funéraire*, 1913 and was appointed Prof. of Eg. Philology at the École in 1919 ; he specialized in texts of late periods and in demotic at the Éc. du Louvre ; he edited texts and made many contributions to journals ; in 1914 he rejoined his regiment, and after being severely wounded, was attached to the Intelligence Service ; he died of influenza early in 1927.

JEA. 13, 81 ; *Chron*. 2, 97.

SPENCER, Paul (*d*. 1767)

Irish antiquary ; travelled considerably in the East, and " in the year 1721 he drew with his own hand draughts of all the Egyptian Pyramids, obelisks, etc. and most of all the curious remains of antiquity in these foreign countries, which are greatly valued "; died at Muff, Co. Londonderry, 11 Sept. 1767 ; his drawings etc. have not been traced.

Lloyd's Evening Post, 21, 318 (1767).

SPIEGELBERG, Wilhelm (1870–1930)

German Egyptologist ; born 25 June 1870 ; educ. Strassburg Univ. and Paris ; studied under Dümichen and Maspero ; his earlier work was mainly on hieratic papyri, especially the juristic, on which he did valuable research ; he later turned chiefly to Coptic and demotic, of the latter he became the leading exponent in Germany, publishing a demotic grammar and numerous editions of texts ; in 1921 he pub. his *Koptisches Handwörterbuch*, a work of great value and superseded only by the great Coptic Dictionary of Crum ; he made many shorter communications on Eg. archaeology, philology and art, and several times visited Egypt ; he was Professor of Egyptology successively at the Universities of Strassburg (1898), Heidelberg (1918) and Munich (1923) ; died 23 Dec. 1930.

ZÄS. 66, 74 (Portr.) ; *JEA*. 17, 144 ; *Chron*. 7, 116 ; *Newberry Corresp.*

SPITTA, (*Bey*) **Wilhelm** (*d.* 1883)

German orientalist ; Librarian of the Vice-Regal Library, Cairo ; retired 1882 and returned to Germany ; pub. many Arabic works, incl. *Grammatik des Arabischen Vulgardialectes von Aegypten,* 1880 and *Contes Arabes Populaires,* 1883, a collection of stories with many ancient Eg. parallels ; died 6 Sept. 1883.

Centralblatt f. Bibliothekwesen, 1884, 105–12 ; *Wilbour*, passim (see index) ; *Hilmy*, ii, 256.

SPOHN, Friedrich August Wilhelm (*d.* 1824)

German orientalist ; Professor of Oriental Languages at Leipsic ; he claimed to have discovered the interpretation of hieroglyphic writing ; an elaborate work with plates, *De Lingua et Literis veterum Aegyptiorum* was posthumously edited by Seyffarth, 1825–31.

Champollion, i, 166, 255, 264, 390 ; *Hilmy*, ii, 256.

SPURRELL, Flaxman Charles John (1842–1915)

Geologist and antiquary ; son of Flaxman S., surgeon of Bexley Heath ; born 1842 ; educ. Epsom College, 1855–6 ; he was not a medical man as stated in error by Petrie ; collected flint implements and fossils, a large collection of which from the Crayford Deposits he gave to the B.M. (Nat. Hist.) in 1895 ; spent several seasons in Egypt as assistant to Petrie, and contributed to his *Neqada* and *Tell el-Amarna* ; pub. papers in *Arch. Journ.*, and *QJGS* ; retired to Norfolk, where he died 28 Feb. 1915.

JEA. 2, 251 ; *Anc. Eg*. 1915, 93 ; *Epsom Coll. Registers* ; *Petrie*, 17, 107, 128 ; *Newberry Corresp.*

STANTON, (*Sir*) **Edward** (1827–1907)

Army officer and diplomatist ; born 19 Feb. 1827 ; educ. Woolwich Acad. ; entered Royal Eng., 1844 ; served at the Cape, 1847–53 ; Crimea, 1854–5 ; retired, 1859 ; General, 1881 ; Consul-General at Warsaw, 1860 and Egypt, 1865–76 ; Chargé d'aff., Munich, 1876 ; C.B., 1857 ; K.C.M.G., 1882 ; K.C.B., 1905 ; he had a collection of Eg. antiquities which was sold in 1894 ; the B.M. bought the hieratic papyrus of Queen Nedjme (10490) ; he procured for the Duke of Sutherland the mummy unrolled by Birch at Stafford House in 1875 ; died 24 June 1907.

WWW. i, 671 ; *Wilbour*, 148 ; *Khedives and Pashas*, 167, 169, 214–8.

STEFANI, Antonio (*fl.* 1815–1835)

Albanian merchant settled at Khartûm about 1815 ; in 1834 he entered into partnership with Giuseppe Ferlini (q.v.) to excavate at Meroë.

Budge, *Eg. Sudan*, i, 285.

STEINBÜCHEL von RHIEINWALL, Anton (1790–1883)

Austrian orientalist and antiquary ; born Krems, Lower Austria 4 Dec. 1790 ; appointed Assistant Keeper of the private collection of antiquities of the Emperor, 1809 ; Professor of Archaeology and Numismatics, Vienna Univ., 1817 ; Keeper of Coins and Antiquities, and also of the Ambras collection, 1819–40 ; member of the Academies of Vienna, Rome, Naples, and others ; pub. an account of the scarabs in the museum, 1824, and a handbook of the Eg. collection, 1826 ; died 1883.

Oesterr. Nat.-Enzyc. 5, 138 ; *Hilmy*, ii, 259.

STEINDORFF, Georg (1861–1951)

German Egyptologist ; born Dessau, 12 Nov. 1861 ; educ. Berlin and Göttingen Univs. ; Ph.D., Gött., 1884 ; Assistant in Berlin Museum, 1885–93 ; Professor of Egyptology, Leipsic, 1893, and remained there until the Nazification of the University when he emigrated to America ; continued his studies in the museums of New York, Boston and Baltimore and the Oriental Inst. of Chicago ; explored the Libyan Desert, 1899–1900 ; excavated at Gizeh, 1909–11 ; in Nubia, 1912–14 and 1930–31 ; made many contributions to *ZÄS* (of which he was editor for some years) and other journals and pub. many technical monographs ; his *Koptische Grammatik*, 1894 (2nd ed. 1904) has been much used by students ; died Hollywood, California, 28 Aug. 1951.

Kürschner ; *Newberry Corresp.* ; *The Times*, 30 Aug. 1951.

STERN, Ludwig Julius Christian (1846–1911)

German orientalist and Celtic scholar ; born Hildesheim, 12 Aug. 1846 ; educ. Hildesheim and Göttingen Univ. ; had great aptitude for languages and in his youth, in addition to the modern languages taught at school, he mastered, self-taught, Italian, Spanish and the Slavonic languages, especially Russian ; at Göttingen he studied under Lotje, Teichmüller, Wiesler and Th. Müller, but specialized in oriental languages under Ewald, Berteau and Benfey ; in addition to Hebrew, Arabic and Ethiopic, in 1868 he turned to Egyptology under Brugsch, and from 1869 onwards continued his studies in the Eg. Dept. of the Berlin Museum ; in 1872 accompanied Ebers to Egypt, and was appointed librarian of the Viceregal Library at Cairo ; in 1874 he was appointed to the staff of the Eg. Dept. at Berlin Museum, and at the same time prepared a catalogue of the oriental MSS. in the Royal Library ; after the death of Lepsius in 1884, Stern found himself unable to work under his successor, and he thereupon completely gave up Egyptology, became Keeper of Manuscripts in the Royal Library in 1886, and began the study of Celtic languages in which he became a recognized authority and was a co-founder and joint-editor of the *Zeitschr. fur Celtische Philologie* ; in Egyptian, Stern's best-known work is his valuable *Koptische Grammatik,* 1880, he also compiled the glossary of the Ebers Papyrus and made many contributions to *ZÄS.* ; died 9 Oct. 1911.

Zeitschr. f. Celt. Philol. 8, 583–587 (Portr.) ; *Zentralbl. f. Bibliothekswesen,* 1912, 36–41 ; *Erman,* 168–9, states that S. *returned* to Celtic studies after he left the museum, but he *began* to study Celtic only after abandoning Egyptian ; *Hilmy,* ii, 260.

STEUART, John Robert (1780–1848)

Numismatist and collector of antiquities ; pub. *Description of the Anc. Monuments in Lydia and Phrygia,* Folio, 1842 ; his numismatic collections were sold in three sales at Sotheby's, 30 Jan. 1840 (15 days), 19 July 1841 and 3 May 1844, the last was anonymous ; many specimens were bought by the B.M. ; his library was sold 25 Nov. 1846 and his antiquities, which included many Egyptian items, in June 1849 ; he travelled in the East, 1826 and was elected F.R.S., 1829 ; died 1848.

STOBART, (*Rev.*) **Henry** (1824–1895)

Second s. William Stobart of Chester-le-Street, Co. Durham ; born 1824 ; Queen's Coll. Oxon., 1842 ; B.A., 1847 ; M.A., 1848 ; ordained, 1849 ; held various curacies 1849–64 ; Rector of Warkton, Northants, 1865–81, where he completely restored the church ; visited Egypt, 1854–5 and brought back some important antiquities ; some of these were pub. in a folio vol. without letterpress, Berlin, 1856 ; most of the antiquities were bought by Joseph Mayer of Liverpool, including the papyri, now famous as *Mayer A & B* ; the B.M. bought the Coptic and Greek papyri, one of which had on the *verso* the Funeral oration of Hypereides, edited by Churchill Babington ; retired to Wykeham Rise, Totteridge in 1881, and died there, 30 Dec. 1895.

Inf. by relatives ; *JEA.* 35, 163 ; 19, 143 ; *ZÄS.* 38, 71 ; *Hilmy,* ii, 261.

STOREY, Samuel (1840–1925)

Of Chester-le-Street, Co. Durham ; born 13 Jan. 1840 ; M.P., Sunderland, 1881–95 and 1910 ; J.P. ; D.L. ; visited Egypt in 1884 and bought antiquities, including two mummies ; died 18 Jan. 1925.

WWW. ii, 1004 ; *Wilbour,* 292.

STRACHAN-DAVIDSON, James Leigh (*d.* 1916)

Balliol Coll. Oxon., M.A., LL.D. ; Master of Balliol 1907–16 ; visited Egypt 1886–7 ; presented to Pitt-Rivers Museum a cup with a hieratic inscription, 1887, pub. by Griffith, *PSBA.,* 14, 328 ; died, unmarried, 28 Mar. 1916.

WWW. ii, 1006.

STRATON, (*Sir*) **Joseph** (*d.* 1840)

Army officer ; son of Col. Muter but assumed the name of Straton about 1816 on succeeding to the property of his aunt, near Montrose ;

an officer in the 6th Enniskilling Dragoons ; at Waterloo commanded the Union Brigade on the death of Sir Wm. Ponsonby and was wounded ; Lieut.-Col., 1814 ; C.B. ; K.C.H. ; F.R.S.E. ; left about £70,000 to Edinburgh University ; visited Salt after a tour in Palestine, 1817 ; accompanied Irby and Mangles to the Pyramids, Sept. 1817 and proceeded as far as Assûan ; pub. *Account of the Sepulchral Caverns of Egypt* (*Edinb. Philos. Inst.* 3, 345) ; died, a Lieut.-General, 23 Oct. 1840.

C. Dalton, *Waterloo Roll Call*, 2nd ed. 62 ; *Irby*, 49, 51, 58 ; *Salt*, ii, 45 ; *Finati*, 215 ; *Hilmy*, ii, 262.

STROGANOFF, (*Comte*) **Gregor** (*fl.* 1856–1880)

Russian nobleman, collector of antiquities ; a catalogue of his collection was pub. at Aachen in 1880, without author's name, but it is known to be by Émile Brugsch : *Catalog der Sammlung ägyptischer Alterthümer des Grafen Gregor Stroganoff.*

Vapereau, 1682 ; *Hilmy*, ii, 263.

STUART, Henry Windsor Villiers (1827–1895)

Politician and traveller ; born 1827 ; ordained 1850 but seceded from the Church, 1873 ; M.P. for Waterford, 1873–4, 1880–5 ; went to Egypt on a social and political mission, 1883–4, on which his reports were pub. as a blue-book ; pub. also *Nile Gleanings*, 1879, *The Funeral Tent of an Egyptian Queen*, 1882 and other works ; died by drowning, 12 Oct. 1895.

DNB. 55, 85 ; *Wilbour*, 212, 246, 287, 295.

STURROCK, John (1832–1888)

Scottish engineer and surveyor to Lloyd's Registry of Shipping ; born Slap, 20 Dec. 1832 ; in private life an enthusiastic antiquary and formed a private museum of antiquities he had personally excavated or purchased at sales ; the collection was sold in 1889 and many items were bought by the Soc. of Antiquaries of Scotland ; of the Egyptian items, the finest specimen was the sword of King Kamose which was acquired by Sir John Evans, who presented a cast of it to the B.M. (36808) ; the sword was exhibited at the Burlington Fine Arts Club in 1922 (see *JEA*. 10, 263, *n*. 7) ; Sturrock died at Oakbank, Monikie, 25 Dec. 1888.

Inf. by C. Aldred.

TABERNA, Vincenzo (*fl.* 1800–1815)

Of Piedmontese origin ; served as an officer in the Mameluke Cavalry in Egypt ; treasurer to Ali Pasha ; interpreter to Sir Sidney Smith ; secretary to Col. Missett, Brit. Consul-General in Egypt ; rendered much assistance to British travellers in Egypt.

Legh, 16, 132, 154 ; *Hamilton*, 344–5 ; *Valentia*, iii, 405.

TANO, Nicolas (*d.* 1924)

Of Greek origin and French nationality ; dealer in antiquities in Cairo ; after his death his business has been continued by his son Georges Tano and his nephew Phocion Jean Tano at 51 Sh. Ibrahim

Pasha, formerly at 7 Sh. Kamel, opposite Shepheard's Hotel ; he died in Cairo in 1924.

Inf. by Dr. L. Keimer.

TATTAM, (*Rev.*) **Henry** (1789–1868)

Coptic scholar ; born 1789 ; Rector of St. Cuthbert, Bedford, 1822 ; Rector of Great Woolstone, Bucks, 1831 ; held both livings until 1849 when he was presented to the benefice of Stanford Rivers, Essex ; Archdeacon of Bedford, 1845–66 ; Chaplain-in-Ord. to Queen Victoria ; F.R.S., 1835 ; Hon. LL.D., T.C.D., 1845 ; D.D. Göttingen ; Ph.D., Leiden ; visited Egypt and Syria 1838–9 to obtain oriental MSS., and brought back a considerable number of Coptic MSS., and also antiquities for Dr. John Lee ; he pub. a Coptic grammar, 1830 and Lexicon, 1835 ; also published a number of Coptic Biblical texts, 1829–52 ; his own Coptic MSS. were acquired by the B.M. (MSS. Or. 422–42) ; his library was sold at Sotheby's, 16 June 1868 ; died at Stanford Rivers, 8 Jan. 1868.

DNB. 55, 386 ; *Hincks*, 13, 69, 160, 179 ; Edwards, *Lives of the Founders*, 613 ; *Hilmy*, ii, 277.

TAYLOR, (*Baron*) **Isidore Justin Séverin** (1789–1879)

French archaeologist and author ; Inspecteur des Beaux Arts ; founder of Société des Gens de Lettres ; sent to Egypt by Charles X and Louis Philippe to arrange for the transfer of the Luxor Obelisk to Paris and to acquire antiquities for the Louvre ; presented by Mimaut to Mohammad Ali in 1830, he gave him a copy of the *Description de l'Égypte* and other gifts ; the removal of the obelisk having been authorized, it could not be effected owing to the revolution of July, 1830 ; he returned in 1833 and secured the obelisk which arrived in Paris in December of that year ; pub. *L'Égypte*, a descriptive work, under the pseudonym of R. P. Laorty Hadji, 1857, and previously collaborated with Louis Reybaud in *La Syrie, l'Égypte, la Palestine et la Judée*, 2 vols., 1839.

Carré, i, 208 ff. ; *Hilmy*, ii, 278.

TEMPLE, Frederick, 1st Marquis of Dufferin and Ava (1826–1902)

Statesman and diplomatist ; born 21 June 1826 ; succeeded as 5th Baron, 1841 ; created Earl, 1871 ; Marquis, 1888 ; P.C. ; G.C.B. ; D.C.L. ; LL.D. ; F.R.S. ; visited Egypt as a young man and was responsible for the demolition of the wall in the Temple of Dêr el-Bahri depicting the so-called "Hottentot Venus" immediately after its discovery by Mariette in 1858 ; the picture was afterwards recovered and is now in Cairo Museum ; special commissioner in Egypt, 1882–3 ; collector of antiquities ; collection sold at Christie's, 31 May 1937 (Eg. lots 15–42) ; died 12 Feb. 1902.

WWW. i, 212 ; *Bibl. Ég.* 18, p. xcvii.

TEXTOR DE RAVISI, (*Baron*) **Anatole Arthur** (1822–1902)

French Colonial Administrator ; served at Réunion, 1847–52 and in India, 1853–63 ; much interested in oriental studies and pub. works on Hindu and Buddhist architecture ; in later life much interested in Egyptology, and made many communications to the Congress of Orientalists at Paris, 1880 and St. Étienne, 1883.

Hilmy, ii, 281.

TEYNARD, Félix (1817–1892)

French engineer ; educ. at Grenoble ; visited Egypt in 1851 and 1869 ; pub. in 1858 in 2 vols. a large and sumptuous collection of photographs of monuments, etc., in Egypt and Nubia intended as a supplement to the *Description de l'Égypte*.

Carré, ii, 313 ; *Hilmy*, ii, 282.

THÉDÉNAT-DUVENT, Pierre Paul (1756–1822)

French diplomatist ; Consul for France at Alexandria ; he made two large collections of Eg. antiquities which were sold in Paris in 1822 (cat. by Dubois) ; he wrote a history of contemporary Egypt, *L'Égypte sous Méhémed Ali*, which was posthumously pub. by F. J. Joly ; the important stela, Louvre C.14, was found by him at Abydos, at the sale it was acquired by Rollin for Cousinéry, by whom it was sold to the Louvre ; a papyrus in the Bibl. Nat. bears his name.

TSBA. 5, 555 ; *Hilmy*, ii, 283.

THOMPSON, (*Sir*) **Henry Francis Herbert** (1859–1944)

Coptic and demotic scholar ; s. Sir Henry Thompson, Bt., F.R.C.S. ; born 1859 ; educ. Marlborough and T.C.C. ; studied Law and was called to the Bar, but finding it uncongenial, he turned to medicine ; biological work in the laboratories at Univ. Coll. London, and especially the use of the microscope brought on eye trouble, and the second career was thus ended ; succeeded as 2nd Bart., 1904 ; at the age of 40, he took up Egyptology and studied under Griffith and Crum at Univ. Coll. ; after a general grounding in the subject, he specialized on Coptic and demotic in which he became one of the foremost scholars of his generation ; he published many independent works and edited many texts, and gave great assistance to Crum in the completion of his Coptic Dictionary ; he was a generous supporter of archaeology and presented his library to the E.E.F. in 1919, retaining only a few books, mostly Coptic and Demotic, for his own use ; he was a Fellow of Univ. Coll. London, Hon. D.Litt. Oxford and F.B.A. ; he died in Bath, 25 May 1944 ; by his will he founded a Chair in Egyptology at Cambridge.

JEA. 30, 67 (Portr.) ; Glanville, *Growth and Nature of Egyptology* (1947), 12 ff.

THURBURN, R. (*fl.* 1810–1830)

Secretary to E. Missett, Consul-General, and afterwards a partner in the house of Briggs & Co., Alexandria ; he was very helpful to English travellers and explorers in Egypt.

Travels of Lady H. Stanhope, i, 134, 138 ; Madden, *Travels*, i, 214, 269 ; ii, 396 ; Hogg, *Visit to Alexandria*, 123, 127, 139 ; *Light*, 23 ; *Salt*, ii, 276–80 ; *Westcar Diary*, 6, 8, 13 ; *Madox*, i, 125 ; *Vyse*, i, 197 ; *Richardson*, i, 25.

TIELE, Cornelis Petrus (1830–1902)

Dutch scholar ; wrote much on the history of religions ; his work on the comparative religions of Egypt and Mesopotamia was translated into English, 1882, as were other works of a similar nature ; his largest work was on the ancient religions from the time of Alexander the Great.

OLZ. 5, 77 ; *Hilmy*, ii, 287.

TIGRANE PASHA (*d*. 1904)

Egyptian statesman ; of Armenian origin ; Foreign Minister and member of the Comité d'Archéologie, Cairo ; he was son-in-law of the celebrated Nubar Pasha ; visited England in 1885 ; he made a collection of Eg. antiquities, some of the stelae and larger stone monuments being displayed in the garden of his house ; presented a fine bas-relief from Heliopolis to the Museum of Alexandria ; some years after his death a catalogue of his collection by Daninos Pasha was pub. in Paris, 1911, *Collection d'Antiquités ég. de Tigrane Pacha d'Abro* (20 pp. 64 plates) ; he died in 1904.

Lord Cromer, *Modern Eg*. ii, 221–5 and *Abbas II*, 44, 46, 58 ; *Wilbour*, 174 ; Maspero, *Rapports sur . . . le Serv. des Antiq*. p. vi.

TILL, William (*d*. 1845)

Dealer in coins and antiquities of 17 Gt. Russell St., London ; he supplied many Eg. antiquities to Dr. John Lee and other collectors ; was agent for Belzoni who left in his charge a number of mummies and other antiquities for disposal ; his coins were sold after his death at Sotheby's in 1845 and 1846 ; died, 1845.

Hartwell Registers.

TIMSAH (*c*. 1788–*c*. 1865)

Arabic تمساح, "Crocodile," the sobriquet given to a native of Luxor who rendered great services to Champollion and acted as his *reis* in 1829, as he had previously so acted for Drovetti ; on the recommendation of Mimaut, the French Consul-General, Timsah and his family were made French protégés, and exempted from corvés, etc. ; Timsah held a certificate from Champollion of which he was very proud ; Brugsch met him at Thebes in 1854, when he recalled many reminiscences of Champollion ; Timsah was still living in 1863, his sons and grandsons were employed by Mariette and for many years after by the Service des Antiquités : two of them, Dieb and Aguil, had more than thirty years' service.

Champollion, ii, 248 ; Brugsch, *Mein Leben*, 183 ; *Rec. Trav*. 12, 218 ; *Wilbour*, 498.

TIRARD, (*Lady*) Helen Mary (1854–1943)

Née Beloe ; born 1854, d. Rev. R. S. Beloe ; married in 1885 Dr. (later Sir) Nestor Tirard, F.R.C.P. (1853–1928) ; she was an early member and zealous supporter of the E.E.F. and served for many years on the Committee ; translated Erman's *Aegypten und aegyptisches Leben* under the title *Life in Ancient Egypt*, 1893, for many years one of the most popular general works on Egypt ;

although in her last years she became blind, she maintained her interest to the end, at nearly 90 years of age.

Private information.

TODOROS (THEODOROS) (*fl.* 1857–1887)

Dealer in antiquities ; a Copt, Consular Agent in Luxor for Prussia ; according to Rhind, he had been trained as a silversmith and used his knowledge of metal-working in the fabrication of forged antiquities ; many genuine antiquities passed through his hands, some of which were bought by Maspero for the Bulak Museum.

Rhind, *Thebes, its Tombs,* etc. 248, 253 ; Lady Duff-Gordon, *Letters,* 221, 306 ; *Wilbour,* 48 and often.

TOMKINS, (*Rev.*) **Henry George** (*d.* 1907)

Biblical archaeologist ; of Weston-super-Mare, a friend of Amelia Edwards and an early member of the E.E.F. which he joined in 1883 and served on the Committee until 1902 ; much interested in Biblical archaeology and pub. many papers thereon in *PSBA., JAI.* and other journals ; translated into English Maspero's communication to the Victoria Institute on the names relating to Judaea in the lists of Tuthmosis III ; died in 1907.

JEA. 33, 88 ; *Hilmy,* ii, 290.

TOMLINSON, (*Rev.*) **George** (1801–1863)

Born 1801 ; St. John's Coll. Cantab., B.A., 1823 ; M.A., 1826 ; D.D. 1842 ; consecrated Bishop of Gibraltar, 1842 ; contributed to the *Trans.* of the R. Soc. Literature several papers on Egyptian archaeology, quite good for their time ; these included a paper on the astronomical ceiling of the Memnonium (Ramesseum) at Thebes ; died at Gibraltar, Jan. 1863.

Hilmy, ii, 291.

TRIANTAPHYLLOS, Thomas (*fl.* 1824–1832)

Greek merchant of Gurneh who shared house with Giovanni d'Athanasi whose operations he superintended in his absence. He is often mentioned by contemporary travellers and diarists, with much variation in the spelling of the name—Triantafelas, Threantopholos, Triantophalos, etc.,—the correct form is Τριαντάφυλλος. Hoskins describes him as " a worthy honest merchant " and as " an immensely stout man mounted as usual on a spirited donkey "; he is probably Thomas T., one of the Archontes in Egypt ; another man of the same name, Pandelis T., was a partner of Mohammad Ali in the tobacco trade at Cavalla.

Hoskins, *Oasis,* 2, 28 ; *Hay Diary,* 1826 ; *Westcar Diary,* 221 ; *Inf. by Dr. Mosconas, Librarian of the Patriarchal Library, Alexandria.*

TRIST, John William (*d.* 1913)

Antiquary and numismatist ; F.S.A., 1887 ; F.R.N.S. ; his collections, which included many Egyptian antiquities, were sold at Sotheby's in July 1895 ; died 24 Oct. 1913.

TURAEFF, Boris (1870–1920)

Russian Egyptologist ; studied first at Petrograd and later under Erman at Berlin ; returning to Russia, he was appointed Professor of Ancient History in the Univ. of Petrograd ; on the acquisition of the Golenischeff Collection, he was made Keeper of the Egyptian Antiquities in the Museum of Moscow ; in 1918, elected member of the Russian Acad. of Sciences ; he had a large private collection of antiquities ; died in Petrograd, in starvation and distress, early in 1920.

JEA. 7, 109 ; *Erman*, 283.

TURNER, (*Sir*) **Tomkyns Hilgrove** (1766–1843)

Army officer ; entered the Army, 1782 ; served in Holland, 1793–4 ; in Egyptian campaign, 1801 ; Colonel of the 19th Foot ; K.C.H. ; Hon. D.C.L. ; he was entrusted with the difficult task of recovering and transporting to England the Rosetta Stone and other antiquities ceded to the British on the capitulation of Alexandria ; died, a General, in 1843.

DNB. 57, 361 ; Edwards, *Lives of the Founders of the B.M*., 364 ; Budge, *The Rosetta Stone* (B.M., 1913), 1–2.

TYLOR, Joseph John (1851–1901)

Engineer and archaeologist ; born 1851 ; A.M.I.C.E., 1877 ; retired from business in 1891 in consequence of ill-health contracted while professionally engaged in Mexico ; in association with Somers Clarke and others he undertook much work at El-Kab, and financed the publication of a fine series of memoirs on the wall-drawings and monuments there ; bequeathed his library to Univ. Coll., London, with duplicates to Oxford ; died at Cap d'Ail in 1901.

E.E.F. *Arch. Rep*. 1900–1, 52, 53.

TYSZKIEWICZ, (*Comte*) **Eustach** (1814–1873)

Polish archaeologist of Vilna ; carried out researches into the tombs of Lithuania and western Ruthenia, the results of which were pub. in 1868 ; travelled in Egypt and Nubia in 1862–3 ; formed a large collection of antiquities, many Egyptian objects being acquired by the Louvre in 1863, and more when the remaining collections were sold in 1898.

Rev. de l'Art, 43, 168, 284.

TYTUS, Robb de Peyster (1876–1913)

American traveller in Egypt ; born Asheville, N. Carolina, 2 Feb. 1876 ; educ. St. Mark's School, Southboro, Mass., and Yale Univ. ; B.A., 1897 ; M.A., 1903 ; studied art in London, Paris and Munich ; went to Egypt in 1899–1900 and again in 1901–2 when he worked with Newberry on the site of the Palace of Amenophis III at Thebes, of which he pub. a preliminary report in 1903 ; in 1904–6 he pub. a number of poems and stories relating to Egypt, some of them in collaboration with his wife ; after his death, his mother, Charlotte Mathilde Tytus (née Davies) financed the publication of a fine series of volumes on the Theban Tombs, five of which have appeared ;

these volumes known as the "Robb de Peyster Tytus Memorial Series," are a worthy monument to his memory; died at Saranac Lake, N.Y., 14 Aug. 1913.

N. de G. Davies, *Tomb of Nakht*, pref. x; *Newberry Corresp.*; *Inf. by Dr. Ludlow Bull.*

UHLEMANN, Maximilian Adolf (*fl.* 1850–1860)

German scholar; a disciple of Seyffarth whose system of hieroglyphic decipherment he defended and expounded in a number of lengthy works.

Renouf, *Life-Work*, i, 1–31; *Hilmy*, ii, 298.

VALENTIA, (*Viscount*)—*See* ANNESLEY

VALERIANI, Domenico (*fl.* 1823–1837)

Writer of Florence; he violently attacked Champollion's system of decipherment in *Antologia* (No. 33, Sept. 1823) to which C. rejoined in the *Rev. Encyc.* (21, 225, 1823); he also pub. *Nuova Illustrazione istorico-monumentale del Basso e dell' Alto Egitto*, 2 vols., with 2 vols. of plates, mostly copied from the works of Denon, Cailliaud, Rosellini, and others, Florence, 1835–7.

Hilmy, ii, 301; *Rec. Champ.* 768, No. 25; *Champollion*, i, 227, 245.

VASSALLI, (*Bey*) **Luigi** (1812–1887)

Italian Egyptologist; born Milan 8 Jan. 1812; studied painting; being involved in a political plot in 1848, he was condemned to death, but was afterwards released; took refuge in Switzerland, France and England where he lived by teaching Italian and selling his pictures; returned to Milan, 1848, but again went into exile in 1849, and travelled to Constantinople and Smyrna, where he married; his wife having died a few months later, he migrated to Egypt and lived as a portrait-painter until he became acquainted with Mariette in 1859; after a short service in Garibaldi's army in 1860, he returned to Egypt as assistant to Mariette and conducted many of his excavations; conservator of the Bulak Museum, 1859–84; retired to Rome in 1884, and died there 13 June, 1887; there is a marble bust of him in the Cairo Museum; in 1856 he sold some important papyri to the B.M. (10068, 10083, 10383).

ZÄS. 25, 111; *Hilmy*, ii, 306; *Bibl. Ég.* 18, p. cxi; Brugsch, *Mein Leben*, 207.

VIDAL, Robert Studley (1770–1841)

Antiquary; Barrister, Middle Temple, but practised little, spending most of his time on his estate in Devonshire; F.S.A., 1804; contributed two papers to *Archaeologia*, vol. 15; had an extensive library and a large collection of coins, medals and antiquities, including Egyptian; the former was sold at Sotheby's, 18 July 1842, the latter in a nine days' sale the same year; he was a benefactor of St. John's Coll. Cambridge; died 21 Nov. 1841.

DNB. 58, 303.

VIDUA, (*Count*) **Carlo** (1785–1830)

Italian traveller ; born Casalo Monferrato, 1785 ; travelled in Greece and Syria, 1816–22, visiting Egypt in 1820 and proceeding as far as the Second Cataract ; his name is carved on the rock of Abu Sir and the Temple of Abu Simbel ; met Champollion in Italy and offered to join his expedition to Egypt, but eventually withdrew ; travelled to Mexico, 1826–7 and afterwards to the Dutch East Indies where he died near Amboyna in 1830.

Enc. It. ; *Champollion*, i, 393 ; ii, v ; *Westcar Diary*, 134.

VIREY, Philippe (1853–1922)

French Egyptologist ; born 1853 ; studied Egyptology first under Chabas and then under Maspero in Paris ; joined the Mission Archéologique au Caire and was employed chiefly in copying Theban Tombs many of which were pub. in the *Mémoires* of the Mission, but his standard of cipigraphic accuracy was a poor one ; pub. *Étude sur le Papyrus Prisse*, with a complete translation, commentary and glossary, 1887, a popular book on Eg. religion and many shorter articles ; wrote the biographies of Chabas, Lefébure and Horrack for the collected edition of their works in the *Bibl. Ég.* ; after his return from Egypt he lectured on Egyptology at the Institut Catholique, Paris ; died 1922.

JEA. 33, 81.

VIVIAN, Hussey Crespigny, 3rd Baron (1834–1893)

Diplomatist ; e. s. 2nd Baron Vivian ; born 19 June 1834 ; clerk in the Foreign Office, 1851–72 ; Agent at Alexandria, 1873 ; Consul-General in Egypt, 1876 (10 May)–1879 ; Agent at Bucharest, 1874–6 ; Ambassador at European Courts, 1879–93 ; Plenipotentiary to the Slave-trade Conference at Brussels, 1889 ; G.C.M.G., 1889 ; succeeded as 3rd Baron, 1886 ; died 21 Oct. 1893.

Burke's Peerage ; Cromer, *Mod. Eg.* i, passim ; *Khedives and Pashas*, 217–20.

VOLNEY, (*Comte de*) **Constantin François Chasseboeuf** (1757–1820)

French savant and traveller ; born Craon (Maine-et-Loire) 3 Feb. 1757 ; he spent four years in Egypt and Syria studying their history and political and social institutions, and pub. a descriptive work *Voyage en Égypte et en Syrie*, 1787 (new ed., 1799) ; was a member of the States-General and of the Constituent Assembly ; in 1792 he bought an estate in Corsica where he attempted to put into practice his social and economic theories ; he was imprisoned by the Jacobins, but escaped the guillotine ; after being for some time Professor of History at the École Normale, in 1795 he visited America, but was accused of being a spy and had to return to France in 1798 ; although not a partisan of Napoleon, he was pressed unto his service and made a Comte, and under the restoration, a Peer of France ; elected Membre de l'Institut, 1795 ; died in Paris, 25 Apl. 1820.

EB. ; *Carré*, i, 90 (Portr.) ; *Hilmy*, i, 186.

VYSE—*See* HOWARD-VYSE

WADDINGTON, (*Rev.*) **George** (1793–1869)

Born Tuxford, Notts., 7 Sept. 1793 ; educ. Charterhouse, 1808–11, T.C.C. ; Fellow, 1817 ; M.A., 1818 ; D.D., 1840 ; travelled in Nubia with the Rev. Barnard Hanbury in 1821 and in Greece, 1823–4 ; pub. a narrative of his Nubian journey, 1822, transl. into German, 1823 ; he was the first to attempt to describe the Egyptian occupation of the Sudan ; Vicar of Masham, 1833–40 ; Dean of Durham, 1840–69 ; died at Durham, 20 July, 1869.

DNB. 58, 410 ; Cailliaud, *Voyage à Méroé*, i, 395 ; Budge, *Eg. Sudan*, i, 34–8 ; *Hilmy*, ii, 314.

WALKER, James Herbert (*d.* 1914)

Medical practitioner ; M.A. ; M.R.C.S. ; L.R.C.P. ; retired early from medical practice and studied Egyptology, attending the classes of Griffith at Univ. Coll., London, from 1892 ; succeeded as teacher of Egyptian and Coptic, 1903 ; translated the inscriptions in many of Petrie's excavation memoirs and took charge of the Eg. Dept. at Univ. Coll. in Petrie's absence ; died 21 July 1914.

JEA. 1, 295 ; *Anc. Eg.* 1914, 190.

WALLIS, Henry (1830–1916)

Artist ; his best-known picture, " The Death of Chatterton," was exhibited R.A., 1856, now in the Tate Gallery ; for some years he visited Egypt annually where he bought antiquities and sold them to museums and private collectors to pay his expenses ; he was an authority on the ceramics of the Near East, and pub. *Eg. Ceramic Art : the Macgregor Collection*, 1898 ; his drawings of the tombs of Assûan are pub. in monochrome, *PSBA*, 10, plates facing pp. 26, 30, 34 ; he had a collection of oriental ceramics, embroideries and antiquities which was dispersed after his death.

Inf. by P. E. Newberry ; Budge N & T. i, 82, 109, 132 ; *Petrie*, 120, 121.

WALMAS, Francis (*fl.* 1810–1840)

Banker of Alexandria ; partner in the house of Samuel Briggs (q.v.) ; very helpful to European travellers in Egypt.

Belzoni, i, 401 ; *Athanasi*, 17 ; *Salt*, ii, 144 ; *Westcar Diary*, 40 ; *Richardson*, i, 52, 115 ; ii, 174.

WALNE, Alfred Septimus (*c.* 1803–1893)

Surgeon ; born about 1803 ; M.R.C.S., 1828 ; L.S.A., 1828 ; practised in London, at Chancery Lane 1829–34 and at Bloomsbury Square, 1834–7 ; in 1837 went to Egypt and was appointed British Vice-Consul in Cairo, and Consul from about 1850 to 1868 when he was succeeded by Rogers-Bey ; practised as a surgeon in Cairo, 1837–1883 ; whilst there, he established a library and museum ; retired 1883 ; died 1893.

R.C.S. Records ; *Vyse*, i, 198, 264 ; ii, 34, 75 ; G. Melly, *Khartoum*, i, 78 ; ii, 89, 267 ; *Romer*, i, 79.

WALPOLE, (*Rev.*) **Robert** (1781–1856)

Traveller and author ; born 8 Aug. 1781 ; T.C.C. ; M.A., 1809 ; B.D., 1828 ; Rector of Mannington, Norfolk, 1809–56 ; travelled in

Greece and countries of the Near East ; pub. *Fragments of the Greek Comedians,* 1805 ; his *Memoirs relating to European and Asiatic Turkey and other Countries of the East, edited from Manuscript Journals,* 1817 (2nd ed. 1818), contains much valuable matter including the journal of Nathaniel Davison (q.v.) ; died in London, 16 Apl. 1856.

DNB. 59, 207 ; *Light,* pref., xi.

WARBURTON, Bartholomew Elliott George (1810–1852)

Irish lawyer, traveller and novelist ; born 1810 ; T.C.C. ; M.A., 1837 ; called to the Bar, 1837 ; in 1843 made an extensive tour in Syria, Palestine and Egypt, and pub. *The Crescent and the Cross,* 1845 ; also wrote historical novels and memoirs of Prince Rupert ; died at sea while on a mission to Darien, 4 Jan. 1852.

DNB. 59, 294.

WARBURTON, (*Rt. Rev.*) **William** (1698–1779)

Ecclesiastic and litterateur, one of the most prominent in his time ; born 1698 ; trained in an attorney's office ; ordained 1723 ; held various benefices ; Bishop of Gloucester, 1759, author of numerous literary and ecclesiastical works ; his connection with Egyptology is his *Legation of Moses* which contains an essay on the decipherment of hieroglyphs, first pub. 1738, several later editions, and transl. into French, 1744.

DNB. 59, 301 ; Nichols, *Lit. Anecd.* ii, 144, 165 ; v, 568 ; *BIFAO.* 5, 82 ; *Hilmy,* ii, 319.

WARD, John (1832–1912)

Artist and traveller ; J.P. ; F.S.A. ; born Belfast, 7 Aug. 1832 ; pub. many works on art ; travelled extensively in Greece and the Near East ; pub. *Pyramids and Progress,* 1900 ; *The Sacred Beetle,* 1901 ; *Greek Coins,* 1902 ; *Our Sudan,* 1905 ; died 20 Feb. 1912.

WWW. i, 741.

WARDI, Antoun (*c.* 1800–*c.* 1877)

Dragoman ; the correct form of the name is uncertain : it is spelt Wardi in the journal of Comte de St. Ferriol, who states that the man was a Greek, established in Gurnah from 1823 as a dealer in antiquities and from whom he made purchases in 1842 ; Vyse, who saw him in 1837, spells the name Werdie, and also says he was a Greek ; elsewhere he is spoken of as Antoûn Ouardé : all these forms are evidently mere vocalizations of an oriental name ; Wardi became in his later years a dragoman to European travellers and so acted for Archibald Campbell (later Lord Blythswood, q.v.), when he visited Egypt in 1874 ; it was from Wardi that Campbell bought the papyrus of the high-priest Pinodjem from the cache of Royal Mummies ; in 1875 he was at Beyrût and had then in his possession the papyrus of Queen Nodjme (part of which is now in the B.M. and part in the Louvre), from the same source : it is therefore evident that he was an accomplice of the Abderrassûl family and helped to dispose of the papyri from the cache before its secret was made known ; Maspero speaks of him as " un drogman syrien," and Dr. T. D. Mosconas, Patriarchal Librarian at Alexandria, states that Wardi must have been of Syiian extraction and was not a Greek.

Tresson, 32 ; *Chabas*, 147 ; *Vyse*, i, 85, 88 ; Maspero, *Momies Royales*, 512 ; *Letter from Dr. Mosconas*, 15 June 1951.

WARREN, John Collins (1778–1856)

American surgeon ; first Professor of Anatomy and Surgery at Harvard ; when surgeon of Massachusetts General Hospital, he unrolled and described a Ptolemaic mummy in 1821 presented to the museum of the hospital by A. O. van Lennep, a Smyrna merchant.

Mem. Inst. Eg. 13, 47 ; N.Y. Hist. Soc. *Bull.* 4, 4 ; *Hilmy*, ii, 321.

WATTIER DE BOURVILLE, Charles Joseph Auguste Désiré (*fl.* 1839–1842)

French Consul in Cairo, 1839–42.

Carré, i, 328 ; ii, 28.

WEIDENBACH, Ernst (1818–1882)

German artist and draughtsman ; born Naumburg, 4 Dec. 1818 ; accompanied the expedition of Lepsius to Egypt, 1842–4 and executed the drawings for most of the plates of the *Denkmäler* ; on his return was on staff of Berlin Museum until 1878 when he resigned in ill-health ; executed many drawings for the illustrations of other works by Lepsius, and by Ebers, Mariette and others ; died Merseburg, 14 Sept. 1882.

Lepsius, 12 and often ; *Chabas*, 70, 72, 74 ; *Bibl. Ég.* 18, pp. clii, clxxiii ; *Inf. by Prof. Weidenbach of Giessen* (grandson).

WEIDENBACH, Max (*d. c.* 1893)

German artist and draughtsman ; younger brother of last, with whom he worked during Lepsius's expedition ; in 1848 emigrated to Australia ; died at Adelaide about 1893.

Inf. by Prof. Weidenbach of Giessen.

WEIGALL, Arthur Edward Pearse Brome (1880–1934)

Journalist and author ; born 20 Nov. 1880 ; educ. Wellington Coll. ; worked under Petrie for E.E.F. 1901 ; Inspector-General of Antiquities in Egypt, 1905–14, in which post he showed great efficiency ; pub. with Gardiner, *Topographical Cat. of Private Tombs at Thebes*, 1913 ; and alone, *Antiquities of Lower Nubia*, 1907 ; *Guide to the Ant. of Upper Eg.*, 1910 and many popular books on Egypt ; died 2 Jan. 1934.

WWW. iii, 1431 ; *Newberry Corresp.*

WEILL, Raymond (1874–1950)

French Egyptologist ; born 1874 ; studied Egyptology in Paris under Maspero ; accompanied Petrie to Sinai ; excavated at Coptos, Kom el Ahmar, Tûneh and other sites ; Director, École des Hautes Études from 1928 ; President, Soc. Franç. d'Égyptologie ; published many important works and contributions to journals ; died 13 July 1950.

Chron. 26, 115.

WELLSTED, James Raymond (1805–1842)

Naval officer and surveyor ; Lieut. in E.I. Co.'s surveying-ship in the Red Sea, 1830–3 ; visited Upper Egypt and made measurements of the temples of Thebes and Dendera, 1834 ; surveyed Socotra Island, 1834 ; travelled in Oman, 1835–7 ; retired through ill-health, 1839 ; pub. *Travels in Arabia,* 2 vols. 1938 (Province of Oman ; Peninsula of Sinai ; Red Sea Coast) ; *Travels in the City of the Caliphs,* 1840 ; died 1842.

DNB. 60, 236 ; St. John, *Eg. and Moh. Ali,* i, 318 ; ii, 38, 133, 135 ; *Hilmy,* ii, 324.

WESSELY, Carl Franz Josef (1860–1931)

Austrian papyrologist ; born Vienna, 27 June 1860 ; Vienna Univ., Ph.D., 1883 ; until 1889 he was a schoolmaster in Vienna, and between 1883 and 1888 he visited Paris, Leipsic, Dresden and Berlin studying Greek papyri ; from 1883 he was a voluntary unpaid assistant in the Archduke Rainer's collection which in 1899 was incorporated in the Hofbibliothek, Vienna ; Privatdocent in Palaeography and Papyrology, Vienna Univ., 1919 ; Corresp. Member, Bologna Acad. ; Member Vienna Acad., 1893 ; he made many contributions to the literature of papyrology, of which his two memoirs on the magical papyri (1888, 1893) are perhaps the best known ; died 21 Nov. 1931.

Kürschner, 1931 ; *Ægyptus,* 12, 250 ; *Archiv f. Papyruskunde,* 10, 314 ; *JEA.* 18, 104 ; C. R. Gregory, *Die Schriften von K. Wessely zu seinem 50 Geburtstag,* Leipsic, 1910.

WESTCAR, Henry (1798–1868)

Born 26 June 1798 ; Exeter Coll. Oxon., 1817 ; B.A., 1820 ; M.A., 1826 ; travelled in Egypt 1823–4 as far as Wady Halfa, in company with F. Catherwood, J. J. Scoles and H. Parke (qq.v.) ; he kept a full journal of the tour, the MS. being now in the possession of Dr. L. Keimer of Cairo ; while in Egypt, he bought horses and some antiquities ; although it is not specifically mentioned, it is probable that he acquired the papyrus, afterwards in the possession of Lepsius, now famous as the Westcar papyrus ; the journal is of great value for the information it supplies of the movements of other travellers, collectors and dealers ; died at Hill House, Souldern, Oxon., 1868. See next entry.

MS. Journal ; *Alumni Ox.* ; *Madox,* i, 404 ; ii, 34 ; *Inf. by G. Rowland* (*descendant*).

WESTCAR, Mary (1781–1844)

Only child of John and Mary Westcar of Creslow Manor, Bucks ; she was baptized 27 Feb. 1781, her mother dying soon after (14 Mar.) ; her father, who lived till 1833, was a large landowner and breeder of pedigree cattle, and was a friend and neighbour of Dr. John Lee of Hartwell ; there are monuments to both parents in the parish church of Whitchurch, Bucks. ; she married, 3 June 1819, Edmund Turberville, R.N. ; Lepsius alleged that the papyrus known as the Westcar Papyrus was given to him in 1838 by Miss Mary Westcar, but this is impossible as she had ceased to be Miss Westcar on her marriage nearly 20 years before and she was living in Italy at the time of his visit to England in 1838; it is much more likely that the papyrus was brought to England in 1824 by her cousin Henry Westcar (q.v.), the only member of the family who had been to Egypt, and that he gave it to Dr. Lee; Lepsius visited Lee at Hartwell in 1838, and he probably then borrowed the papyrus from him and did not return it; this would account for the fact that he never published it nor deposited it in the Berlin Museum, but kept it in his private possession all his life; it was found amongst his papers and presented to the museum by his son after his death; the statements in the preface to Erman's edition of the text are therefore erroneous, and the papyrus cannot be in any way associated with Mary Westcar (Turberville); she died 12 Mar. 1844.

Whitchurch Parish Registers; *Inf. by G. Rowland* (*descendant*); O'Byrne, *Naval Biogr.*, 1214; Erman, *Die Märchen des Papyrus Westcar*, preface; G. Lipscomb, *Hist. Bucks*, iii, 520.

WHITEHOUSE, Frederic Cope (1842–1911)

American lawyer; born Rochester, N.Y., 9 Nov. 1842; studied in France, Germany and Italy; called to the Bar, 1871; made a prolonged stay in Egypt and discovered the Wady Raiyan in the Fayûm, a depression which he connected with the ancient Lake Moeris, and wrote many papers thereon; he also wrote on ethnology and geology; died 1911.

WWWA. i, 1337; *Wilbour*, 373; *Hilmy*, ii, 326, 457.

WHITTEMORE, Thomas (1871–1950)

American archaeologist; born Cambridge, Mass., 2 Jan. 1871; educ. Tuft's Coll.; lectured at Columbia and New York on Byzantine and Coptic art; excavated for E.E.S. at Balabish, Amarna, and elsewhere and contributed to excavation reports; Keeper of Byzantine Coins in the Fogg Museum, Harvard; Director of the Byzantine Institute of America; in 1931 preserved the mosaics of St. Sophia by permission of the Turkish Govt.; died in Washington, 8 June 1950.

The Times, 9 June 1950; *Numismatic Circular*, 58, col. 378.

WIEDEMANN, Karl Alfred (1856–1936)

German Egyptologist; younger s. Gustav Heinrich W. (1826–1899) a well-known physicist; born Berlin, 18 July 1856; a pupil of Ebers and Maspero; Professor of Egyptology at Bonn, 1891–1928; retired, 1928; wrote numerous books and papers on every branch of Egyptology in all the oriental journals; his *History* and *Religion of Anc. Eg.* were translated into English.

ZÄS. 73 (unnumbered page at beginning); *Chron.* 12, 232; *Hilmy*, ii, 328.

WILCKEN, Ulrich (1862–1944)

German papyrologist; born Stettin, 1862; studied under Mommsen; Privatdocent, Berlin, 1888; between 1889 and 1915 he held lecturerships or professorships successively at Breslau, Würzburg,

Halle, Leipsic, Bonn and Munich ; Professor at Berlin, 1917–31 and on his retirement became Professor Emeritus ; Ph.D. ; D.Jur. ; Hon. D.Litt., Oxford ; Member of Berlin Acad., and Foreign or Corresponding member of the Acads. of Saxony, Bavaria, Göttingen, Vienna, Turin (Lincei), Oslo, Leningrad, Cracow, Amsterdam, Athens and London (Brit. Acad.) ; he was the foremost papyrologist of his generation and his publications are both numerous and important ; died at Baden-Baden, 10 Dec. 1944.

Gnomon, 21, 88 ; *Chron.* 23, 250 ; *JEA*. 31, 2 ; *Kürschner*, 1931 ; *Erman*, 194, 201, 220, 283 ; *Bildnisse berühmter Mitgleider der Deutschen Akad. der Wiss. zu Berlin*, 1950, 105 (Portr.).

WILBOUR, Charles Edwin (1833–1896)

American Egyptologist ; born 1833 ; he studied Egyptology under Maspero in Paris and also in Berlin ; the last twenty years of his life were spent alternately in Egypt and in France ; whilst he had much knowledge of the Egyptian language and archaeology, he published nothing, and was a spectator rather than a worker in Egypt ; he was an accurate copyist of texts and supplied many of his colleagues with material ; for several winters he had the privilege of being Maspero's guest on the steamer attached to the Service des Antiquités, and of the observations he made on these voyages, he has left a very full account in his letters, which were pub. by the Brooklyn Museum in 1936 ; he formed a valuable collection of antiquities, and these, together with his library, are now in the Brooklyn Museum, where his family have established a Wilbour Memorial Hall ; his name is particularly associated with the great papyrus of Ramesses V, edited by Sir Alan Gardiner, which was purchased as a memorial to him ; Wilbour died in Paris, 17 Dec. 1896.

Capart, *Travels in Egypt* [Wilbour Letters], 1936 (Portr.) ; *Sphinx*, i, 254 ; Maspero, *L'Égyptologie*, 1915.

WILD, James William (1814–1892)

Architect, a pupil of George Basevi ; born 9 Mar. 1814 ; accompanied as a volunteer the expedition of Lepsius to Egypt in 1842 and remained during the exploration of Lower Egypt, but then stayed in Cairo to study Arabic architecture ; returned to England in 1848, he designed many buildings and was decorative architect to the Great Exhibition of 1851 ; he was curator of Sir John Soane's Museum in London from 1878 until his death, 7 Nov. 1892, and was then the last survivor of Lepsius's expedition ; his notebooks and drawings are in the Griffith Inst., Oxford.

E.E.F. *Arch. Report*, 1892–3, 27 ; *DNB*. 61, 221 ; *Lepsius*, 12, 35, 56.

WILKINSON, (*Sir*) John Gardner (1797–1875)

Egyptologist and traveller ; born 5 Oct. 1797 ; educ. Harrow, 1813 and Exeter Coll. Oxon., 1816, but owing to ill-health left without taking a degree ; at Harrow, he came under the influence of the head master, Dr. George Butler, himself a student of hieroglyphs and a friend of Dr. Thomas Young ; visited Italy in 1820 where he met Sir William Gell and took up the study of Egyptian ; went to Egypt in 1821 and spent 12 years there, and carried out excavations at Thebes in 1824, 1827–8 ; pub. *Materia Hieroglyphica*, Malta, 1830 ; *Topographical Survey of Thebes*, 1832 ; returned to England, 1833 ; F.R.S., 1834 ; pub. *Topography of Thebes*, 1835, and his best known work, *Manners and Customs of the Anc. Eg.*, 3 vols. 1837, of which there were several subsequent editions ; Knighted, 1839 ; returned to Egypt in 1842 and pub. *Modern Egypt*, 1843 ; travelled in Eastern Europe 1842 and pub. account of his travels, 1843 ; visited Egypt again, 1848–9 ; spent the following winter in Italy, studying the Turin Canon of Kings, of which he pub. a new facsimile ; D.C.L. Oxon., 1852 ; visited Egypt for the last time, 1855 ; took a prominent part in all archaeological movements and collected natural history specimens, on which he made many contributions to zoological and geological journals ; a benefactor to the B.M., to which he presented many antiquities and two large collections of papyri (mostly demotic) in 1834 and 1835 ; gave his own collection of classical and Eg. ant. to Harrow School ; he left a large mass of MSS. and drawings, most of which are now deposited in the Griffith Inst., at Oxford ; died at Llandovery, 29 Oct. 1875 and buried there.

DNB. 61, 274 ; frequently mentioned in contemporary diaries, e.g. *Hay*, *Bonomi*, *Westcar* ; *Hilmy*, ii, 330.

WILLIAMS, John (1797–1874)

Astronomer, Egyptologist and sinologist ; born 1797 ; in early life much interested in Egyptology ; invented a process of taking rubbings of inscriptions and a method of taking impressions of seals, scarabs, etc. ; pub. *Essay on the Hieroglyphics of the Anc. Eg.*, 1836 ; lent his rubbings to Samuel Sharpe who made use of them in his *Eg. Inscriptions* ; much associated with Dr. John Lee both in Egyptology and astronomy ; F.S.A. ; F.R.A.S., but resigned fellowship on joining the staff as Asst. Secretary, 1848–74 ; member of the Chronological Inst. ; studied Chinese ; pub. *Observations of Comets B.C. 611 to A.D. 1640 from Chinese Annals*, 1871, and many papers on Chinese history, archaeology, astronomy and numismatics in R.A.S. *Monthly Notices*, *Journ. Num. Soc.* and other journals ; died 3 Dec. 1874 ; his collection of Egyptian rubbings presented to Griffith Inst., by his grandson in 1941.

Proc. Soc. Ant. 2nd ser. 6, 354 ; R.A.S. *Monthly Notices*, 35, 181 ; P. W. Clayden, *Life of Samuel Sharpe*, 70 ; *JEA*. 27, 7 ; *Hartwell Reg.*

WILSON, Edward Livingstone (1838–1903)

American photographer ; he took a large series of photographs of Philae and other temples in Egypt, many of which were published ; went with Maspero and Emile Brugsch to make a final exploration of the tomb in which the Royal Mummies were found, in Jan. 1882 ; he pub. an account of this in an illustrated American magazine, *The Century*, 34, 1 (May 1887) ; also pub. " The Temples of Egypt " in *Scribner's Mag.* 4, Oct. 1888, 387.

Wilbour, 125 ; Maspero, *Les Momies Royales*, 520.

WILSON, (*Sir*) William James Erasmus (1809–1884)

Surgeon ; born 25 Nov. 1809 ; studied at Barts and was Demonstrator of Anatomy at Univ. Coll., London ; founded a Chair of

Dermatology, R. Coll. Surg.; M.R.C.S., 1831; F.R.C.S., 1843; F.R.S., 1845; President, R.C.S., 1881; Knighted, 1881; much interested in Egypt and in 1877 defrayed the cost of bringing Cleopatra's Needle from Egypt to London; pub. *Egypt of the Past,* 1881 and other works; took a leading part with Amelia Edwards in founding the E.E.F. in 1882, and gave much financial assistance; died, Westgate-on-Sea, 8 Aug. 1884.

DNB. 62, 148; *JEA.* 33, 71; *Hilmy,* ii, 337.

WILSON, William Rae (1772–1849)

Traveller; a lawyer by profession; born Paisley, 7 June 1772; Hon. LL.D., Glasgow; F.S.A.; travelled in Europe, Egypt and Palestine; pub. *Travels in Europe, Egypt and the Holy Land,* 2 vols., 1823 (4th ed. 1847); died 2 June 1849.

DNB. 62, 150; *Hilmy,* ii, 338.

WINLOCK, Herbert Eustis (1884–1950)

American Egyptologist; born Washington, 1 Feb. 1884; educ. Harvard, Ph.D., 1906; excavated in Egypt for the Metropolitan Museum, N.Y.; from 1906 he worked at Lisht, the Oasis of Khargeh and Thebes where many valuable discoveries were made which enriched the museums of Cairo and New York; wrote or edited many valuable publications and contributed to *JEA* and other journals; Director of the Metrop. Museum from 1929; died Florida, 27 Jan. 1950.

The Times, 30 Jan. and 7 Feb. 1950; *Newberry Corresp.*

WOLFF, (*Rt. Hon. Sir*) **Henry Drummond** (1830–1908)

Diplomatist; born 1830; educ. Rugby; entered the Foreign Office as a clerk, 1846; employed in many diplomatic missions in France, Bulgaria, Turkey, Egypt, Persia and elsewhere; P.C., 1885; G.C.B., 1889; G.C.M.G., 1878; was in Egypt when the Royal Mummies were discovered and was present at the unrolling of some of them; died 11 Oct. 1908.

WWW. i, 776; Maspero, *Momies Roy.* 525, 765.

WRESZINSKI, Walter (1880–1935)

German Egyptologist; born Moglino, 18 Mar. 1880; studied at Königsberg and Berlin under Erman; Professor at Königsberg, 1915; visited Egypt several times and made a photographic survey, the results of which are embodied in his *Atlas zur altaegypt. Kulturgeschichte*; pub. also three parts of his unfinished work on the medical papyri, comprising the Berlin, Hearst, London and Ebers Papyri, 1909–13, the inscriptions in the Vienna collection, and other works; editor of *OLZ*; died 9 Apl. 1935.

Kürschner, 1931; *ZÄS.* 71 (unnumbered page).

YATES, William Holt (1802–1845+)

Physician and traveller; born 1802; M.D. Edinb., 1825; Senior Physician of the General Dispensary, London; Pres. Royal Med. and Phys. Soc., Edinburgh; travelled in Egypt and Nubia, 1829–30;

pub. medical works, and *Modern Hist. and Condition of Egypt*, 2 vols. 1843 ; member of Syro-Egyptian Soc. for which he pub. a memoir on obelisks, 1845 ; not traced after 1845.

Lancet, 1832–3, ii, 477, 790, 821 ; 1833–4, i, 76 ; 1842–3, i, 867 ; 1843–4, i, 755 ; *Hilmy*, ii, 345.

YEATES, Thomas (1768–1839)

Orientalist ; born 9 Oct. 1768 ; All Souls Coll. Oxon., 1802 ; employed by Claudius Buchanan to catalogue and describe the oriental MSS. brought by him from India, *c.* 1808–15 ; Assistant in Dept. of Printed Books, B.M., 1823–39 ; pub. a dissertation on the Pyramids, 1833 and the history of Egypt, 1835 ; died 7 Oct. 1839.

DNB. 63, 311 ; *Hilmy*, ii, 347.

YOUNG, Thomas (1773–1829)

Physician and physicist ; of Quaker stock, born Milverton, Somerset, 13 June 1773 ; precocious in languages, by the age of 14 he was acquainted with Greek, Latin, French, Italian, Hebrew, Persian and Arabic ; studied medicine in London, 1792, Edinburgh, 1794, and Göttingen, 1795 where he became Dr. of Physick, 1796 ; F.R.S. 1794 ; entered Emmanuel Coll. Cantab., 1797 ; practised as physician in London from 1799 ; Prof. of Physics, R. Inst., 1801–3 ; made important discoveries in physics, especially in the undulatory theory of light and the physiology of vision ; in 1814 began his attempts to decipher hieroglyphics, and although his results were small and only partial, they are not negligible, though they have been much exaggerated ; in 1819 formed an Egyptian society to publish hieroglyphic inscriptions, plates of which appeared in parts and were continued under the auspices of the R. Soc. of Literature ; in 1823 pub. *Discoveries in Hieroglyphical Literature* ; his Egyptological papers are now in the B.M. (Add. MSS. 27281–5) ; died in London, 10 May 1829.

Life, by Dean G. Peacock, in vol. i of *Collected Works*, 1855 ; *Life*, by F. Oldham, 1933 (Portr.) ; *DNB*. 63, 393 ; *Hilmy*, ii, 348 ; for his part in decipherment, see CHAMPOLLION, J. F.

ZINCKE, (*Rev.*) **Foster Barham** (1817–1893)

Antiquary ; born Jamaica, 5 Jan. 1817 ; Wadham Coll. Oxon. ; B.A., 1839 ; Vicar of Wherstead, 1847 ; one of Queen Victoria's chaplains ; travelled extensively and pub. works on the countries visited ; his *Egypt of the Pharaohs and of the Khedive* (1871, 2nd ed., 1873), enjoyed great popularity ; died 23 Aug. 1893.

DNB. 63, 409 ; *Hilmy*, ii, 367.

ZOËGA, Georg (1755–1809)

Danish scholar ; son of a Lutherian minister ; born Duhlen, Jutland, 20 Dec. 1755 ; educ. Göttingen Univ., 1773 ; he had a bent for archaeology which arose out of the study of the writings of Winckelmann ; visited Rome, Venice, Dresden and Leipsic, returning home in 1777 ; became tutor to a family in Fühnen, 1778 ; again travelled in Italy, 1780, but his operations were suddenly stopped by the death of his father ; employed on classifying the coins in the national collection at Copenhagen ; in 1782 he was sent on a mission in connection with numismatics, but the journey became a prolonged residence abroad and he never again returned to his native land ; in 1783 he came under the notice of Borghia in Rome who became his patron and employed him in archaeological work ; he married in 1783 Maria, d. of the painter Pietruccioli and was received into the Church of Rome ; in 1787 he pub. a catalogue of the Egyptian coins in the Borghia collection ; this attracted him to Egyptology which he studied with avidity, spending seven years in the preparation of his *De Origine et usu Obeliscorum*, Rome, 1797 ; he interested himself in hieroglyphic decipherment and learned Coptic, and produced the work by which he is best known, the *Catalogus Codicum Copticorum* ; died in Rome, 10 Feb. 1809.

Enc. It. 35, 972 ; *Hartleben* (see index) ; *Hilmy*, ii, 368.

ZOUCHE, (*Baron*)—*See* CURZON

ZUENDEL, Johannes (1813–1871)

Swiss Egyptologist ; son of Konrad Z. (1789–1853), banker, and President du Tribunal de la Ville, Berne ; born 30 Aug. 1813 ; Professor of Greek and Literature, Acad. of Lausanne ; master of Greek and Latin, École Reale, Berne ; studied Egyptology ; pub. a few independent works and some articles in *ZÄS* and *Rev. Arch.* ; a correspondent of Chabas, to whom he introduced Naville ; died 9 June 1871.

Dict. Hist. et Biogr. de la Suisse ; *Chabas*, 45, 49, 71, 73, 110 ; *Hilmy*, ii, 370, 459.

MADE IN GREAT BRITAIN
BY HARRISON AND SONS LIMITED
PRINTERS TO HIS MAJESTY THE KING
LONDON, HAYES (MIDDX.), AND HIGH WYCOMBE